Paddling and Hiking
THE GEORGIAN
BAY COAST

Paddling and Hiking
THE GEORGIAN BAY COAST

Kas Stone

The BOSTON
MILLS PRESS

A BOSTON MILLS PRESS BOOK

First Printing

LIBRARY AND ARCHIVES CANADA CATALOGUING IN PUBLICATION
Stone, Kas, 1959-
Paddling & hiking the Georgian Bay coast / Kas Stone.

Includes bibliographical references and index.
ISBN-13: 978-1-55046-477-1 (pbk.)
ISBN-10: 1-55046-477-9 (pbk.)
1. Hiking—Ontario—Georgian Bay Region—Guidebooks.
2. Trails—Ontario—Georgian Bay Region—Guidebooks.
3. Canoes and canoeing—Ontario—Georgian Bay Region—Guidebooks.
4. Kayaking—Ontario—Georgian Bay Region—Guidebooks.
5. Georgian Bay Region (Ont.)—Guidebooks.
I. Title. II. Title: Paddling and hiking the Georgian Bay coast.
GV199.44.C22O58 2008   796.5109713'15   C2007-906819-7

PUBLISHER CATALOGING-IN-PUBLICATION DATA (U.S.)
Stone, Kas, 1959-
Paddling & hiking the Georgian Bay coast / Kas Stone.
[224] p. : col. photos., maps ;   cm

Includes bibliographical references and index.
Summary: Guidebook includes the trails as well as the lore and history of the region.
ISBN-13: 978-1-55046-477-1 (pbk.)
ISBN-10: 1-55046-477-9 (pbk.)
1. Hiking—Ontario—Georgian Bay Region—Guidebooks.
2. Trails—Ontario—Georgian Bay Region—Guidebooks.
3. Canoes and canoeing—Ontario—Georgian Bay Region—Guidebooks.
4. Kayaking—Ontario—Georgian Bay Region—Guidebooks.
5. Georgian Bay Region (Ont.)—Guidebooks. I. Title.
796.5109713'15 dc22   GV199.44.C22O58.S766   2008

Published by Boston Mills Press, 2008
132 Main Street, Erin, Ontario, Canada N0B 1T0
Tel: 519-833-2407 • Fax: 519-833-2195
e-mail: books@bostonmillspress.com • www.bostonmillspress.com

IN CANADA
Distributed by Firefly Books Ltd.
66 Leek Crescent
Richmond Hill, Ontario, Canada L4B 1H1

IN THE UNITED STATES
Distributed by Firefly Books (U.S.) Inc.
P.O. Box 1338, Ellicott Station
Buffalo, New York, USA 14205

Design by Sue Breen and Chris McCorkindale, McCorkindale Advertising & Design
All photographs by Kas Stone unless otherwise noted.

Front Cover: The Bustard Islands light station.
Page 1: (top left) Tarvat Bay, Killarney; (top right) Niagara Escarpment cliffs at Lion's Head; (bottom) Tanvat Island, The Bustards.
Page 2-3: The Massasauga Provincial Park shoreline at Moon Bay.
Page 5: Henrietta Point, Franklin Island.
Back Cover: (top left) Overhanging Point, Bruce Peninsula National Park; (top right) Indian Falls; (bottom right) Kas and Skye on a paddling and hiking expedition.

Printed in China

The publisher gratefully acknowledges the financial support for our publishing program by the Government of Canada through the Book Publishing Industry Development Program (BPIDP).

With thanks to all my travelling companions,

especially Rick Chuchra and Skye, for their patience, support

and good humour during the writing of this book.

CONTENTS

Western Shore: The Bruce Peninsula   167

Never underestimate Georgian Bay's navigational challenges. Before you set out, buy the appropriate maps and be sure you really know how to use your compass and GPS.
PHOTO BY RICK CHUCHRA

What This Book is About

This book explores the coastal landscape of Georgian Bay — Ontario's sixth Great Lake. With its tremendous scenic diversity and hundreds of fascinating years of human history, Georgian Bay seems at times to defy exploration. Around every headland and island, along every beach and cliff, another unexpected treasure reveals itself — a fragment of shipwreck, a twisted rock, an abandoned village, a breathtaking view. Whether you are paddling and hiking along its shores for a summer's holiday or a whole lifetime, you will never feel that you have "done" Georgian Bay; there will always be something else to discover.

Georgian Bay was first surveyed and charted by the British Royal Navy in the early 1800s. Captain William Fitzwilliam Owen made a preliminary survey in 1815 and his protege Henry Bayfield continued the work with rigorous mapping expeditions in the years that followed, producing a complete set of marine charts in 1823. With only a few alterations in the intervening centuries as mapping technology improved and water levels fluctuated, these charts still serve as the foundation for navigation around the bay today. It was during Bayfield's hydrographic explorations that Georgian Bay acquired both its name (in honour of King George IV) and its surprising designation as a bay of Lake Huron rather than as a separate Great Lake.

Georgian Bay, regardless of its name, is not a body of water to be trifled with. Measuring 200 km in length, 80 km in width and oriented northwest to southeast, perfectly aligned to receive the maximum battering from prevailing winds, its magnitude and moods command respect and its navigational challenges are legendary. For the outdoor enthusiast armed with common sense, good maps and solid paddling and hiking skills, however, the bay provides exceptional opportunities for adventure.

When planning an excursion on Georgian Bay, it is worth considering the geography of the coast and the type of outdoor activity best suited to each location. The northern and eastern shores from Killarney to the French River delta and the Thirty Thousand Islands are rugged in character, encompassing quintessential Canadian Shield landscape dominated by rock, water and windswept pines. Significant tracts of the shoreline are contained within provincial parks, conservation reserves and First Nations territories where the wilderness is protected. Bays and rivers cut deeply into the mainland, pushing major highways as far as 30 km away from the coast and making road access to Georgian Bay only intermittent. Some wonderful hikes can be enjoyed here, but these shores are really the realm of the paddler. With many thousands of islands and shoals and all the channels between them, as well as numerous backcountry campsites, the routes for canoeing and kayaking are limited only by the time available.

On the western side of Georgian Bay, the coast is shaped by the formidable cliffs of the Niagara Escarpment snaking up the Bruce Peninsula. The cliffs plunge deeply into the bay, providing few coves or islands for shelter. Paddling is not impossible here; in fact, some splendid trips can be had investigating the coast's many shipwrecks and admiring the escarpment from the unusual perspective of a canoe or kayak. But the routes are often dangerously exposed, and backcountry campsites are difficult to find, as roads run closer to the shore and much of the land is privately owned. The hiking, on the other hand, is magnificent. The Bruce Trail, Canada's oldest and longest hiking trail, runs for 840 km along the escarpment corridor. Almost 250 km of that distance — the most challenging and picturesque segment — traverses the Bruce Peninsula between Owen Sound and Tobermory. Sometimes the trail makes its way along the brow of the escarpment, clambering to clifftop ledges to take in a stunning view. Sometimes it follows a shingle or cobble beach at the bottom, enticing hikers into the bay for a refreshing swim. Some sections of the trail ramble through pleasant woodlands and across farm fields, while others scramble over cliff-base rockfalls and into caves and potholes. With its scenic appeal and environmental significance, the Bruce Trail has become a popular destination, drawing more than 400,000 hikers annually from around the world.

Georgian Bay's south shore offers some surprising opportunities for outdoor enthusiasts. With its gentle terrain, luxurious sandy beaches, long stretches of private property and proximity to the urban centres of southern Ontario, wilderness experiences can be difficult to find here. But they *can* be found, or they can be *created* by visiting this busy coast during the off-season — snowshoeing along a beach in February, hiking to the summit of a ski hill in July or paddling around an island as the ice retreats in early spring.

OVERVIEW OF PADDLING AND HIKING EXCURSIONS

(green numbers correspond to locations on the adjacent map, and to chapter numbers in this book)

1	George Island Trail	20	Hibou
2	Tar Vat Trail	21	West Rocks
3	Chikanishing Trail	22	Indian Falls
4	Collins Inlet, Philip Edward Island and The Foxes	23	Skinner's Bluff
		24	Bruce's Caves
5	French River Hike	25	Historic Wiarton
6	French River Delta and the Bustards	26	The Wrecks of Colpoy's Bay
7	Byng Inlet to the Churchill Islands	27	Hope Bay
8	Dillon to the McCoys ... and Beyond	28	Cape Dundas
9	Snug Harbour to the Minks	29	Lion's Head
10	Killbear's Hiking Trails	30	White Bluff and Reed's Dump
11	Depot Harbour	31	Smokey Head
12	The Massasauga's Moon and Wreck Islands	32	Devil's Monument
13	Beausoleil Island	33	Cabot Head and Wingfield Basin
14	Awenda	34	Halfway Log Dump and Storm Haven
15	Giants Tomb Island	35	Little Cove to Halfway Rock Point
16	Wasaga Beach and the *Nancy*	36	Burnt Point
17	Collingwood and Nottawasaga Island	37	Flowerpot Island
18	Craigleith	38	Fathom Five National Marine Park
19	The Blue Mountains		

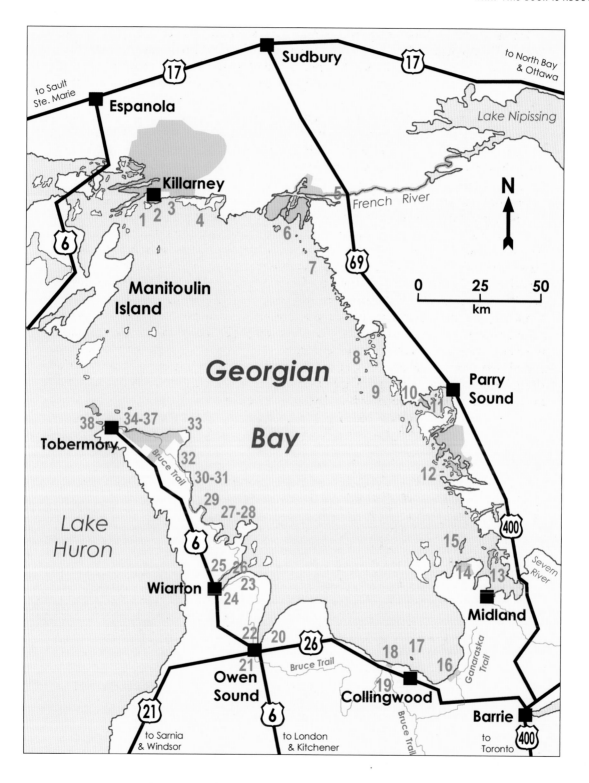

This book introduces you to 38 of the best places for paddling and hiking along the mainland coast of Georgian Bay from Killarney to Parry Sound to Collingwood to Tobermory. The excursions range from hour-long strolls to strenuous hiking and multiday paddling expeditions, and each excursion explores some interesting feature of the area's natural environment or human heritage. The book is intended as a practical guide, so every chapter includes information about access points and route planning, and provides a list of maps available for the area and recommendations about useful publications and websites for further research. And for the armchair traveller, there are many tantalizing landscape photographs and stories about the bay's history that can be enjoyed from the comfort of the living room.

A few words of caution must temper your enthusiasm, however: just because an excursion appears in this book does *not* mean that you should grab your paddle and hiking boots and head for Georgian Bay. While most of the routes described here can be undertaken by any reasonably fit person with solid basic paddling and hiking skills, other routes are more demanding, both physically and technically. The hiking can be extremely rugged, especially along the remote trails of the northern Bruce Peninsula, and the hobbling distance for help seems interminable in an emergency. Rattlesnake bites are extremely rare but cannot be dismissed; poison ivy is abundant, and allergic reactions to it are uncomfortable.

Paddling excursions on Georgian Bay, though pleasantly portage-free, are subject to significant risk from wind and waves that can leave you stranded for days, miserably contemplating your existence on a barren rock. As for the incessant canoe-versus-kayak debate, do not allow yourself to be frightened away from Georgian Bay if you paddle an open canoe, and more importantly, resist overconfidence merely because you travel by kayak. The wrecks of much larger and more powerful vessels than these are scattered liberally across the floor of Georgian Bay! The best and safest boat is the one you know how to paddle.

Some excursions in this book require superior navigation skills, particularly along the eastern coast, where thirty thousand islands can feel like thirty million when you are lost! Every chapter includes an overview map of the excursion route and sometimes, if the route is long, additional maps showing portions of the route in greater detail. However, these are intended only as general guides and must not be used for navigation. Before you set out, obtain the appropriate maps for the area. National Topographic Survey (NTS) "topo" maps, at a scale of 1:50,000, include comprehensive

Maps Legend

	land/parkland
	water/marshland
	urban/Native land
6	highway
39	county/secondary road
⫴⫴⫴	railway
⌇	trail
• • • •	paddling/hiking route
• • • •	alternative route
P	parking
←	lookout
△ ⛺	campsite/campground
⛩	picnic site
⬛👥	building/washroom
⛪	lighthouse
🎿	ski hill
ABC	route references

information about terrain contours, natural features and human installations found on land. Nautical charts (popularly "marine charts" or simply "charts") produced by the Canadian Hydrographic Service provide similar information about the aquatic geography, showing water depth, coastal landmarks and navigation fixtures such as lighthouses, buoys and channel markers. Georgian Bay's marine charts range in scale from a 1:200,000 overview of the entire bay to 1:50,000 and 1:20,000 close-up charts of small sections of its coast. Paddlers usually prefer to use marine charts rather than topo maps, as they provide the most accurate, up-to-date information about the complex shoreline. For hikers on the Bruce Peninsula, *The Bruce Trail Reference: Trail Guide and Maps* contains an excellent set of maps showing the trail's route and much supplementary information about natural features, historical sites, trail access points, and locations for parking and camping nearby. At the local level, detailed maps of specific areas of the Georgian Bay shore are available from national and provincial parks, conservation authorities, tourist associations and private mapping companies. Sources for maps and charts are listed at the end of each chapter. Whichever map you use, follow your progress across it closely during your journey, and be sure that you really know how to use your compass. A GPS (global positioning system) can be a great aid and comfort but, like all electronic toys, is subject to failures that your brain usually is not.

In short, it is your responsibility to ensure that you have the appropriate emergency gear, navigation tools, and requisite paddling and hiking experience for the big water and rugged terrain of Georgian Bay. Properly equipped, you will enjoy all the glorious landscapes and historical treasures that the bay has to offer — only a fraction of which will fit in this already lengthy book!

"Leaves of three, let them be!" Poison ivy flourishes along Georgian Bay's western and southern shores. You can identify the plant by its leaves, which are usually glossy green or red and have smooth or slightly toothed edges. The leaves grow out from the stalk in groups of three, with the central leaf protruding on a longer stem than the two outer leaves. Urushiol, a resin produced by poison ivy, causes an allergic reaction in many people that results in intense itching, skin rashes and blisters.

MEASUREMENTS & CONVERSIONS

Distances and areas in this book are referred to using metric measurements, which may be converted to imperial units as follows:

1 kilometre (km) = 0.62 miles (mi)
1 metre (m) = 1.1 yard (yd) or 3.25 feet (ft)
1 square kilometre (km²) or 100 hectacres (ha) = 247 acres (ac)

GPS references are given in UTM coordinates (eastings and northings) for Zone 17T using map datum WGS84.

Introduction to Georgian Bay

NATURAL LANDSCAPE

A crow flying around the Georgian Bay shoreline, clockwise from Killarney to Tobermory, might be amazed by the variety of landscapes passing beneath him. In the north, where the La Cloche Mountains descend to the Killarney coast, sparkling white quartzite is strikingly juxtaposed with rich red granite and turquoise water. On the eastern shore, thousands of tiny islands and shoals, with Parry Sound nestled in their midst, have been sculpted into the shapes of smooth, giant whalebacks. Farther south the terrain becomes tamer in the sheltered bays of Severn Sound and the sweeping, sandy crescents of Nottawasaga Bay. And on Georgian Bay's western side, the shoreline gives way to the jagged cliffs of the Niagara Escarpment winding north towards the tip of the Bruce Peninsula.

This 600 km coast (as our crow flies) and the medley of landscape features along it are the culmination of more than 2 billion years of the Earth's history. Small continents have collided here and merged to form supercontinents. Mountain ranges rivalling the Himalayas have been pushed up, and erosive agents have worn them down again. Tropical seas have lapped across coral reefs along these shores, and glaciers have locked the bay in ice more than 2 km thick. Rocks now resting at the water's edge were once buried at depths of more than 30 km. They have been melted and squeezed, scraped and polished, and carried far from their places of origin. The result of this geological activity — all the tectonic and glacial manoeuvring — is the splendid array of landscapes we enjoy along the Georgian Bay coast today.

The core of the North American continent is an ancient chunk of the Earth's crust called the Canadian Shield. It began to form more than 3 billion years ago when a group of volcanic islands melded into a single land mass northwest of Lake Superior.

About a billion years later, that original continent collided with another along what is now the north shore of Georgian Bay. The rocks along the continents' outer edges, together with the quartz-rich sediment on the ocean floor between them, were compressed and uplifted to form the massive Penokean mountain range. The impact of this and subsequent collisions forced magma from the Earth's mantle up into the subterranean cavities along the mountains' southern margin, where it solidified into granite. Many millennia and several ice ages later, the overlying rock has been eroded away, revealing the quartzite roots of the Penokean Mountains in the sparkling La Cloche hills and exposing the rich red granite along the Killarney shoreline. These are Georgian Bay's oldest rocks, dating back almost 2 billion years.

(Left) Georgian Bay's oldest rocks are the brilliant white quartzite and rich red granite found on the Killarney shore.

Over the next billion years, the landscape was jostled repeatedly as a succession of small continents, collectively known as the Grenville Province, piled up against the edge of the older continent, pushing up another mountain range, the Grenville Mountains, along what is now the eastern shore of Georgian Bay. The rocks at the base of these mountains were buried 20 to 30 km deep, heated to extremes of 500 to 750° C and squeezed so intensely that they were profoundly altered. Chemically, their component minerals separated and realigned themselves into parallel bands, and structurally, they became pliable enough to bend and fold like Plasticine. The resulting rock, gneiss (pronounced "nice"), is characterized by its twisted, multicoloured ribbons. Like the Penokean Mountains before them, the Grenville Mountains eventually wore away, unearthing these billion-year-old rocks along the Georgian Bay shore between Collins Inlet and the Severn River.

Meanwhile, on the western side of Georgian Bay, the cliffs of the Bruce Peninsula arose — from a coral reef in a tropical sea! Between 570 million and 300 million years ago, the slow-motion dance of continents across the globe positioned fledgling North America close to the equator. During that time the tectonic choreography also caused three major collisions between North America and the forerunners of modern Europe and Africa. The impact pushed up mountain ranges along North America's east coast and created sags and bulges in the Canadian Shield bedrock behind the mountains. The bulges became arches of high land. The sags became basins of seawater such as the Michigan Basin, which covered what is today southwestern Ontario and the adjacent state of Michigan. Following each collision, large quantities of sediment washed down from the newly

Gneiss is the bedrock of eastern Georgian Bay, characterized by twisted, multicoloured ribbons.

The Niagara Escarpment was once a coral reef in a tropical sea. Physical and chemical processes have gradually transformed the reef into a jagged dolostone battlement, which stands today along Georgian Bay's western shore.

forged mountains and settled in the basins to form layers of shale and sandstone (like the reddish Queenston shale and the Whirlpool sandstone found today across south-central Ontario). Then, as the mountains wore down and the sediment supply diminished, the basin waters became clear and coral reefs began to grow.

Hard-shelled marine creatures, able to mineralize external layers of tissue into a protective covering of calcium carbonate, first made their appearance on the evolutionary stage about 560 million years ago, flourishing in the tropical waters of the Michigan Basin. The shell remained after the death of the creature inside, and the accumulated shells of generations of reef creatures consolidated over time to form limestone. During a prolific period about 425 million years ago, the reefs of the Michigan Basin rivalled Australia's Great Barrier Reef, and the resulting limestone ridge was more than 725 km long and as thick as 100 m in places. Submerged for millennia in magnesium-rich seawater, the limestone underwent a chemical transformation. Magnesium molecules from the seawater replaced some of the calcium molecules in the limestone to produce a dense, durable rock called dolostone. The ridge still stands today as the caprock of the Niagara Escarpment.

The tectonic upheavals that caused all the collisions along the eastern edge of North America and welded together a supercontinent began to change direction about 300 million years ago and tear that supercontinent apart again. A watery wedge was driven between North America and Europe, gradually widening to form the North Atlantic Ocean. The continent also drifted northward, away from the equator into the mid-latitudes.

Ice and water wore away Ontario's ancient mountain ranges, reducing the topography, once measured in thousands of metres, to the gently undulating Canadian Shield landscape that is familiar to us today.

Geological stretch marks appeared across the landscape, creating in the bedrock the fractures that are today's valleys and riverbeds. Released from the pressure of collisions and the weight of mountain ranges, the eastern margin of North America was gradually uplifted. The Michigan Basin began to dry up, and its floor tilted, causing the dolostone ridge to slope gently downward from northeast to southwest. By 150 million years ago, North America's tectonic activity had shifted to mountain building in the western part of the continent, and Georgian Bay was left in relative peace.

The most recent chapter in Ontario's geological history is the erosion of all the dramatic topographic features that were created in previous millennia. The agents of this erosion are ice and water — on a grand scale, the continental glaciers and their meltwater and, on a smaller scale, the seasonal and daily fluctuations in weather that continue to wear away the land today.

Glaciers have scoured the landscape many times in the province's 4-billion-year history, but evidence of their passing has been largely erased by subsequent geologic events. Only the most recent ice age left any significant visible record. The Wisconsin glacier (also called the Laurentide Ice Sheet) began its advance about 70,000 years ago. It reached its maximum extent about 20,000 years ago, stretching into the northern United States and burying Ontario under ice to depths of 3 km. The glacier then retreated between 14,000 and 8,000 years ago, sliding eventually into the Arctic waters north of Labrador.

As the ice withdrew, pools of meltwater accumulated at its rim, creating vast glacial lakes across southern Ontario — precursors of the modern Great Lakes. Glacial Lake Algonquin, at its height about 11,000 years ago, covered much of the area of present-day Lakes Superior, Michigan and Huron, including Georgian Bay, and inundated the adjacent low-lying areas. As the glacier moved northward, the

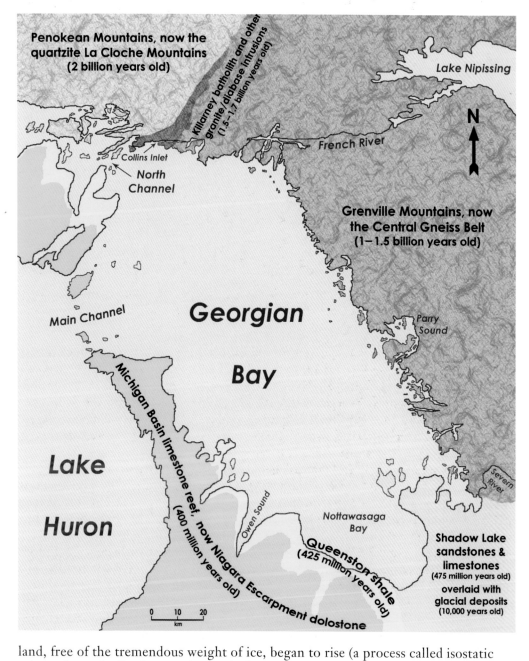

Penokean Mountains, now the quartzite La Cloche Mountains (2 billion years old)

Killarney batholith and other granite/diabase intrusions (1.5–1.7 billion years old)

Lake Nipissing

French River

Collins Inlet

North Channel

N

Grenville Mountains, now the Central Gneiss Belt (1–1.5 billion years old)

Parry Sound

Main Channel

Georgian

Bay

Michigan Basin limestone reef, now Niagara Escarpment dolostone (400 million years old)

Lake

Huron

Owen Sound

Nottawasaga Bay

Severn River

Queenston shale (425 million years old)

Shadow Lake sandstones & limestones (475 million years old) overlaid with glacial deposits (10,000 years old)

0   10   20
km

land, free of the tremendous weight of ice, began to rise (a process called isostatic rebound), gradually altering the level of the lake and the drainage patterns of its waterways. Initially, Lake Algonquin drained south into the Mississippi River system. Then, as the retreating ice uncovered more northerly channels, drainage was directed eastward, at first through what is now the Trent-Severn Waterway into glacial Lake Iroquois (forerunner of Lake Ontario) and eventually across the French, Mattawa and Ottawa river channels towards the Atlantic Ocean. Finally, as the northern lands rebounded and the modern Great Lakes took shape, the flow turned to its present course through the St. Clair, Niagara and St. Lawrence rivers.

Glaciation left a profound legacy of erosion on the Georgian Bay landscape. Like coarse-grit sandpaper, the debris that was trapped in the glacial ice scratched across the land, and massive floods of meltwater washed over it, stripping away hundreds of metres of surface material, gouging deep grooves and etching fine striations, sculpting pits in porous rock and polishing hard rock smooth.

Along the shore of northern and eastern Georgian Bay, the Penokean and Grenville mountain ranges were levelled and their remains carried away. The topography, once measured in thousands of metres, was reduced to undulating outcrops of bald rock interspersed with boggy lowlands and barren islands — the Canadian Shield landscape that is familiar today in the cottage country of the Thirty Thousand Islands, the French River delta and Killarney.

The glaciers carried the debris from the mountains and dumped it across southern Ontario and the northern United States. Some of this debris was deposited on the south shore of Georgian Bay, burying the older layers of shale, sandstone and limestone that had formed in the early days of the Michigan Basin. Glacial till, an unsorted mixture of sediment ranging in size from particles of clay and grains of sand to pebbles and boulders, created a gently rolling terrain that has sustained the area's economy with its deciduous woodlands, farm fields, aggregate quarries and brick works, golf courses and ski hills, and the many miles of sandy beaches along Nottawasaga Bay.

On the Bruce Peninsula shore of Georgian Bay, glaciers stripped away the overlying sediment to reveal the jagged battlement of the Niagara Escarpment. Though durable, the escarpment's dolostone bears significant scars of erosion nonetheless. Fierce torrents of glacial meltwater carved potholes and tunnels into the rock. Waves crashing on the shore of Lake Algonquin excavated caves and chiselled columns (called stacks or, popularly, flowerpots) from the cliff face. At the base of the cliffs, the softer layers of sandstone and shale wore quickly away, undermining the dolostone caprock (a process known as sapping). The seasonal cycle of freeze and thaw and the persuasive force of gravity pried chunks of the dolostone loose, leaving jumbles of rock (talus) along the foot of the escarpment. Today, small streams and Georgian Bay storms continue the work. Over the centuries, one small rockfall at a time, the escarpment is receding westward.

Chemical processes have accelerated the escarpment's erosion. Carbonate in the dolostone reacts with water to form a weak carbonic acid that dissolves the rock, leaving a pockmarked (karst) landscape with small pits and channels etched across the surface and larger cavities and channels in subterranean fractures.

The escarpment's environment is one of inhospitable extremes. Along the winding cliffs and exposed dolostone pavements (alvars) of the Bruce Peninsula, the natural inhabitants are subjected to scorching droughts and icy floods, desiccating winds, fire and rock slides. Only the hardiest species can survive here, among them a collection of

(Right) Deposits of glacial debris have shaped a pastoral landscape along Georgian Bay's southern shore.

ancient, twisted cedars, some more than 500 years old, which cling to barren crevices in the rock, astonishing botanists with their perseverance. The Bruce Peninsula also boasts an extraordinary abundance of orchids (43 species) and ferns (more than 20 species) and is one of the last refuges for Ontario's only venomous snake, the endangered and shy massasauga rattlesnake. Persecution and habitat destruction in the wake of human development around Georgian Bay have restricted the rattlesnake's territory to just a few isolated pockets on the Bruce Peninsula, the Thirty Thousand Islands and the French River delta.

The remarkable landscape of the Georgian Bay coast attracts widespread recognition — locally, provincially, nationally and even internationally — for its environmental significance. Three national parks, eight provincial parks and dozens of nature reserves, conservation areas, land trusts and municipal parklands have been created around the bay in an effort to protect this natural heritage. UNESCO added international sanction to these efforts by designating two areas of Georgian Bay as World Biosphere Reserves. Biosphere reserves, of which there are only 13 in Canada and about 500 worldwide, are managed so as to promote a balanced relationship between humans and the environment.

Glacial ice, wind and waves created the sweeping, sandy beaches of Nottawasaga Bay.

UNESCO supports scientific research and monitoring in these areas and encourages sustainable development and responsible recreational use to safeguard their unique ecosystems.

The Niagara Escarpment Biosphere Reserve was the first to be established, in 1990, a tribute to its significance as the ecological spine of southern Ontario. The Georgian Bay Littoral Biosphere Reserve, the world's largest freshwater archipelago, was added in 2004, encompassing the many islands between Severn Sound and the French River as well as the adjacent mainland back to Hwy 400/69.

When we are paddling and hiking along the Georgian Bay coast today, reminders of the landscape's ancestry can be found everywhere — in the rocks, in the water, in the communities of plants and animals on the shorelines, and even in the human activities shaped by those shorelines. Keep in mind, however, that while today's landscape seems solid enough, geology is never idle and Nature is forever improving itself. The process of transformation continues beneath our feet!

HUMAN LANDSCAPE

The beauty of Georgian Bay's natural landscape makes it appealing, and its proximity makes it accessible to the large, city-weary populace of southern Ontario. In the last century, this has led to the bay's widespread development for human enjoyment. Cottages and resorts, from rustic camps to extravagant chalets, dot the shoreline and islands. Summer visitors crowd its beaches and parks. Marinas are tucked into every cove, and navigation channels criss-cross the waterways, buzzing with boating traffic of all descriptions.

In an earlier day, only the sound of paddle against birchbark canoe disturbed the natural rhythm of wind and waves. Native people moved into the Georgian Bay area about 9,000 years ago, soon after the glaciers moved out. The Ojibwe and other Algonkian-speaking tribes occupied the northern part of the bay, and Iroquoian-speaking tribes — like the Petun and the Wendat (the latter known as Huron by the French) — settled along the southern shore. They subsisted by hunting and fishing, trapping and trading, gathering sap and berries, and (where soil made it possible) cultivating corn, squash and beans.

The first European to see Georgian Bay was Étienne Brûlé. He was sent in 1610 by the governor of New France, Samuel de Champlain, to scout exploration routes westward and to pave the way for trade with local Native people. Full of youthful bravado, Brûlé (then only 18) quickly adapted to life among the Huron, with whom he lived for most of his remaining years. Initially, he acted as Champlain's emissary, travelling extensively throughout southern Ontario and serving as interpreter and mediator between Native tribes and the French. After years among the Huron, however, he became increasingly disenchanted with his own countrymen, and ultimately his loyalty strayed so completely that in 1629 he assisted a British force against Champlain at Quebec City. Brûlé then retired to Huronia (the Europeans' name for Huron territory) and largely disappeared from the French record. He died in 1632 at the age of 40 and was buried in a Huron village on the Midland peninsula, though the precise location of his grave and manner of his death — murdered by the French or killed and eaten by the Huron — continues to be the subject of fanciful debate.

Brûlé had opened the floodgates. Down the French River during the seventeenth and eighteenth centuries came legions of European explorers, traders and missionaries in search of, respectively, a route to the Orient, a wealth of beaver pelts, and a flock of heathen souls in need of conversion.

The Huron of southern Georgian Bay, already allied with the French and boasting a sophisticated trading network of their own, initially prospered from the fur trade. But their success drew unwelcome attention from the Iroquois to the south, whose beaver populations were already in decline. Competition for pelts led to skirmishes between the tribes and to Huron casualties along the trade routes. Another threat to the Huron came from the French themselves, whose missionaries brought Christianity and, unwittingly, smallpox to the villages, weakening the Native cultural fabric with their religion and the health of the Native population with their disease.

Jean de Brébeuf was one of the first and certainly the best known of Georgian Bay's Jesuit missionaries. He arrived in Huronia in 1626 and remained there, with only brief

Father Jean de Brébeuf lived among the Huron people at the Jesuit mission of Sainte-Marie from 1626 until his martyrdom in 1649.

sojourns in Quebec and France, until his death in 1649. Brébeuf was an intelligent and perceptive man, educated well in France and self-taught in Native languages and culture. His missionary fervour was tempered with a flexible and compassionate approach to his Native parishioners that won him their grudging acceptance and even admiration. In the two decades he spent in Huronia, Brébeuf converted many souls to Christianity and established several religious houses, including the Sainte-Marie mission, built in 1639 on the banks of the Wye River. Iroquois raids intensified during the 1640s. In 1649 a large force overcame the Huron villages of St. Ignace and St. Louis, near Sainte-Marie. Refusing to escape, Brébeuf and his junior missionary, Gabriel Lalemant, were captured with the Huron villagers and tortured and executed. Their remains are buried in Sainte-Marie's Church of St. Joseph.

Following these attacks the Huron people, decimated by warfare and disease, abandoned their villages. Their population, which had numbered 30,000 in the early 1600s, was reduced by the end of 1649 to a few scattered groups. The largest of these (about 3,000 people) accompanied the handful of French remaining in the area to Christian Island in Georgian Bay, burning Sainte-Marie upon their departure to prevent its takeover by the Iroquois. The winter of 1649/50 was one of extreme deprivation for the colony, and most of its members succumbed to starvation, disease or roving Iroquois. The following spring the survivors (a mere 300!) fled Christian Island and made their way to New France, effectively closing the history book on the nation of Huronia. Three centuries later, during the mid-1900s, the mission site was excavated and restored as a historic park: Sainte-Marie-Among-the-Hurons. The original French and Native buildings have been carefully reconstructed, and the park is staffed with interpretive guides dressed in period costume. In 1930 Jean de Brébeuf was canonized in recognition of his work among the Native people. His relics are preserved in the Martyrs' Shrine Church across the road from Sainte-Marie.

Meanwhile, the fur trade prospered for the Europeans and the Ojibwe tribes of northern Georgian Bay. During the seventeenth and early eighteenth centuries, trade was dominated by the French. Their traditional St. Lawrence–Ottawa–Mattawa–Nipissing–

French river route bustled with voyageurs' canoes bringing European trade goods west from Montreal in the spring and beaver pelts east from the interior before the autumn freeze-up. When New France fell to Britain under the 1763 Treaty of Paris, this route was taken over by British and loyalist American traders operating under the banner of the North West Company.

By the mid-1800s, the dwindling supply of beaver pelts, the remoteness of the remaining trapping areas and the changing fashions in Europe (silk replacing beaver as the favoured fabric for gentlemen's hats) gradually brought the fur trade to an end. Its legacy, however, was profound. The search for beaver pelts and safe trade routes had stimulated exploration and opened the interior of the continent to European travel and colonization. The French River route into Georgian Bay was the first and for a long while the most important artery into the interior. However, shifting allegiances and conflicts between the French, English, Americans and Native peoples led to the development of other approaches. The voyage over the open water of the Great Lakes was one means of access, though not the preferred — at least until the advent of larger merchant vessels on the lakes made it less dangerous. Another was the arduous Toronto Portage from Lake Ontario up the Humber River, across to Lake Simcoe and then along either the Severn River or the Nottawasaga River into Georgian Bay. The fur trade, in short, made Georgian Bay a major hub of transportation during the country's formative years.

The fur trade also spawned trading posts at strategic sites along the Georgian Bay shore — at the mouths of rivers and the entrances to channels, and in the protection of sheltered bays. These places, where Native trappers and European traders once met to exchange pelts and trade goods, became the townsites where now we stop for fuel, camping supplies and ice cream cones.

Penetanguishene was the first European town to appear on the Georgian Bay shore. During the War of 1812, its sheltered harbour and strategic position between the Severn and Nottawasaga rivers made the site an obvious choice for a naval base so the British could defend their northern territories against marauding Americans. However, by the time buildings were raised and a road pushed through from Lake Simcoe (the first to Georgian Bay from the south, back-breakingly cleared during the winter of 1814/15), the war was over. The town quickly became a civilian rather than a military centre, populated by merchants and innkeepers, lumbermen and shipbuilders.

The land for the Penetanguishene base was acquired by treaty in 1798 from the Ojibwe who had drifted into the southern part of the bay region following the Huron's departure. In the half century that followed, First Nations relinquished much of their traditional territory to the British — the region between Georgian Bay and Lake Simcoe in 1815, the area from Georgian Bay to Lake Ontario in 1818 and most of the Bruce Peninsula through treaties signed in 1836 and 1854. In exchange, like Native peoples all across North America, they were granted Indian reserves. The legitimacy of this process and the boundaries of the reserves became matters of profound ethical debate and protracted legal wrangling during the twentieth century; indeed many Native land claims against the Canadian government have yet to be settled.

British surveyors moved in, neatly apportioning the land and establishing the lines for future roads and railways. They set the course for settlement of the bay during the second

(Above left) The Martyrs' Shrine Church in Midland celebrates the lives and work of those who died in Huronia for their Christian beliefs. (Above right) Exploration and trade in North America was driven by the European fashion for beaver felt hats. PHOTO COURTESY OF SAINTE-MARIE-AMONG-THE-HURONS, ONTARIO MINISTRY OF TOURISM, MIDLAND

half of the nineteenth century. Transportation routes, economic activity and towns grew up rapidly together around the shore. It was, after all, the era of the Industrial Revolution, the age of steam and progress, when engines replaced sails and railway tracks were laid along ancient footpaths.

Two more roads were built between Lake Simcoe and Georgian Bay during the 1830s and 1840s — one through Coldwater to Sturgeon Bay and the other alongside the Nottawasaga River to Wasaga Beach. Then, in 1855, the first railway line to the bay was laid. Collingwood was selected as its terminus, and the town was quickly transformed from an isolated outpost to a busy port. In subsequent decades the extension of the railway up both sides of the bay led to similar growth in other places; the tracks reached Midland in 1872, Sydenham (now Owen Sound) in 1873, Wiarton in 1882, and Parry Sound and Byng Inlet during the 1890s. These towns became major centres, where steamships transferred their cargoes of northern timber, fish and Prairie grain to rail lines bound for markets in the south and returned with mail, manufactured goods and immigrants with their household effects. Lumber mills, shipbuilding yards and communities of merchants developed around the ports, stimulating local economies and providing townspeople with employment.

Georgian Bay's commercial boom lasted through the latter half of the 1800s and into the first decades of the 1900s. By the 1920s, however, timber resources were becoming exhausted, cut for lumber or cleared for farming. The fishery declined dramatically during the 1940s and 1950s, due in part to overfishing of the bay's stocks of trout and whitefish and in part to the introduction into the Upper Great Lakes — accidental or otherwise — of the parasitic sea lamprey and other non-native species. The increasingly efficient network of roads and railways and the opening of the St. Lawrence Seaway for large freighter traffic in 1959 made the ports of Georgian Bay less vital to the country's transportation system. By the mid-twentieth century, the bay's economy had come to depend largely on tourism instead.

The beauty of Georgian Bay's landscape had not escaped the notice of early explorers, but limited access prevented widespread travel until the late 1800s. Then, as steamship routes, railway lines and roads developed around the bay and as the twentieth century brought increasing leisure and affluence to Ontario's population, Georgian Bay's shoreline and islands became a vacation mecca. Urbanites snapped up land for cottage properties, and tourist facilities sprouted up along the shore. The sandy southern section of the bay became especially popular and increasingly commercial. Wasaga Beach, with its 14 km beach and its amusement parks, now hosts upwards of 50,000 visitors on a typical summer

Georgian Bay is a much-loved recreation destination. On a typical summer weekend, Wasaga Beach hosts upwards of 50,000 visitors!

Like Collingwood, pictured here, many towns that were hubs of industry and transportation in the early 1900s became hubs of tourism and recreation by the end of the century.

weekend; popular Killbear Provincial Park has recorded more than 360,000 guests in recent years at its campgrounds and day-use facilities!

For the outdoor enthusiast wishing to explore Georgian Bay's natural landscape in peace, however, there are still many opportunities for paddling and hiking along the bay's shoreline — if you know where (and when!) to go. The excursions in this book will introduce you to some of these wonderful places.

CHAPTER 1

George Island Trail

OVERVIEW

George Island is a large triangular slab of granite that lies on the south side of Killarney Channel. A marvellous hiking trail winds across the island's interior and along its western shore, introducing the visitor to the extraordinary natural and geological history of the Killarney landscape. The day's excursion also explores the area's human history. It begins and ends at the hub of that history, the village of Killarney, and touches on several other sites of importance to the village's economic development.

Killarney's landscape is arguably the most scenic in the province, and its geological history is long and complex. Examples from every phase of that history are visible today from the hummocks and headlands along the George Island Trail. The white quartzite of the La Cloche Mountains sparkles on the northern horizon, reminding us that a sandy sea floor was pushed up here 2 billion years ago to form the Penokean mountain range. Hiking across the outcrops of red granite on George Island, our boots are treading on the Killarney batholith, a large bubble of magma that oozed into a subterranean cavity deep beneath Killarney between 1.7 billion and 1.5 billion years ago. Looking out from the trail's main viewpoint, we see tiny offshore islands in the waters to the southeast — humps of gneiss, twisted ribbons in shades of pink and grey that were squeezed from the granite when the Grenville Province collided with Killarney between 1.5 billion and 1 billion years ago. Across Killarney Bay, shelves of shale from the bottom of the Michigan Basin and limestone from its tropical reefs lend a youthful (400- to 425-million-year-old) aspect to the shores of Badgeley Island. And, arriving on George Island's western shore, we discover a raised cobble beach left behind by glacial Lake Algonquin just a few thousand years ago. For geology buffs, the region's exciting geomorphology is described in the Natural Landscape section of this book's introduction. Even if you are not much interested in their origins, you cannot help being impressed by the sheer beauty of Killarney's rocks!

The rocks have contributed to the human history of Killarney by creating landforms and fostering natural ecosystems that have influenced the comings and goings of its people. The fracture in the granite batholith that created Killarney Channel, for instance, was long regarded by travellers as a sheltered paddling route — Killarney's original Ojibwe name, Shebahonaning, means "safe canoe passage." The channel was used by Native

(Left) Smooth granite outcrops on George Island's western shore.

Smelly tar vats, wooden barrels, and the skeleton of an old fishing tug — relics of the George Island fishing station.

people and then by European explorers and voyageurs in the fur trade, and its shore provided a welcome camp at the midpoint of the lengthy journey between Montreal and the western terminus of the Upper Great Lakes trading route at Fort William.

It was to this camp that Killarney's first permanent residents came. Étienne Augustin de la Morandière, a fur trader from Quebec, set up a trading post here in 1820 and, with his Native wife, Joesephite Sai-sai-go-no-kwe, established a farm with crops and cattle imported from Manitoulin Island. The post's success attracted other settlers to the area and soon turned Shebahonaning, by then renamed Killarney, into a thriving community. By 1850 the fur trade had given way to logging. The pines that flourished on the sun-drenched granite and quartzite slopes supported a busy log drive in Killarney every spring — until timber resources began to dwindle in the early 1900s. Then the fishery picked up the economic slack, and Killarney became one of the most productive of Georgian Bay's many fishing stations. In a sheltered cove on George Island's western shore, you will still find the remains of a tar vat operation that fishermen once used to preserve their cotton nets.

Beginning in 1911, on the other side of Killarney Bay, silica was mined from Badgeley Point for use in the ceramic and the glass- and steel-refining industries. The mining equipment was moved to Badgeley Island in 1970 to extract a particularly rich deposit of orthoquartzite on the island's northeast side. Unimin Corporation's open-pit quarry continues at the site today, startling George Island hikers occasionally with the blast of explosives and the rumble of heavy machinery.

Though primary resources have been Killarney's traditional economic backbone, in recent decades the village has relied on the service industry. Tourists came initially with the steamships that carried lumber, fish and trade goods between ports on Georgian Bay and the North Channel. Killarney's glorious scenery soon made it a destination in its own right, visited in the early 1900s by the growing affluent class who cruised the bay by steamer or yacht — and by painters, most notably members of the Group of Seven, whose admiration for Killarney's landscape gave rise to a stunning body of artistic work. Without road or rail access, however, Killarney remained too remote for the general populace. That changed in 1961, the year Hwy 637 opened, giving Killarney residents easy access to the province's expanding network of roads and, in the other direction, presenting southern Ontarians with a superb opportunity for ecotourism. Killarney Provincial Park, established in 1964, was a further draw for outdoor enthusiasts, who came in growing numbers to hike the park's trails and paddle its clear turquoise lakes. Cottages sprang up along the shoreline outside the park, together with hotels, restaurants, marinas and supply shops, to cater to the influx of visitors. On a sunny summer day, Killarney now bustles with activity, and Killarney Channel is as busy with cruising tourists as it once was with fur-laden canoes, logging barges and fishing tugs.

Distance: **7 km loop hike, 100-500 m access paddle each way**

Access

- Drive to the end of Hwy 637 in Killarney.
- Until recently, access to the George Island Trail has been from the Sportsman's Inn, directly across Killarney Channel from the trailhead. The inn accepted a small fee for permission to launch a canoe or kayak from its dock. For people without a boat of their own, the inn operated a ferry shuttle service across the channel. As this book goes to press, however, the future of this venerable inn — built in 1903 but failing both financially and structurally a century later — is sadly uncertain.
- If access is not possible at the inn, you may launch from one of the other marinas along Channel Street or from the public dock at the end of Hwy 637.
- Parking is available behind St. Bonaventure Church, entering from Commissioner Street. Leave your donation in the box behind the church.

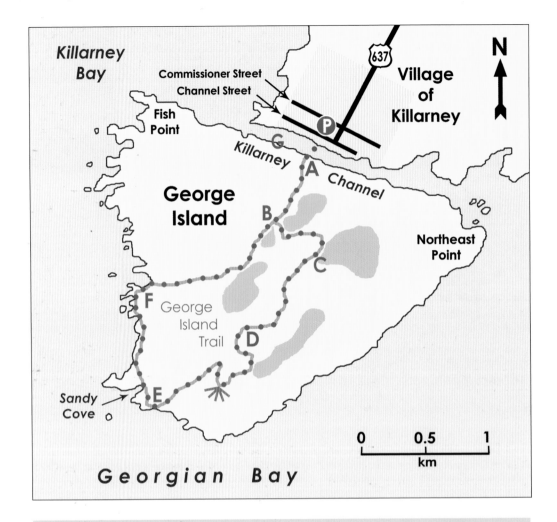

Route Description

1st Segment: Across Killarney Channel (100-500 m paddle, depending on launch site)

Paddle from your launch site across Killarney Channel to the tiny beach **A** opposite the Sportsman's Inn, and pull your canoe or kayak ashore.

2nd Segment: Trailhead to Trail Junction (0.5 km hike)

Climb the bluff behind the beach. At the top an overgrown lawn and a crumbling chimney mark the location of a former cottage — and the start of the George Island Trail (red plastic arrows nailed to trees and red painted arrows on the rocks will guide you clearly along the route). Follow the trail inland as it winds through a mixed woodland to a junction **B**. Take the left-hand fork towards the beaver pond; you will return along the other branch.

Overlooking one of George Island's beaver ponds.

3rd Segment: Trail Junction to Western Shore (3.2 km hike)

The trail skirts the corner of the pond on an old beaver dam, its sticks now cemented with mud and grass into a solid walkway. On the other side, a large rock gives a pleasant view across the beavers' territory. This is the first of several ponds and marshlands you will see along the trail. Beavers are active in some, their dams and lodges fortified with recently chewed branches. Others have been abandoned and are becoming overgrown with marsh grasses. The marshlands will turn into "beaver meadows" and gradually accumulate enough organic material to form soil in which saplings can take root and begin to grow into trees. When there are enough trees to support a beaver population, the beavers will return to build their dams and drown the forest again. So, in cyclical fashion, "succession" unfolds in the wetlands.

Between the beaver ponds, the trail crosses the red rock of the Killarney batholith, scoured and polished smooth by glaciers. Some of the granite outcrops are as flat as tabletops; others erupt as knobby hills from the landscape. Much of the rock is bare, though if you look closely, you will see that lichens are slowly claiming the surface and pines are penetrating the cracks. All three native species of pine — white, red and Jack — are represented on George Island. The straggly Jack pines are found on the more southerly outcrops of granite, while red and white pines are scattered liberally along the route, producing needle-strewn woodlands where the trail is pleasantly soft underfoot.

About 400 m past the first beaver pond, the trail skirts a second pond and passes among charred stumps **C** where fire has claimed some of the trees. The trail then crosses a beautiful flat slab of granite, climbs over a rocky knob **D** and, after passing a third beaver pond, scrambles up a rocky crevice. At the top, on a clear day, a veritable smorgasbord of islands lies before you. Badgeley Island can be seen (and maybe heard!) immediately to the west, across Killarney Bay. Manitoulin Island stretches its impressive bulk down the western horizon. Towards the south and east are scattered smaller islands — The Foxes, the Hawk Islands, Green, Papoose — and the isolated outpost of Squaw Island, which, like Killarney, was once one of the bay's busiest fishing stations. You may even imagine that you can see the cliffs of the Bruce Peninsula on the southern horizon, but they are almost 80 km away.

Turning sharply back from the lookout, the trail makes its way down the hill, across a jumble of fallen rock where the footing is very uneven. After 750 m it emerges onto the shore at the southwestern edge of George Island **E**.

4th Segment: Western Shore to Tar Vat (1.3 km hike)

The first thing you will notice upon reaching the shore is the cobble beach that extends almost 50 m inland from the water, up a series of rough terraces. This is a "raised" beach, common along all the rocky shorelines of Georgian Bay and Lake Superior. It was left behind by Lake Algonquin, a vast glacial lake that formed along the retreating edge of the Laurentide Ice Sheet about 12,000 years ago, filling the Great Lakes basin with meltwater to depths many metres greater than the present-day level of the lake. Waves crashed on the lake's beaches and battered its cobbles, just as they do today. The smooth, rounded rocks were left high and dry when the shores of Lake Algonguin receded; at the upper reaches of the beach, they are becoming encrusted with lichens.

Turn right and follow the red markers along the western side of George Island. The trail ducks across several tiny headlands, but for much of its distance, it hugs the shore, making its way over smooth slabs of granite that slope gently into the water and around small coves lined with weeds or cobbles (but not with sand, despite the name, Sandy Cove, printed on the map). You will see large, weathered logs in some of these coves — timber that strayed from the log drives many decades ago. Another reminder of yesteryear awaits in the final cove — the remains of a tar vat operation **F**, where you will find two large metal vats, wooden barrels, the partially submerged hull of an abandoned tug and smelly rocks smeared with tar. Fishermen used to bring their cotton nets here to preserve them, soaking them in hot tar and spreading them across the rocks to dry. (For more information about Killarney's fishery, see Chapter 2.) Before leaving the site, be sure to turn your binoculars west across Killarney Bay, where the silica quarry can be seen cutting into the quartzite hump of Badgeley Island.

5th Segment: Homeward (2 km hike, 100-500 m paddle)

Continue along the shore from the tar vat for 200 m. At the base of the cove, the trail climbs inland across the rocks and meanders back through the pines for 1.5 km, past two more wetlands, to the trail junction **B**. Turn left and retrace your outward route to your canoe or kayak on the beach at Killarney Channel. With all the history you have absorbed and all the scenery you have admired along the trail, you may find yourself quite exhausted — but thoroughly satisfied — by the time you reach your launch site across the channel in Killarney!

Another Way to See George Island

While the George Island Trail boasts a splendidly varied landscape and many scenic and historical highlights, its abundant wetlands bring forth a vigorous crop of biting insects each spring that might, at least between mid-May and the end of June, dampen your enthusiasm for an inland hike. An excellent alternative approach is by canoe or kayak — *if* the forecast is calm, as the island's outer shore is dangerously exposed. The 11 km circumnavigation of George Island reveals three distinct aspects, one for each side of its roughly triangular shape.

The north shore is lined with cottages and marinas, and Killarney Channel is often busy with boat traffic. A distinctive feature along this shore — one that can only be visited by boat — is the Lourdes Grotto **G**, located slightly to the west of the George Island trailhead. There you will find a shrine established by the St. Bonaventure Roman Catholic parish in 1947 and restored in 1984. It is a spiritual site where offerings are left and prayers are said to cure ailments of the body and soul.

On the island's western shore, smooth sloping rocks create many headlands and tiny islands, and the coves between them are shallow and sheltered. It is not difficult to see why the tar vat operation was located here **F**. Its big black vats are easy to spot from the water, but paddlers with a GPS may wish to aim for the site's UTM coordinates: 0458686E, 5089779N. Farther down this shore (at UTM coordinates 0458900E, 5088900N) you will find the raised cobble beach **E**.

Rounding the corner beyond the beach, you will be astonished by the change in terrain — the angular red rocks, rough cobble coves and scrubby vegetation of George Island's exposed southeastern shore. There are no safe landing places along this coast, and it is 3.5 km to the shelter of Killarney Channel around Northeast Point. In good weather, however, your journey will be rewarded with fascinating shoreline scenery and beautiful views towards the La Cloche hills on the northern horizon.

Maps, Publications & Information
- NTS map 41 H/13: Little Current.
- Nautical chart 220501: Killarney to Little Current.
- *Geology and Scenery: Killarney Provincial Park Area*, Ontario Geological Survey Guidebook No. 6, written by R. L. Debicki and published by the Ministry of Natural Resources in 1982.
- *Georgian Bay Jewel: The Killarney Story*, by Margaret E. Derry and published by Poplar Lane Press in 2007.
- Village of Killarney Tourism: (705) 287-2424, www.municipality.killarney.on.ca.
- Killarney Museum: 29 Commissioner Street, Killarney; (705) 287-2424.

CHAPTER 2

Tar Vat Trail

OVERVIEW

The village of Killarney has had many incarnations in its nearly 200 years of history. It began as a fur-trading post, and in recent decades it has blossomed as a tourist haven. But it was during the heyday of Georgian Bay's commercial fishery that Killarney enjoyed its era of greatest prosperity and growth. From the 1870s until the collapse of the fishery in the late 1950s, Killarney was one of the most productive of the bay's many fishing stations. Each year families would travel from their winter homes

(Above) One of the many glorious views along the Tar Vat Trail.

in communities on southern Georgian Bay and even from as far away as Saugeen Shores on Lake Huron to spend the summer months at Killarney. They fished for lake trout, whitefish, sturgeon and herring, and some families stayed on year-round, supplementing their income with farming, trapping and berry picking.

Gillnets were the traditional gear of the Killarney fishery. Suspended between cork or wooden floats at the surface and stone or lead sinkers at the bottom, these fine-filament nets would entangle fish by their gills when they tried to swim through the mesh. Pound nets also came into use in the early 1900s. Their design was highly efficient, funnelling fish down a leader net into a trap-like chamber where they were held, alive, until they could be harvested. Fishermen originally hauled their nets using open-decked rowboats, but as gear became increasingly sophisticated, the ships required to collect the bigger catches became sturdier and more powerful. Oars and sails gave way to tugs powered first by steam and later by diesel.

Whether the net was of the gill or pound design and whether hauled by rowboat or tugboat, the material used in the construction of Killarney's nets was — until the advent of nylon in the mid-1900s — cotton. And cotton is prone to rot. Part of a fisherman's routine, therefore, included regular visits to the local tar vats. These large basins were jacked up on rocks, filled with tar, and heated from below with wood fires until their contents liquefied. Fishing nets were soaked in the protective ooze and then spread across the rocks to dry.

The telltale whiff of tar gives away the location of these operations, even today, more than half a century after the last fire was lit under the last vat of tar. The fishery failed in Killarney, as it did all across Georgian Bay, by the end of the 1950s. The growing efficiency of fishing gear and greater numbers of people engaged in the industry had led to overfishing. To make matters worse, debris from the logging industry had polluted many spawning grounds and parasitic sea lamprey and other non-native species had invaded the Great Lakes–St. Lawrence Seaway, contributing to a severe decline in Georgian Bay's fish populations that no amount of regulation or restocking was ever able to reverse. Today Killarney's only commercial fishery is Herbert's, which runs a busy fish and chip eatery from a converted school bus at the end of Hwy 637, its cheerful red and white paintwork providing a beacon for hungry paddlers and hikers!

The smell of tar lingers, and the vats and other detritus of the tarring operation can still be found at two sites near Killarney — one on the west side of George Island (see Chapter 1) and the other along the mainland shore at Tarvat Bay. This chapter follows a popular hiking trail from the Killarney East Light to the Tarvat Bay operation and continues east along the trail to admire some of Killarney's glorious natural scenery — the red shoreline granite set against the glittering quartzite of the La Cloche hills.

Distance: **3.5 km linear hike (7 km return)**

Access
- In Killarney exit Hwy 637 east onto Ontario Street (signposted to the Killarney airfield).
- After 800 m take the right-hand fork onto a rough, one-lane road. Follow it 700 m to the Killarney East Light on Red Rock Point.
- Park on the left side of the road in the small gravel area just before the gate.

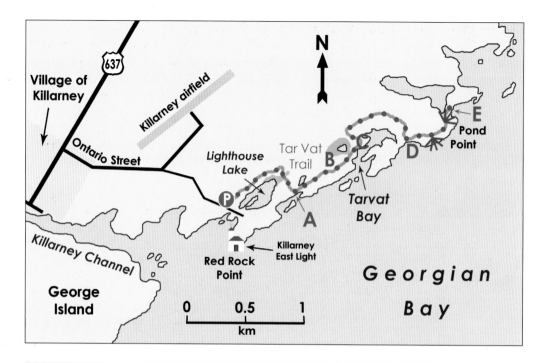

Route Description

1st Segment: Around Lighthouse Lake to Georgian Bay Shore (1 km hike)

Follow the yellow markers (plastic arrows nailed to trees and painted arrows on the rocks) that lead east from the parking area, across a damp patch to a granite ridge behind Lighthouse Lake. At the end of the lake, the trail crosses a marshland. The rickety boardwalk here may prove more of an obstacle than an aid as you slither and squelch your way across it to solid ground on the other side. The trail then climbs over a rocky headland to a granite knob at the shore of Georgian Bay **A**.

2nd Segment: Along Shore to Tar Vats (0.8 km hike)

Turn left and follow the shoreline rocks across a spillway from a tiny pond. Beyond the spillway the trail makes its way up a ridge for 300 m. It can be hard to follow over open ground, so watch for cairns and yellow paint on the rocks. The summit of the ridge **B** is an outcrop of quartz-rich rock, whose white and grey colouring stands out strikingly against the surrounding red granite. The trail descends from the ridge, through a small woodland, to the shore of Tarvat Bay. Crossing a tiny stream that empties from a beaver pond (the beaver's dam can be seen at the top of the stream), the trail climbs over another rocky headland and emerges at the site of the tar vat operation **C**. One vat is obvious at the edge of Tarvat Bay, and you will see discarded drums and crumbling pilings in the water below. A second vat is tucked behind the rocks a few metres to the northwest, at the edge of what would once have been an inlet of Tarvat Bay but now is overgrown with trees. Smears of tar blacken the rocks all along the shore, permeating the air with their odd petroleum perfume.

3rd Segment: Tarvat Bay to Georgian Bay Shore (1.7 km hike)

Many hikers turn back after visiting the tar vats, but the trail continues farther east. It passes a ledge overlooking the beaver pond and then turns inland, making its way through a mixed woodland where oaks and other deciduous trees are scattered among the pines. After 1 km the trail swings back to Georgian Bay **D**. Turn left at the shore and clamber along the ragged granite ridge that runs slightly back from the water's edge. This portion of the trail is less frequented, so you may find that some of the cairns have collapsed and the yellow arrows are more difficult to locate. But the views from the ridge into Georgian Bay amply compensate for these navigational challenges. On the other side of Pond Point, the trail comes to a rocky lookout over a series of headlands, with the La Cloche hills visible in the northeast. From there it continues 100 m down the hill to a rough cobble beach **E**. Just a few metres behind the cobbles, you will find a primitive old campsite at the edge of a tranquil pond. This makes an excellent place to stop for a picnic lunch and a rest in preparation for the return leg of your hike.

4th Segment: Homeward (3.5 km hike)

As this is a linear trail, you will have to retrace your outward route back to the car. With all the splendid views along the shores of Georgian Bay, Tarvat Bay and Lighthouse Lake and another chance to reflect on Killarney's fishing history, it is unlikely you will find the journey dull!

Killarney East Light

A short stroll from the Tar Vat Trail parking area to the end of the road brings you to the Killarney East Light. The present tower was built in 1909, replacing the original lighthouse that had graced the site since 1866. Aluminum siding was added to the structure many decades later to

Killarney East Light on Red Rock Point.

protect it from storm spray, giving the tower's exterior its modern appearance. The East Light was one of two that guided the procession of fishing boats, cargo vessels and passenger ships that once passed through Killarney Channel. The other is the Killarney West Light on Partridge Island, 1.5 km off the channel's western entrance. Killarney's lightkeepers were responsible for *both* lights, so their residence was located midway between the two in the village of Killarney itself — an unusual luxury for lightkeepers, whose occupation usually obliged them to spend months in isolation on windswept rocks out in the bay. The lights became fully automated in the early 1980s and continue to guide the many pleasure craft that use Killarney Channel today.

Maps & Information
- NTS map 41 H/14: Collins Inlet.
- Nautical chart 2204B05: Beaverstone Bay to Killarney.
- Village of Killarney Tourism: (705) 287-2424, www.municipality.killarney.on.ca.
- Killarney History: www.killarneyhistory.com.

CHAPTER 3

Chikanishing Trail

OVERVIEW

Killarney Provincial Park, the "crown jewel" of Ontario's park system, has become a magnet for outdoor enthusiasts. Every year thousands of canoeists are drawn to its inland lakes (and challenging portages!) and hikers to more than 100 km of backpacking and day-use trails. The park is famous for the stunning scenery and variable topography produced by its remarkable geology — the sparkling white quartzite of the La Cloche Mountains, bordered by the rich red granite of the Killarney batholith and dotted with clear turquoise lakes.

Sometimes forgotten is the wonderful terrain at Killarney's southern margin, the location of one of the park's shortest but most interesting hiking trails. The 3 km Chikanishing Trail follows the Chikanishing River downstream to Georgian Bay and continues along the shore to the Western Entrance of Collins Inlet. It winds through stands of windswept pine and across smooth outcrops of granite, pausing at sites steeped in the human history of the area. The Chikanishing River and Collins Inlet were at one time, after all, among the busiest fur-trade and log-drive corridors in all Ontario!

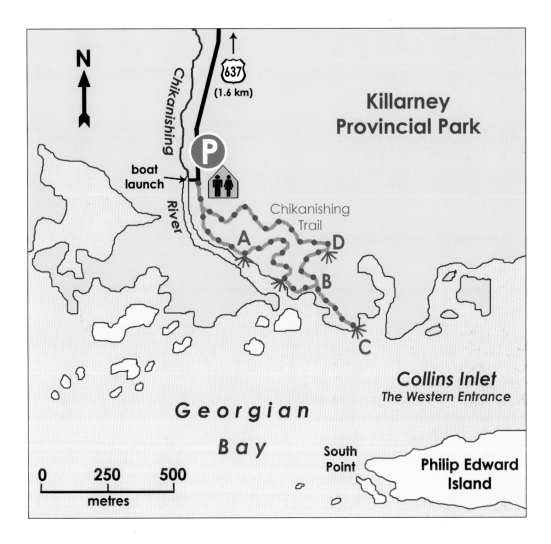

Distance: 3 km loop hike

Access

- If you are camping at Killarney Provincial Park, your campground registration gives you free access to the park's hiking trails. Otherwise, your first stop must be at the George Lake park office to buy a day-use vehicle permit.
- Drive west on Hwy 637 for 1.4 km and turn left onto the Chikanishing Road.
- The road twists over rough terrain for 1.6 km to the Chikanishing River boat launch, where there is a large gravel parking lot and a convenient outhouse.

(Left) View across Collins Inlet from a ridge on the Chikanishing Trail.

Route Description

1st Segment: Along Chikanishing River to Lookout (0.5 km hike)

The trail begins at a large wooden sign bolted to the rocks east of the parking lot and makes its way past a series of interpretive panels that introduce hikers to various aspects of life on the Killarney shore, from early Native settlement and European exploration to present-day tourism. Red arrows — plastic ones nailed to trees and painted ones on the rocks — mark the route. Follow them across the granite outcrops above the Chikanishing River and up the hill to a lookout **A** over the mouth of the river.

2nd Segment: Chikanishing Lookout to Trail Junction (0.7 km hike)

From the lookout the trail turns inland through a wooded area, then emerges at another rocky knob with a view over the islands and shoreline beyond the Chikanishing River mouth. Continue along the trail as it curves around the edge of a small bay to a trail junction **B**. The bay was once filled with water, but it is now becoming overgrown with grasses and shrubs. A few large, weathered logs can be seen here — fugitives from log drives more than half a century ago. Rusting rings on the shore of the nearby islands are other reminders of that time. Each spring in those days would bring a flood of pine timber, cut during the winter around George Lake and other lakes upstream, surging with the meltwater down the Chikanishing River. The logs were then corralled into booms tethered to the shore until they could be towed to lumber mills.

3rd Segment: Trail Junction to Collins Inlet Shore (0.3 km hike)

Turn right and follow the boardwalk and bridge across the bay to a granite headland on the other side. Another 100 m brings you to the water's edge **C** at Collins Inlet, a narrow channel that runs for 20 km straight along a geological fault separating Philip Edward Island from the mainland. For Native paddlers and for voyageurs of the fur trade, the channel provided a sheltered alternative to the exposed and shoal-strewn Georgian Bay shore on Philip Edward Island's south side. In fact, these travellers sometimes journeyed even farther inland, choosing (remarkably!) to paddle and portage up the Chikanishing River and across the quartzite hills of the La Cloche range in order to avoid the wave-battered western headlands between Killarney, Frazer and McGregor bays.

A century later Collins Inlet became a highway for the booms of logs destined for the mill village of the same name, 16 km east of Chikanishing. The mill operated from 1868 until its buildings were destroyed by fire in 1917. By then timber resources in the area had been depleted to such an extent that the mill owners sold the timber rights and land rather than incur the expense of rebuilding. The village was abandoned. Small-time local logging continued until the 1940s, the timber rafted into booms and towed all the way to mills in Midland at the southern end of Georgian Bay.

Fortunately, sufficient time has now elapsed for the pines to re-establish themselves here, providing a picturesque backdrop for the ribbon of quartz that cuts across the red granite of the shoreline rocks.

4th Segment: Collins Inlet Shore to Collins Inlet Lookout (0.5 km hike)

Retrace your route from the shore, back across the bridge to the trail junction, and follow the trail straight ahead. This takes you along a boardwalk and then up a bare ridge of rock **D** overlooking Collins Inlet's Western Entrance and South Point on Philip Edward Island. The birchbark canoes of Native travellers and the *canots de maître* of the voyageur brigades that once traversed the inlet have been replaced by motorboats that buzz back and forth to fishing camps and cabins and by the high-tech canoes and kayaks of modern explorers like ourselves.

5th Segment: Homeward (1 km hike)

From the open rock, the trail runs down the hill into shady woods where the terrain is softer underfoot and where boardwalks over the marshy sections keep your feet dry. After 500 m the trail completes its loop back to the trailhead sign beside the parking lot.

Maps & Information

- Killarney Provincial Park map at a scale of 1:50,000, published by the Friends of Killarney Park, is widely available from outdoor stores across the province and from The Outpost store at the George Lake park office.
- NTS map 41 H/14: Collins Inlet.
- Nautical chart 2204B05: Beaverstone Bay to Killarney.
- Killarney Provincial Park: (705) 287-2900, www.ontarioparks.com.
- Friends of Killarney Park: (705) 287-2800, www.friendsofkillarneypark.ca.

Quartz slashes across the granite at the midpoint of the Chikanishing Trail.

CHAPTER 4

Collins Inlet, Philip Edward Island and The Foxes

OVERVIEW

Collins Inlet slices through the Killarney landscape, creating an almost perfectly straight, 20 km long, east-west channel. Emptying directly into Georgian Bay at the inlet's western end, near the mouth of the Chikanishing River, and into Beaverstone Bay at its eastern end, the channel has provided safe passage for many centuries of travellers. Native paddlers with their birchbark canoes, voyageurs in the fur trade and then lumbermen during the log drives, freighters and passenger vessels on the Georgian Bay coastal run, and today's tourists in their pleasure boats have all welcomed the shelter of the inlet over the exposed waters of the open bay.

To the south of Collins Inlet lies a large, triangular wedge of rock called Philip Edward Island and, farther offshore, a collection of smaller islands with evocative names like Scarecrow Island, Mocking Bird Island, The Foxes and the Hawk Islands. The ancient humps of rock that make them up are worn smooth and streaked with bands of pink and red and grey. They are part of a large chunk of gneiss that formed at the leading edge of the Grenville Province when it slammed into Killarney about 1.5 billion years ago. Except, that is, for Green Island at the southern edge of the archipelago — an anomalous block of limestone that is a billion years younger.

The remoteness of this area has kept it largely undeveloped. Some logging roads criss-cross the mainland interior, and Hwy 637 cuts through the landscape farther north, but the only access to the coast is by water, either from the village of Killarney or from the Chikanishing River in Killarney Provincial Park (or, many kilometres to the east, from the French and Key rivers). A few cottages and fishing camps are scattered along the shore, most of them nestled in the shelter of Collins Inlet and Beaverstone Bay. Otherwise the land is gloriously wild.

It is, in fact, a paddler's paradise. Whether simply a day paddle at the Western Entrance to Collins Inlet, a longer journey among the offshore islands or a full circumnavigation of Philip Edward Island, the opportunities for canoeing and kayaking here are exceptional. The gently hilly terrain, which has large areas of open rock, offers possibilities for hiking too. On many of the islands, you may pull your boat ashore and poke along the coastline for hours on foot or climb to a barren hilltop to admire the view — always a dazzling panorama that includes either the broad expanse of Georgian Bay or the sparkling hills of Killarney's La Cloche range, often *both*.

(Left) Hilltop view from Solomons Island.

Log booms were tethered to large iron rings at the mouth of the Chikanishing River.

Only a small proportion of the land is privately owned — some scattered cottage properties that are easily identified by their buildings, and the land on the eastern shore of Beaverstone Bay, which forms part of the Point Grondine Indian Reserve. The status of the remaining land is in transition. Negotiations that began during the 1990s under Ontario's Living Legacy Land Use Strategy and culminated in the 2006 Provincial Parks and Conservation Reserves Act have attempted to reconcile the widely divergent interests of forestry and mining companies, government and environmental agencies, local residents and visiting tourists. Increased protection has been promised for the area's wild spaces, and Killarney Provincial Park has been slated for significant expansion — by as much as 50% — to include many of the islands and coastal waters between Killarney and the French River. The precise boundaries have yet to be determined, however, and designated campsites and fees have not been established. As this book goes to press, most of the land on Philip Edward Island and the other offshore islands remains Crown land, where Canadian residents may camp free of charge and visitors from abroad may camp with a permit purchased from the local office of the Ontario Ministry of Natural Resources, in Sudbury. This will likely change in years to come, so be sure to check at the Killarney Provincial Park Office at George Lake for current regulations.

Your exploration of the shoreline and islands will begin at the Chikanishing River access point, but beyond the mouth of the river, your route should be determined by the weather, by your paddling skills and by the amount of time available. Rather than describe a particular route in step-by-step detail, therefore, this chapter lists four possibilities ranging from 10 km in length to 55+ km. It also pinpoints sites of natural interest and historical significance (labelled **A** to **R** on the accompanying maps) that you may wish to incorporate into your route planning. Be sure to use the most detailed, up-to-date maps available (marine charts are usually best), but don't panic if they fail to match reality when you get there, as shrinking water levels in Georgian Bay have altered the shoreline greatly in some places.

The islands and headlands on the Georgian Bay side of Philip Edward Island provide many beautiful sites where you may pitch your tent for the night. Campsites are harder to find (and generally less attractive) on the Beaverstone Bay and Collins Inlet sides, where the terrain is rougher and there is more privately owned land. Killarney Provincial Park offers two designated campsites on the north shore of Collins Inlet towards the Western Entrance; a permit is required to use them. Wherever you camp during your travels, bear in mind the exposed nature of many of these sites and the fragility of their environments, and practice responsible, low-impact camping to ensure their continued viability. To avoid their overuse, specific campsites have not been recommended in this chapter, and only the park's two designated campsites are shown on the map.

Distance: 10-20 km, 20-30 km, 35-45 km or 55+ km paddle

Access

- Stop by the George Lake office at Killarney Provincial Park to buy a vehicle parking permit for the planned duration of your trip.
- Drive west on Hwy 637 for 1.4 km and turn left onto the Chikanishing Road.
- Follow the road, which twists for 1.6 km beside the Chikanishing River, to a large parking lot and boat launch at the end.

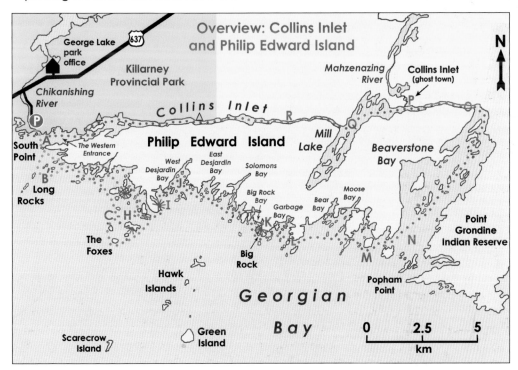

Route Description

SHORT: Collins Inlet's Western Entrance and Philip Edward Island's South Point (see Western Area map)

- Distance: 10–20 km paddle
- Minimum time: day trip
- Route on map: orange dots
- Features of interest: A-B
- Extensions: east into the mouth of Collins Inlet, west among the islands between the Long Rocks and the mainland

MEDIUM: Philip Edward Island's Southwest Shore to The Foxes (see Western Area map)

- Distance: 20–30 km paddle
- Minimum time: 3–5 days
- Route on map: orange dots plus green dots
- Features of interest: A-H
- Extensions: east into West Desjardin Bay (I-J), southeast to the Hawk Islands and Green Island

LONGER: Philip Edward Island's Southwest Shore to Big Rock (see Overview map)

- Distance: 35–45 km paddle
- Minimum time: 4–6 days
- Route on map: orange/green dots plus purple dots
- Features of interest: A-K
- Extensions: east towards Beaverstone Bay (L-M)

LONGEST: Circumnavigation of Philip Edward Island (see Overview map)

- Distance: 55+ km
- Minimum time: 7–10 days
- Route on map: orange/green/purple dots plus red dots
- Features of interest: A-R

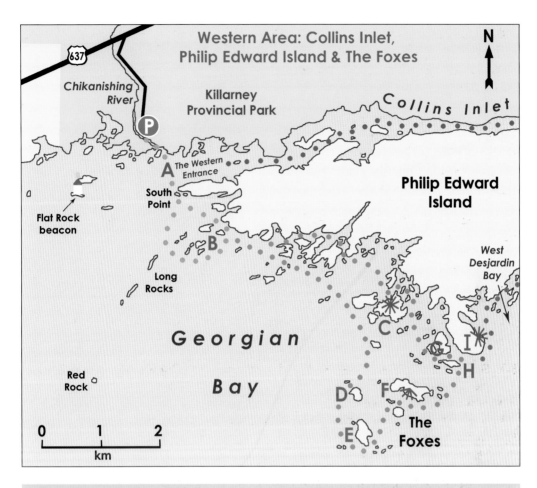

Features of Interest

A Chikanishing River and Collins Inlet's Western Entrance

Paddling lazily on these waterways on a sunny summer's day, you may find it difficult to envision their importance to travellers in centuries past. Eighteenth-century fur traders preferred Collins Inlet to the treacherous waters of the open bay, sometimes even choosing to paddle and portage their enormous canoes and heavy cargoes up the Chikanishing River and across the La Cloche Mountains rather than risk the wind and waves along the exposed headlands to the west. A century later, loggers used the Chikanishing River to drive logs down from the Killarney highlands each spring, gathering them into booms at the river mouth, where they were tethered to the shore by iron rings and spikes driven into the rocks. Collins Inlet became a highway for these booms, which were towed either to the sawmill town of Collins Inlet, 16 km to the east (see P for details), or across Georgian Bay to larger mills in the south. You will still find iron rings and spikes along the shore; one conspicuous ring can be seen on the southeast side of the island at the mouth of the Chikanishing River.

B South Point and Nearby Islands

The landscape at the western tip of Philip Edward Island (with the geographically confusing name South Point) is characterized by low-lying topography and many bare outcrops of smooth pink rock. This is gneiss (pronounced "nice"), which forms when extreme pressure is applied to existing rocks, typically during collisions between large blocks of the Earth's crust. Compression causes the component minerals in the rocks to realign into parallel bands with alternating stripes of granular material (commonly quartz or feldspar) and mica. When the Grenville Province collided with Killarney almost 1.5 billion years ago, two types of gneiss were created by the impact: *ortho*gneiss (in bands of pink and red) from Killarney's red granite, and *para*gneiss (in pink and grey) from the sedimentary rocks that had been on the sea floor in front of the Grenville Province. Orthogneiss, like the granite from which it came, is a durable rock. So, when glaciers scoured the landscape in more recent millennia, ridges of orthogneiss were left behind, becoming Philip Edward Island's prominent headlands and the many offshore islands and shoals. The sedimentary-based paragneiss eroded more deeply to form depressions, many of which are now filled with water — Beaverstone Bay, West Desjardin Bay, Mill Lake and the Mahzenazing River. The boundaries between the two gneisses are not always precise, and you will find examples of both types of rock on South Point and the nearby islands, their twisted, multicoloured ribbons polished by waves and ice.

C Solomons Island

Solomons Island, with its open rock and sparse vegetation, is an excellent place to pull ashore and explore the landscape on foot. A bare hill on the island's north side gives stunning views in all directions. You may also notice a wind-torn flag and a rustic cabin on the island across the channel to the north — a fragment of human presence in an otherwise wild landscape.

D Unnamed Fox Island

This small, nameless island at the western edge of The Foxes island group has been exquisitely sculpted by water and ice. You must leave your canoe or kayak and follow the shoreline on foot to appreciate the island's artistry. Pools have been carved into the smooth rock and rivulets etched across its surface. The pink and red gneiss is fringed with lichens in exuberant shades of orange and green. And enormous angular blocks perch incongruously among the rounded cobbles on the beaches. The island is a study in form, colour and texture, worthy of a Group of Seven painting!

E West Fox Island

The varied topography of West Fox Island also deserves exploration on foot. The smooth, bare rocks along its northeastern shore contrast interestingly with the jagged terrain on the south side of the island and with the "beach" on its western shore, where you will find some unexpected chunks of limestone and fossils among the granite and gneiss. Water has shaped a series of fascinating pools in the steep rock face that rises from a narrow cove on the island's east side.

The stunning landscape of Philip Edward Island, framed by Killarney's La Cloche Mountains.

F Martins Island and Neighbouring Shoals

Martins Island is the largest of The Foxes. From the cove on the island's southern shore, you can climb to a bare knoll with views towards Scarecrow, Green and the Hawk islands. Closer at hand, just 125 m off Martins Island's southwestern tip, lies a small cluster of barren rocks carved with impressive channels — more evidence of the erosive power of waves and ice.

G Lowe Island

Lowe Island and the small neighbouring island to its west are privately owned, with modest cottages along the channel between them — a channel that is gradually becoming unnavigable as the water level decreases in Georgian Bay.

H East Fox Island

East Fox Island is one of the smallest in The Foxes island group. Its eastern shore is particularly lovely, with bare rock outcrops sloping smoothly into the water and surfacing, or almost surfacing, as shoals just offshore.

I Used-to-be Island

Perhaps some far-sighted cartographer intentionally left the large island on the map just above East Fox Island nameless, or perhaps the omission was accidental. In either case,

Timbers stand like rows of jagged teeth at the mouth of the Mahzenazing River, once the site of the busy sawmill town of Collins Inlet.

falling water levels and accumulated sediment have closed the channel marked on the map and created an isthmus that now solidly connects the island to the south shore of Philip Edward Island. If you pull your canoe or kayak ashore at what used to be the northeastern corner of the island and scramble up the hill, your efforts will be rewarded with panoramic views to the east and north. From this perspective it is easy to see the difference between Green Island (the appropriately named, heavily treed island in the south) and the other islands in this archipelago. The reason for the difference lies in the nature of Green Island's limestone rocks — their alkaline chemistry and relative softness are better able to support vegetation than the dense, acidic gneisses of the other islands.

J Desjardin Bay

As you paddle across West Desjardin Bay to East Desjardin Bay, Solomons Bay and Big Rock Bay, you will wish you had spent more time scouting the water from the vantage point of the hill on Used-to-be Island. These bays are thick with shoals and tiny islands. Though it is only 4.5 km (as the crow flies) to Big Rock, the journey, weaving through the labyrinth, may take several hours. If the day is blustery, however, you will appreciate the shoals for the excellent shelter they provide when wind and waves would prevent venturing out into the open water of Georgian Bay.

K Big Rock

The shelter of the shoals is interrupted by Big Rock, a large hump of land that juts south into Georgian Bay. Rough conditions are common around this headland, and a 400 m portage provides an alternative passage for paddlers who cannot bear the prospect of a peaceful windbound day spent on shore. For the rest of us, the headland has several tiny coves that provide sheltered anchorages for our boats while we scramble up the hill to admire the view from the Big Rock summit.

L Bateman Island and Hamilton Island

The shoals return on the other side of Big Rock, and your route through the intricate maze of channels in Garbage Bay is (appropriately) littered with navigational challenges. A surprising cluster of cabins on the shores between Bateman Island and Hamilton Island, and a footbridge spanning one of the channels, interrupts the feeling of wilderness.

M Hincks Island

Hincks Island marks the end of your journey along Philip Edward Island's southwestern shore and gives you a last opportunity to clamber ashore and enjoy the views across Georgian Bay's wild and wave-battered coast. Just beyond Hincks Island, a channel opens into Beaverstone Bay and the character of the landscape changes significantly.

N Beaverstone Bay

Beaverstone Bay, 8 km long and as broad as 3 km, is large enough that you will not suffer instant claustrophobia upon leaving the open water of Georgian Bay. Beaverstone Bay is sprinkled with islands — pleasant knobs of rock topped with pine trees — that provide sheltered channels for your route north. Cottages dot the islands and the eastern shore forms part of the Point Grondine Indian Reserve, so opportunities for camping are limited here. The terrain itself is more angular and fragmented, having few smooth, flat rocks upon which to pitch a tent in any case. Towards the top of Beaverstone Bay, the shorelines converge into a muddy narrows and then bend sharply left into Collins Inlet.

O Collins Inlet (the Channel)

Geographically, Collins Inlet will impress you immediately with its straight, narrow, steep-walled channel. The channel follows a fault in the bedrock, created when the landscape was jostled repeatedly by chunks of the Earth's crust piling up one after another between 1.5 billion and 1 billion years ago, welding themselves into the Grenville Province. For the next 20 km — interrupted only by Mill Lake one-third of the way down the fault — Collins Inlet slices through that landscape, one of many such fractures along Georgian Bay's northeastern shore.

After several days of open-water paddling, Collins Inlet feels oddly like an interior river. For most of its length, the banks are lined with cliffs and fallen rock, but in places where small streams feed into the inlet, deposited sediment has formed reedy flatlands. The sheltered shorelines are thickly forested, and deciduous trees grow among the cedars and pines. Scattered along the shore are cottages and fishing camps, and you may have the company of motorboats in the marine channel from time to time. Collins Inlet is, after all, the traditional east-west corridor for travellers in the area. A sense of this history may overtake you during your long paddle, and you may find that your companions become the ghosts of voyageurs and lumberjacks, and your modern canoe or kayak is accompanied by birchbark *canots de maître*, sidewheeled paddle steamers and screw-propeller tugs.

P Collins Inlet (the Ghost Town)

The ghosts are numerous at the confluence of Collins Inlet and the Mahzenazing River, about 3 km west of Beaverstone Bay. In 1868, when the area was just being opened up to logging, a small sawmill was established here to process timber cut along the Mahzenazing River. During the early 1880s, it grew under the ownership of the Midland and North Shore Lumbering Company. Then, in 1886, Toronto businessman John Bertram purchased the timber rights and mill, changing the name to the Collins Inlet Lumber Company. The facility expanded to include storage buildings, a sawdust burner (with its landmark 30 m chimney) and a large infrastructure of support services and lodgings for workers. In addition to basic processing of logs into boards, the sawmill manufactured shingles, laths and pickets for the construction industry and boxes for shipping fruit and fish. It became one of Georgian Bay's largest mills, drawing timber from the vast watershed of the Mahzenazing and Chikanishing rivers.

During the 1890s Canadian lumbermen became embroiled in a dispute with their U.S. counterparts. American logging companies were buying the timber rights to large tracts of Canadian forests and towing unprocessed sawlogs cut from those forests directly to mills in the United States. From the Americans' standpoint, this was the most economic method, as it enabled them to bypass processing costs at Canadian sawmills and avoid the substantial U.S. tariff imposed on processed timber (sawlogs could be imported duty-free). For Canadian mills the practice resulted in decreased revenue for them and reduced employment for their workers. John Bertram, who had been a Member of Parliament between 1872 and 1878, brought his political influence to bear on behalf of Canadian loggers, including his own Collins Inlet Lumber Company. In 1898 the provincial government passed legislation requiring all timber cut on Crown land to be milled in Ontario and refused to renew the annual timber leases of any American logging company that failed to comply. As a result the sawmills on Georgian Bay boomed for another 20 years. Dwindling timber resources during the 1920s and 1930s eventually led to mill closures. At Collins Inlet, however, operations ended abruptly in 1917 when the mill was destroyed by fire. Rather than incur the cost of rebuilding, its owners (Bertram having died in 1904) sold the timber rights to the Chew brothers of Midland, who rafted the logs to their sawmills at the southern end of Georgian Bay. Having lost its raison d'être, the townsite was quickly abandoned.

In 1946 the mill property was purchased for use as a private hunting and fishing camp, activities that continue at the Mahzenazing River Lodge today. Some of Collins Inlet's old buildings have been converted into cabins for guests at the lodge, but otherwise all that remains of the town and its mill is debris — rusting iron rings in the rocks, crumbling pilings from the old wharf at the mouth of the Mahzenazing River, submerged logs lurking in the depths, and rotting timbers littering the shorelines.

Q Mill Lake

Like Beaverstone Bay and many of the other bays in the area, Mill Lake is a water-filled depression created by the erosion of a band of sedimentary-based paragneiss — the same band that forms the Mahzenazing River bed. The lake is 5 km long and almost 1 km wide, and it is dotted with islands, sandy shallows and marshlands that invite exploration.

Among the cottages and fishing camps, you will find remnants of the small sawmilling operations that gave the lake its name.

R Pictograph

Collins Inlet pictograph. PHOTO BY RICK CHUCHRA

Pictographs are the picture writings that the Ojibwe and Cree painted on rocks at important sites along their travel routes. They used red ochre, a pigment made from iron oxide powder mixed with animal fat or fish oil. Pictographs are found across the Canadian Shield, typically in places of spiritual significance where the natural elements of earth, water and air converge, such as on a cliff face beside a waterway. Interpretation of the pictographs today is largely conjectural, as no written records ever existed to explain their meaning and the practice of picture writing ended more than a century ago when the spread of European culture across North America altered the customs of its Native peoples. It is believed that some pictographs relayed messages to travellers, while others commemorated special events or illustrated teachings of the manitous (revered Native spirits).

The pictograph on Collins Inlet is located on the north side of the channel, about 2.2 km west of Mill Lake, on a cliff face 2.5 m above the waterline. Badly faded after centuries of weathering, it can be difficult to find. According to scholars the painting represents a canoe with many paddlers (a common theme in picture writing). This one is unusual because it incorporates a cross into the image, suggesting that it was painted *after* Christian missionaries arrived on the shores of Georgian Bay.

Maps & Information

- Killarney Provincial Park map at a scale of 1:50,000, published by the Friends of Killarney Park, is widely available from outdoor stores across the province and from The Outpost store at the George Lake park office.
- NTS map 41 H/14: Collins Inlet.
- Nautical charts 2204B05: Beaverstone Bay to Killarney (western and central area) and 2204A03: French River to Beaverstone Bay (eastern area).
- Killarney Provincial Park: (705) 287-2900, www.ontarioparks.com.
- Friends of Killarney Park: (705) 287-2800, www.friendsofkillarneypark.ca.

RECOLLET FALLS

These treacherous falls were the scene of many hundreds of portages by missionaries going to and from the missions established in Huronia in 1615. The Recollet Fathers were the first to use the French River, the most direct waterway to the west. Though they were few in number, their work among the Amerindians and as chaplains to exploratory and military expeditions is well recorded in early Canadian history. With the capture of the colony of New France by the Kirke brothers in 1629, the Recollet Fathers were compelled to leave. Though early maps of the French River indicate the falls, in French, as "Sault," the name was changed to Recollet Falls apparently for its association with the Recollet Fathers.

Erected in 1993 by the Friends of the French River Heritage Park with the assistance of the Ontario Heritage Foundation.

CHAPTER 5

French River Hike

OVERVIEW

Perhaps you have come to this page out of curiosity, surprised that the famous French River is paired in a chapter title with hiking rather than with paddling. Or you may be wondering how a book about the Georgian Bay coast has managed to stray so far inland. The answer lies in the French River itself — in its tremendous significance as a natural waterway and as a major artery of human travel into the very heart of Canada. No book about Georgian Bay can ignore the French River. And since many excellent books have been written about the river's paddling routes, *this* book introduces the river by means of a short hike instead.

The French River begins at Lake Nipissing and runs for 111 km in a southwesterly direction, emptying into northeastern Georgian Bay. The river's course takes it along major fault lines in the ancient Canadian Shield bedrock, often flowing down two or more parallel channels and, near its outlet, dividing into four main channels and dozens of secondary ones to form a complex delta among the rocky islands. The drop in elevation from Lake Nipissing to Georgian Bay is 18 m — 1 m down for every 6 km across. Anyone who has paddled the river, however, will testify that the "downs" are more impressive than suggested by this measure, as they are concentrated in some alarming sections filled with rapids and waterfalls.

It was not always so. Some 12,000 years ago, the French River was still locked beneath the retreating Wisconsin glacier. As the ice sheet moved steadily northward and the land gradually rebounded from the immense weight, ever-more-northerly drainage outlets were revealed, and the pattern of water flow changed dramatically several times. About 6,000 years ago, a channel was uncovered roughly following the present-day French–Mattawa–Ottawa river route, and water from the Upper Great Lakes area poured through it — in an *easterly* direction — towards the Atlantic Ocean. Everything changed again about 4,000 years ago. As the northern land continued to rebound, water was redirected south into the St. Clair River and through the Lower Great Lakes to the St. Lawrence River. North Bay, the highest point of land along the French–Mattawa–Ottawa channel, became the watershed divide. Water to the east of North Bay continued to flow down the Mattawa and Ottawa rivers, but water from Lake Nipissing reversed direction and flowed, as it does today, westward down the French River to Georgian Bay.

The Shield Archaic peoples who moved into the French River area as the glacier withdrew and the early Algonkian-speaking Native people who succeeded them might have witnessed these latter changes in the landscape. Certainly the Ojibwe and Huron

(Left) Historical plaque at Recollet Falls.

The French River runs along the steep-walled channel of a geological fault.

who inhabited the Georgian Bay shore when Europeans arrived were familiar with the French River and had already developed sophisticated trading networks along it. Down the French River in 1610 came Étienne Brûlé, credited as the first European to set eyes on Georgian Bay. Brûlé was sent by the governor of New France, Samuel de Champlain, to scout routes westward and to pave the way for trade with Native residents. Champlain himself followed in 1615, and in his wake came legions of explorers, fur traders and missionaries. Indeed, the river disgorged so many French travellers that it came to be known by local Ojibwe as the French River.

During the heyday of the fur trade, when the North West Company controlled the trading route between Montreal and the Upper Great Lakes, the French River became a critical transportation link. Brigades of voyageurs, their canoes laden with European trade goods, left Montreal each spring, paddling and portaging their way up the Ottawa and Mattawa rivers, across the watershed divide into Lake Nipissing, down the French River into Georgian Bay, through the North Channel and along the northern shore of Lake Superior. In Fort William and Grand Portage at the western end of their route and at smaller trading posts along the way, they exchanged their manufactured products, cloth goods and beads for a wealth of beaver pelts. Then they retraced their route to Montreal before the autumn freeze-up. The enormous birchbark canoes they used on the large rivers and open water of the Great Lakes — the *canots de maître* — were 10 to 12 m in length with a carrying capacity of 4 or 5 tons. Crews of eight to fourteen voyageurs paddled long days at an astonishing rate of 40 to 50 strokes per minute, hauling their canoes and cargoes over 36 portages to cover 1600 km each way during a single season. By today's standards their existence was extremely harsh and their life expectancy short; but from an eighteenth-century perspective, the voyageurs enjoyed rewards and adventures not available to the common man.

Changes in European fashions and a decline in beaver populations brought an end to the fur trade within a decade or two of the North West Company's amalgamation with the Hudson's Bay Company in 1821. The French River fell silent — until 1872, that is, when the district's first lumber contract was issued. For the next half century, loggers replaced voyageurs on the river, and the annual spring log drive filled the waterway with pine trees. Downstream, mill towns sprang up along the Georgian Bay shore — like French River Village near the river's Main Outlet — and settlers established homes there. By the time dwindling timber resources forced the sawmills to close during the 1920s, tourism had taken root. At first by boat, then by rail (the Canadian Pacific and Canadian National railways extended lines across the French River in 1908) and finally by road (Hwy 69 was constructed during the early 1950s), hunters and fishermen, cottagers and outdoor adventurers were drawn north by the river's scenic beauty and its opportunities for recreation.

In recognition of the French River's historical significance in the country's development, the Canadian Heritage Rivers Board designated it a Canadian Heritage River in 1986. In 1989 provincial park status was granted by the Ontario government. In recent years management of the park has become more active and access increasingly regulated to ensure greater protection for the waterway and its shoreline. In 2006 the popular rest stop at the junction of Hwy 69 and the French River was replaced with a splendid new visitor centre.

The hike in this chapter begins at the visitor centre and then follows a short trail to Recollet Falls. The second European to make the journey down the French River (following Étienne Brûlé in 1610) was the Récollet missionary Joseph Le Caron, sent from France in 1615 to live among the Huron people of southern Georgian Bay. Other Récollet (and later Jesuit) missionaries followed Le Caron in the years that followed, many ultimately sacrificing their lives while endeavouring to deliver their faith to the New World. Recollet Falls is named in honour of these martyrs.

Distance: **1.75 km linear hike (3.5 km return)**

Access
- Take Hwy 69 towards the point where it crosses the French River, approximately 90 km north of Parry Sound and 60 km south of Sudbury.
- Turn west off the highway just south of the French River bridge, and drive up the hill to the French River Visitor Centre parking lot.

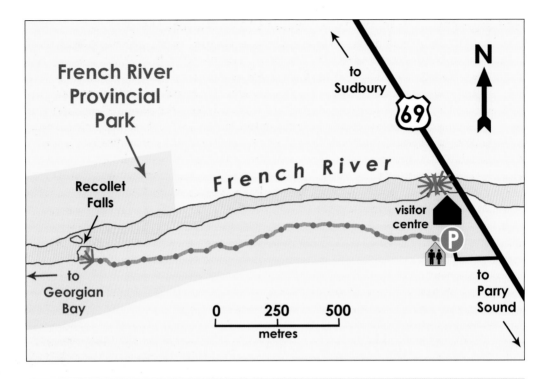

Route Description

1st Segment: Visitor Centre and French River Bridge (0.5 km hike)

Before beginning your hike, be sure to stop by the French River Visitor Centre, located on the north side of the parking lot. Its displays combine historical artifacts and modern technology to introduce visitors to the rich natural and human heritage of the French River area. The centre also serves as the French River Provincial Park office, providing information and issuing permits for backcountry travellers wishing to paddle and camp along the waterway.

After immersing yourself in French River history, walk down the hill behind the visitor centre and across the footbridge (used by snowmobiles in winter) to enjoy the views both upstream and downstream. The French River cuts a straight channel along a steep-walled gorge here. The narrowness of the channel has made it suitable for bridge construction, and you will notice two other bridges — one for Hwy 69 and one for the CPR — spanning the river within a kilometre of the footbridge you are standing on. Before they were built, the only transportation corridor was the river itself. Standing on the bridge, even today, it is not difficult to imagine flotillas of birchbark canoes passing beneath you on their way down the river to Georgian Bay.

Return to the large sign, near the entrance to the visitor centre, that marks the start of the hiking trail to Recollet Falls.

2nd Segment: Visitor Centre to Recollet Falls (1.5 km hike)

The trail heads west, running parallel to and slightly above the river channel and clearly blazed with blue plastic markers. It winds across classic Canadian Shield terrain, the woodlands dominated by pines and the billion-year-old bedrock underfoot polished smooth and fringed with lichens and moss. Occasionally you will catch glimpses of the river and its cliff walls through the trees to your right. Finally the trail emerges onto a hilltop clearing with a lovely view downstream to Recollet Falls, where the French River splits around a small island and slides over a shelf of rock on its way downstream to Georgian Bay. A short scramble brings you down the hill to a plaque honouring the Récollet missionaries and to a portage that skirts the falls. The luxurious wooden boardwalk is a far cry from the rocks and mud that would have greeted the Récollets on their missionary journeys and across which Native paddlers and French voyageurs would have lugged their heavy canoes and packs. An old iron ring in the large bare rock beside the waterfall recalls the river's logging history. This makes a lovely site to enjoy a picnic lunch, or at least a moment's contemplation, before the return journey.

3rd Segment: Homeward (1.5 km hike)

As this is a linear trail, you must return via the outward route.

Maps & Information
- NTS map 41 I/2: Delamere.
- An excellent park map, produced by the Friends of the French River Heritage Park and published by Ontario Parks, is widely available at outdoor stores, local marinas and at the park visitor centre.
- French River Provincial Park: (705) 857-1630, www.ontarioparks.com.

The French River Visitor Centre combines historical artifacts and modern technology to introduce visitors to the rich heritage of the French River.

CHAPTER 6

French River Delta and the Bustards

French River Provincial Park was established in 1989 to protect the river's significant natural and cultural heritage. Classified as a waterway park, it encompasses the French River itself and many of the river's tributaries. The park also includes a large area of adjacent shoreline and the vast delta of channels, shoals and islands at the mouth of the river. Dead Island, a former Native burial ground near the mouth of the Pickerel River, has come under the park's jurisdiction, as have the offshore Bustard Islands, once the site of one of Georgian Bay's busiest fishing stations and still home to one of the bay's most picturesque lighthouses. Scattered throughout the parkland are private cottages, commercial marinas and lodges, and significant tracts of Indian reserve land.

Growing public enthusiasm for outdoor activities in recent decades has increased the stress on the French River's fragile environment. Management of the park, therefore, has had to become more active and access better regulated to protect the river and its shorelines adequately. Beginning in 2004, designated campsites (numbered but largely undeveloped) were established at appropriate sites and permits and fees for camping were instituted.

When outdoor enthusiasts contemplate a holiday in the French River Provincial Park, they typically think of a river trip with portages and rapids, accessed from an upstream marina at Hartley Bay, Wolseley Bay or Dokis Bay. Often forgotten are the tremendous opportunities for flatwater paddling (though "flat" is a relative term when applied to the open water of Georgian Bay!) in the French River delta and offshore islands. This book, in keeping with its focus on coastal Georgian Bay and its portage-free promise, approaches the French River delta from an unconventional direction — the Key River.

The Key River runs (slowly enough not to be a problem) 14 km from Hwy 69 to the cottage community of Key Harbour, formerly an industrial port, at the northeastern corner of Georgian Bay. The boundary of the French River Provincial Park and also its first campsites lie about 5 km due west. This means, of course, that any trip in the French River delta begins and ends with a paddle of at least 19 km, and requires a minimum of three to four days of backcountry travel.

From Key Harbour your exact route among the islands and channels will depend on wind and waves, on your own preferences and on the amount of time available. The possibilities are overwhelmingly numerous. Rather than describe a particular route in step-by-step detail, therefore, this chapter gives four general route suggestions ranging from 50 km long to 100+ km, which are illustrated on the French River Delta Overview map. The Overview map also shows the area's main navigation channels and pinpoints sites of natural interest and historical significance (labelled A to K) that you may wish to incorporate into your route planning. You will find descriptions of these sites and detailed maps, where appropriate, in the accompanying text.

It is worth emphasizing here (at the risk of stating the blindingly obvious) that solid paddling and navigation skills — together with good judgement and a lively sense of humour — are essential prerequisites for a canoeing or kayaking holiday in such a remote corner of Georgian Bay. A reliable weather radio is an invaluable companion, and an accurate map will become your lifeline. If you lack navigational confidence, then stick close to the marked boating channels and follow your progress closely on the relevant marine chart. Marine charts generally contain the most detailed and up-to-date information, but even they may lead you astray in the French River delta, where fluctuating water levels seem regularly to block channel entrances, turn islands into peninsulas and introduce unexpected shoals on your horizon. With these cautionary admonitions in mind, however, you are certain to enjoy the most exhilarating of paddling holidays here!

Distance: **50 km, 65-75 km, 75-85 km or 100+ km paddle**

(Above left) The Bustard Islands light station is a picturesque trio of towers perched on a windswept rock about 5 km from the mouth of the French River.

Access

- Buy your French River Provincial Park permit from the French River Visitor Centre or one of the many local businesses that supply them.
- Exit Hwy 69 at the Key River, approximately 75 km north of Parry Sound and 75 km south of Sudbury.
- Parking and launch facilities are available for a modest fee at the marinas here, the largest being the Key Marine Resort. For information call (705) 383-2308 or visit www.keymarine.com.

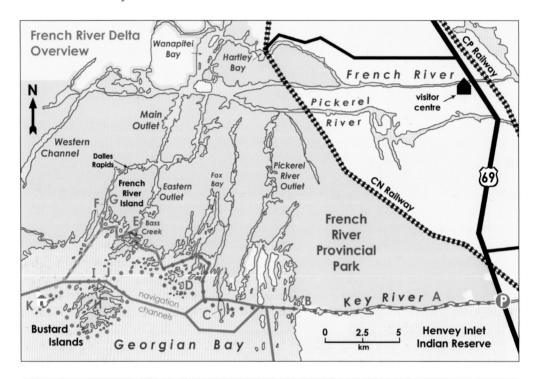

Route Description

SHORT LOOP: Key River to Dead Island and Outer Foxes

- Distance: 50 km paddle
- Minimum time: 3–4 days
- Route on Overview map: red dots
- Features of interest: A-D

MEDIUM LOOP 1: Key River to French River Main Channel and French River Village

- Distance: 65–75 km paddle
- Minimum time: 4–5 days
- Route on Overview map: red dots plus green dots
- Features of interest: **A-G**

MEDIUM LOOP 2: Key River to Bustards

- Distance: 75–85 km
- Minimum time: 5–6 days
- Route on Overview map: red dots plus purple dots
- Features of interest: **A-D** and **H-K**

LONG LOOP: Key River Through French River Delta to Bustards

- Distance: 100+ km
- Minimum time: 7–10 days
- Route on Overview map: red/green/purple dots plus connecting orange dots
- Features of interest: **A-K**

Features of Interest

A Key River

While it may lack the historical significance of its celebrated cousin to the north, the Key River merits our appreciation, not merely for its portage-free access to Georgian Bay, but also for its beautiful rocky scenery. Like the French River, the Key River formed along a geological fault that created a remarkably straight, east-west channel cutting 16 km through the underlying bedrock. As you paddle down the channel towards Georgian Bay, you will enjoy a great variety of landscapes. Some sections of the river run through steep-walled gorges where white pines and cedars enjoy a sun-drenched but rather precarious existence on tiny rock ledges. And you may find turkey vultures eyeing your progress hungrily from clifftop perches. In other sections glacial ice has rounded and polished the shoreline rocks smooth, and Jack pines have taken root — in *what*, though, it is often difficult to tell. There are even a few flat sections of the river where sand and reeds are encroaching on the channel, typically where sediment has been deposited at the mouths of small feeder streams. The right-hand shore, except for small patches of private cottage property, is part of the French River Provincial Park; most of the left-hand shore belongs to the Henvey Inlet First Nation. Near its mouth the Key River widens, and cottages pop up thickly on both sides of the channel. If you are making this journey during the height of the summer season, jostled for 14 km by motorboat wake, you will have had your fill of the river by now.

B Key Harbour

Even today, more than 50 years after the last commercial shipment pulled out of port, the cribbing that remains from the Key Harbour dock makes you realize what an impressive

At Key Harbour modern cottages mingle with the ruins of a century-old port.

structure it once was. More than 350 m in length and wide enough to support three train tracks, the dock was used by the Canadian National Railway to off-load coal destined for the northern supply depots that fuelled the company's steam-powered locomotives.

Before its incarnation as a coal port, Key Harbour was, for a brief period from 1908 until 1918, a shipping centre for iron ore. The story begins with the discovery in the early 1900s of a rich and easily accessible deposit of iron ore at Moose Mountain, about 50 km north of Sudbury. The Moose Mountain Mine was established to extract the ore, but then the ore had to be processed and shipped to markets, mainly in the United States. The harbour at the mouth of the Key River was close to Sudbury and deep enough for Great Lakes freighters, so it was deemed the best site for a smelter and port facility.

In 1905 the Moose Mountain Mine entered into an agreement with William Mackenzie and Donald Mann, owners of the Canadian Northern Ontario Railway, that gave the CNO exclusive rights to transport the ore. In return, the railway agreed to construct a 12 km spur track connecting the new port to the main line at Key Junction and to invest heavily in the smelting and shipping infrastructure. Mackenzie and Mann acquired the land around the Key River mouth and along the spur line from the Henvey Inlet Indian Reserve. The track was laid during the summer of 1907 and the harbour was dredged.

The following year saw construction of the docks, storage hoppers, a vast conveyor system and an electrical powerhouse, together with lodgings and a supply store for employees. The smelter, however, was never built, as it turned out to be more economical to ship the iron ore directly to smelting furnaces in the United States than to ship coal from the United States in sufficient quantities to supply a smelter in Key Harbour.

By 1916, Key Harbour was having trouble accommodating the new, larger breed of Great Lakes iron ore freighter whose turning radius exceeded the harbour's capacity. So, when the newly formed Canadian National Railway took over the ailing CNO in 1918, the ore shipping business was transferred to the more substantial facility 80 km to the south at Depot Harbour, and Key Harbour was used instead for off-loading CNR coal.

Key Harbour's port and the spur line to Key Junction also served the local fishery, which shipped its catches by rail to markets in the south. Even passengers frequented the line. Indeed, resident entrepreneur Arthur Gropp developed an ingenious transportation system by attaching a 1907 Ford Model T engine to a small open flatbed car of the sort normally used to move railway ties and equipment along the track. Gropp's first machine was a primitive, single-car affair for his own needs, but the idea became so popular that he developed more sophisticated versions of the "jitney train" that hauled several cars behind a converted automobile (the train was named after the jitney, a small motorized vehicle that carried people from place to place for a modest fee — the original taxi). Gropp built a thriving business around his invention, which came to be called the Toonerville Trolley by Key Harbour passengers who had to brave wind, rain, mosquitoes and other wildlife during the 12 km trek up and down the line. In 1932 Gropp married the Key Junction postmistress, moved to Moon River and bought a sawmill. His jitney train service continued to operate for more than two decades afterwards, under the ownership of the Gauthier fishery, which hired men to run it for the transport of fish and passengers.

The gradual conversion of CNR locomotives to diesel power made the coal port at Key Harbour obsolete by the end of the 1940s. With the extension of Hwy 69 north during the early 1950s, fishermen were able to send their catches more efficiently by refrigerated trucks from Britt than by jitney service from Key Harbour. In the absence of viable commercial activity at Key Harbour, the community soon folded. The spur rail line was abandoned in 1958, and the tracks taken up soon afterwards.

Key Harbour's modern incarnation, like that of so many former industrial towns on Georgian Bay, is as a summer cottage community with fishing lodges and marine services. The old powerhouse still presides over the river mouth, and the massive timber-and-stone pilings from the CNR's coal docks jut far out into the harbour. There are other scattered remains on shore — lumps of coal, rusting bits of metal and the century-old railbed, now overgrown.

C Dead Island

The story of Dead Island may be entirely apocryphal. Or it may be an unsubstantiated but essentially true account passed down through several generations of storytellers. In either case it is a sad story that undoubtedly has happened somewhere at some time and is therefore worthy of recounting here and reflecting upon as you paddle west to the island from Key Harbour.

In keeping with Native custom, local Ojibwe brought their deceased for "burial" at the sacred site on Dead Island. Cloaked in fur or wrapped in birchbark with a few of their personal effects, the bodies were placed either in trees or under piles of rocks to shield them from roving animals.

Meanwhile, in Chicago during the late 1880s, plans were afoot to host a World Exposition to honour the 400th anniversary of the "discovery" of America by Christopher Columbus. World Expositions had become common during the latter part of the nineteenth century; more than 50 were held between 1850 and 1890, each host city bent on outdoing its predecessor. Philadelphia had put on a successful American Centennial Exposition in 1876, and when the U.S. Congress selected Chicago as the site for the 1893 Columbian Exposition, local businesses pledged more than $5 million towards the event. As it turned out, the total cost of Chicago's Exposition was more than five times that amount, but the fair became touted as the greatest ever held. Dozens of countries participated and attendance exceeded 27 million; 200 state-of-the-art buildings were constructed and an area of more than 600 acres was given over to the display of new and fascinating things — including, it seems, a sideshow containing artifacts and the mummified remains of several North American Indians.

The burial grounds on Dead Island were found empty that year. Although it could never be proved, Georgian Bay's Ojibwe were certain that their sacred island had been plundered and the remains of their loved ones stolen to satisfy the curiosity of fairgoers in Chicago. The bodies disappeared when the Exposition closed in October — rubbish no longer needed.

Today, in a cove halfway up Dead Island's eastern shore, the map innocently shows a picnic site. It is, indeed, an excellent place to enjoy your picnic lunch — *if*, that is, you don't mind sharing it with ghosts!

D Outer Fox Islands

There are no grave secrets on the Outer Fox Islands nor any rusting relics from the past (at least none that we're aware of!). The Outer Fox Islands are noteworthy in this chapter simply by virtue of their windswept natural beauty. Scattered across the mouth of Fox Bay, this small archipelago — the Outer Fox Islands, together with the expressively named Shirt Tails to the south and the nameless islands to the west — is a collection of almost barren rocks and wave-battered shoals. As you paddle through the maze of tiny channels between them, you will notice that some are smooth and rounded and polished like giant cobbles while others are flat slabs of rough-textured rock; some are dominated by pines while others contain a scruffier mix of cedars and shrubs. It is a fascinating pattern, repeated all along Georgian Bay's northeastern coast. Whatever the geological nuances that produced them, the environment of all these islands is fragile, with scant soil and severe buffeting from wind and waves. The only buildings you will find here are the cheerfully painted cabins of a fishing camp on a few privately owned islands at the western end of the archipelago. The other islands fall within the French River Provincial Park and are preserved in their natural state. No designated campsites have been established on the Outer Foxes, but many excellent sites can be found on the sheltered islands in Fox Bay, slightly to the north, and one of them will make a good base for your exploration of the area.

The Bass Creek tramway.

E Bass Creek Tramway (see French River Mouth map)

The smooth boardwalk of tightly spaced planks is considerably more luxurious than a hiker might expect from the P240 (240 m portage) indicated on the French River Provincial Park map. Known as the Bass Creek Tramway, this boardwalk bypasses the rocks and rapids at the lower end of the French River's Eastern Outlet between Bass Lake and Georgian Bay. Used today by paddlers and fishermen, the tramway was originally a narrow-gauge rail line. The line's tracks were fixed to timber cribbing for most of its length but loosely chained at either end where they entered the water so that they could float up and down as water levels fluctuated. The line was built in 1912 by the Pine Lake Lumber Company, which had just purchased the abandoned sawmills at French River Village and wanted to move them upstream to a new location on the Pickerel River. Subsequently the tramway was maintained by the provincial Department of Lands and Forests for transporting firefighting equipment back and forth and also used by local cottagers and fishing camps to move their boats, building materials and even their guests between the French River and Georgian Bay. Indeed, Rainbow Camp was built in the early 1920s at the top end of the tramway to allow its guests easy access to fishing in both the bay and the river.

Eventually the tramway's tracks fell into disrepair and were replaced with a wooden walkway. No longer able to use the small flatbed railcar that had run along the tracks, frequenters of the tramway became inventive and brought baggage carts, wheelbarrows and even furniture dollies to haul their loads along the portage. Although this is a portage-free book, it is worth tying your canoe or kayak to the wharf at the Georgian Bay end of the tramway and walking the 240 m to the other end to appreciate the boardwalk's construction. Although the land around Rainbow Camp is privately owned, the tramway itself is available for anyone to use.

F French River Range Lights (see French River Mouth map)

As you paddle peacefully into the mouth of the French River's Main Outlet, it may be difficult to imagine the traffic that once steamed up and down the channel here. French River Village, just a short distance upstream, was one of Georgian Bay's most productive sawmill towns. From its founding in the mid-1870s until its demise in 1910, the townsite's shore was lined with timber, stacked and waiting to be collected by the Great Lakes steamships. These ships had first to run the gauntlet of shoals and tiny islands at the mouth of the river. A quick glance at the map will tell you why, in 1875, the federal Department of Marine and Fisheries authorized construction of not one but *four* range lights there (range lights are a series of beacons that, when aligned correctly, enable a ship to navigate safely along a precise track). Two of the range lights — the French River *Outer* Range Lights — were built on the Bustard Islands. The other two — the French River *Inner* Range Lights — were built inside the river mouth, the first on Lefroy Island and the second at the end of a tiny inlet behind French River Village. The Lefroy Island light was merely a tapered wooden panel, painted white and topped with a beacon. Today's structure looks much the same, but it is made from modern materials and now sports a bright orange stripe. The original beacon behind the village was mounted on a simple wooden trellis, but in 1893 the trellis was replaced by the square tower you see today.

The French River Range Lights' first lightkeeper was a busy man indeed, as he had to keep the lanterns lit at all four lights, rowing back and forth every day between French River Village and the Bustard Rocks, 5 km offshore. Edward Borron performed the duties from 1875 until his death in 1902; his wife, Emma, continued them (with the assistance of her sons and in the face of considerable opposition from some of the local men) until 1918, when the Department of Marine and Fisheries split the job and appointed a second lightkeeper to tend the lights on the Bustard Islands. Two other lightkeepers succeeded Mrs. Borron at the Inner Range Lights until the beacons were automated in 1935.

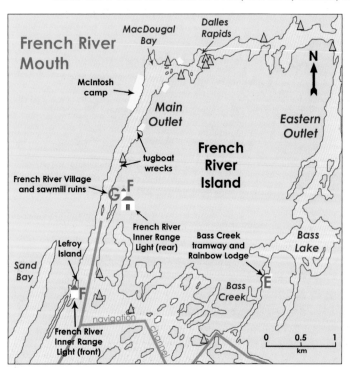

G French River Village

(see French River Mouth map)
During the 1800s, initially to furnish the British navy with masts for its vast fleet of sailing ships and then to supply the burgeoning cities of America with building materials, loggers advanced across Ontario, felling

French River Village is overgrown with trees, perhaps an appropriate fate for a former sawmill town.

its virgin pine forests and providing employment for the province's many new immigrants. The gradual march westward led authorities in 1872 to grant timber rights for an enormous tract of Crown land on the northeastern shore of Georgian Bay that included the French River watershed. Several logging companies set up camps and began cutting in the area, but their operations were small and fragmented until, in 1883, the newly formed Ontario Lumber Company purchased some of the rights and established the mill town of French River Village near the river's Main Outlet. The company built two sawmills and a whole infrastructure of houses and services to support them. At its peak the village stretched far along the rocks down the east side of the river, its roads paved with sawdust and its seasonal population swelling to 1,400. On maps and in written histories, you may see the town referred to as Coponaning or Wabbtown. The first name was given to it by the provincial land surveyor dispatched in 1875 to lay out the townsite; the second was acquired at about the same time that local entrepreneur Sam Wabb set up a trading post nearby and built lodgings that he rented out to some of the mill workers.

The Ontario Lumber Company mills churned out millions of board feet of timber during the next two decades, becoming one of the most productive lumbering operations on Georgian Bay. French River Village, as a result, was a thriving settlement with all the conveniences of the day. However — the "however" that accompanies all resource-based industries — as accessible timber supplies dwindled during the first decade of the 1900s, the company's fortunes began to falter. The final blow came in 1910 when, at the instigation of the local fishery, progressive new environmental legislation was enacted prohibiting the pollution of fish spawning beds with debris from sawmills. The Ontario Lumber Company declared bankruptcy. Its assets were bought two years later by the Pine Lake Lumber Company, which moved the mill equipment to a new site up the Pickerel River. The Village of French River did not survive the loss of its founding business. One by one the shops closed and the residents moved away. By the early 1920s, the townsite

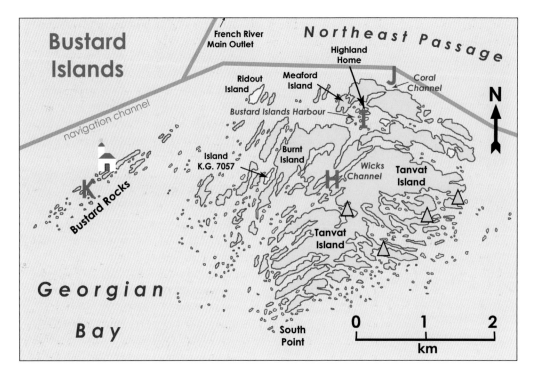

was largely vacant, and most of the buildings had been demolished. Lightkeeper Bob Young stayed on — his post utterly isolated — until 1934.

Paddling up the French River from Georgian Bay today, you will still see the crumbling stone chimney and foundations of one of the sawmills on the right-hand shore. If you pull your canoe or kayak onto the rocky beach here and poke about the ruins, you will find part of a flywheel and some other rusting pieces of machinery and rotting timbers and, farther up the shore, the boilers and wreckage of several old tugboats. But remarkably little evidence remains of the once substantial townsite. It has become — in a final ironic twist — completely overgrown with trees!

H Bustard Islands Landscape (see Bustard Islands map)

At last count the Bustard Islands numbered 559. That count, however, was done more than a quarter-century ago, and in the intervening years, shrinking water levels in Georgian Bay have exposed many formerly submerged shoals, almost certainly increasing the tally. After spending several days paddling among all the islands that make up the Bustards, you will be convinced that there are at least a thousand of them! Tanvat Island, sprawling across the southeastern shore, is the largest; the smallest are little bigger than rocks.

The pattern of geology and vegetation found on the Outer Fox Islands is repeated here: rounded humps of rock and windblown pines on some islands (Tanvat Island and others in the southeast) and craggier, rougher rocks with cedars and shrubs on others (the northern and western islands in the group). Wind and waves in recent times and glacial ice in millennia past have shaped the island landscape seen today. Their erosive power is evident in the smooth spillways and potholes sculpted into the rock in many places on Tanvat Island, in the barrenness of the islands all around the exposed fringes and in the complex maze of channels carved into the interior. Some of these channels are deep and sheltered enough to be navigable in any weather. Others — even some still clearly marked as channels on the maps (Coral Channel and Wicks Channel, for instance) — have become too shallow or are blocked completely at one end, so that you will have to portage or drag your canoe or kayak across them if you are determined to continue.

In the sheltered heart of the Bustard Islands is a deep harbour encircled by small islands. This became the hub of activity for the commercial fishermen who used to spend their summers here. Some of the old cabins now serve as cottages for descendants of those families, and a few other cottages have been added more recently. The old Bustard Island Camp, built as a fishing and tourist resort in the mid-1950s (on a tiny island identified merely as K.G. 7057), is now privately owned, as is Ridout Island, where a modern cottage has been constructed near the former site of the Dominion Fish Company station.

There are several beautiful campsites along the eastern shore of Tanvat Island from which to base your exploration of the Bustards. Another site is tucked into a sheltered interior cove accessible from the west; in fact, it can also be reached by a short portage (marked by cairns) over the rocks from the east if rough weather prevents you from paddling around the exposed and shoal-strewn headland at South Point. From any of these sites it is possible to hike great distances along the open shoreline, giving you the opportunity to stretch your legs on a windbound day and to appreciate the landscape from a different perspective.

I Bustard Islands Fish Station (see Bustard Islands map)

The year 1875 was pivotal for the Bustard Islands. James Pillgrem, a fisherman born in Newfoundland and raised in Meaford, discovered the Bustard Islands Harbour that year and built a fishing camp there. It was also in 1875 that the federal Department of Marine and Fisheries erected a lighthouse on the Bustard Rocks to guide Great Lakes freighters to the mouth of the French River — and, serendipitously, fishing boats into the Bustard Islands.

For many decades James Pillgrem and his sons spent their summers fishing at the Bustards, initially based at Meaford Island (named after their winter home) and then from the tiny island, in the centre of the harbour, that came to be known as Highland Home. The Pillgrems were joined in subsequent years by several dozen other families, and fishing camps sprouted up on islands all around the harbour. The fish — staples of whitefish, lake trout and herring — was packed on ice and shipped from the Dominion Fish Company's station on Ridout Island. In the early years, catches were collected twice a week by the steamship that ran between Killarney and the railway terminals on southern Georgian Bay. Later, as the network of rails and roads developed around the bay, fish was sent by rail from Key Harbour and then by refrigerated truck from Britt.

James Pillgrem died in 1916, but his youngest son, William, continued to fish until his retirement in 1955. By then the Georgian Bay fishery had died. Overfishing, in conjunction with pollution of the spawning grounds by logging debris and invasion of the bay by the parasitic sea lamprey and other non-native species, had irreparably damaged the fish stocks. The last commercial fishermen left the Bustards in the early 1950s.

Many of the Bustard Islands' original fishing shanties are maintained as summer cottages, some still owned by descendants of the islands' first fishermen.

Many of the original fishing shanties on the islands around Bustard Island Harbour have been converted into summer cottages, and some are still owned by the descendants of those first families. One of James Pillgrem's buildings on Highland Home has been restored as a boathouse, and you will see many relics along the shores — cribbing from the old docks, an ice crusher, and rings and cables in the rocks. No trace of the Dominion Fish Company's packing facility remains on Ridout Island. Many of these islands are now privately owned, so please restrict your explorations to the water.

J *Coral* Wreck (see Bustard Islands map)

Little information is available about the *Coral*, except that she was a wooden sailboat that ran aground in the early 1900s at the north end of a small channel between two of the Bustard Islands — subsequently named Coral Channel in her honour. Like the ship, the channel itself is now disintegrating. Accumulations of rock and sand, and falling water levels, have blocked its northern outlet completely. The timber frame of the *Coral*'s hull and scattered pieces of debris are easy to locate and can best be seen from the vantage point of the shoreline rocks.

K Bustard Rocks and Bustard Islands Lighthouse (see Bustard Islands map)

When the federal Department of Marine and Fisheries decided in 1875 that lights were needed to guide the Great Lakes steamships safely through the maze of shoals into French River Village, it authorized the construction of four beacons. Two were built near French River Village. The other two — the French River *Outer* Range Lights — were installed on the Bustard Rocks. A third beacon was added at the Bustard Rocks when the original lights were overhauled in 1893. It is a picturesque trio but puzzling at first glance, as the three towers seem almost randomly placed on the rocks. Not so! Range lights are positioned very precisely so that, when correctly aligned by an approaching ship, they guide it on an exact course through treacherous waters. The Bustard Islands' main lighthouse and the range light to its south align to guide approaching ships on a course that avoids Isabel Rock to the north and a cluster of shoals to the

The wreck of the Coral.

south; the main lighthouse and the range light to its north guide ships past the Bustard Rocks towards the two range lights at the mouth of the French River, 5 km to the northeast.

Of all the Bustards' lightkeepers, Tom Flynn was the best loved and longest serving, taking over the post in 1928 and returning every season until his retirement in 1951, when batteries were installed to automate the lights. During his tenure, Flynn and his wife gradually transformed the barren landscape into a cozy domestic patch. The Bustard Rocks are precisely that — rocks! The Flynns brought soil in baskets from neighbouring islands to make tiny vegetable gardens in sheltered hollows. And they kept chickens, selling the eggs to visitors and slaughtering the flock for meat when the time came to leave the light station each fall.

Following the lights' automation, the lightkeeper's cottage, subjected to fierce storms on the isolated island, deteriorated to such an extent that it was demolished in 1965. Only a cement platform remains, where gulls perch to survey their fishing grounds. The beacons themselves continue to operate — in their original towers, now modernized — for the benefit of travellers along Georgian Bay's northeast shore, though nowadays these travellers often come by canoe or kayak, simply for the pleasure of the scenery.

Maps & Information
- NTS map 41 H/15: Key Harbour.
- Nautical charts 224401: Alexander Passage to Beaverstone Bay (overview), 2204B01: Key Harbour to French River (east & central) and 2204A03: French River to Beaverstone Bay (western corner).
- An excellent park map, produced by the Friends of the French River Heritage Park and published by Ontario Parks, is widely available at outdoor stores, local marinas and at the park visitor centre.
- French River Provincial Park: (705) 857-1630, www.ontarioparks.com.
- *Northeastern Georgian Bay and Its People*, written and published by William A. Campbell in 1982.

CHAPTER 7

Byng Inlet to the Churchill Islands

OVERVIEW

The wild and windswept islands of northeastern Georgian Bay offer some choice opportunities for adventure in your canoe or kayak. From the access point at Byng Inlet, it is possible to visit the historic Gereaux Island lighthouse, poke across the McNab Rocks and then make your way through the archipelago that lies to the north — Cunninghams Island, Champlain Island, Rogers Island, One Tree Island, the Churchill Islands and the multitude of nameless humps of rock that lie between them. Tiny channels cut through the landscape, providing sheltered paddling even when wind and waves are rough on the open bay. You will find a few modest cottages tucked among the islands, and the small-craft navigation channel runs close to the mainland shore, but otherwise you can look forward to many hours — or days — in peaceful solitude.

The excursion described in this chapter takes in some of the key natural features and historical sites along the coast between Byng Inlet and the Churchills. The route is not meant to be followed with pinpoint precision, however, as there are plenty of alternatives to accommodate the variable conditions in weather, the time available, and the interests and expertise of individual paddlers. The length of your journey may range from a leisurely day paddle near the mouth of Byng Inlet (the short loop routes described below) to a more strenuous expedition that extends the route northwards (the long route) and requires overnight gear and solid paddling and navigation skills. Detailed marine charts are essential in this labyrinth of islands, where it is entirely possible to pass within just a few metres of a location you have visited previously and yet not recognize the place! If in doubt stick close to the small-craft marine channel whose red and green markers give comforting assurance, though in exchange you will have to tolerate the increased traffic.

There are many lovely campsites along the shore of Black Bay and on the larger islands between Duffy Island and the Churchills. Most of the land here is Crown land, where Canadian residents may camp free of charge and visitors from abroad may camp with a permit purchased from the local Ministry of Natural Resources office in Sudbury or Parry Sound. Take care to avoid the scattered cottage properties, and do not trespass on

(Left) Rocks and pines dominate the Churchill Islands landscape.

The open rocky shorelines provide many beautiful campsites in this part of Georgian Bay.

the mainland shore between Black Bay and the Key River, as it belongs to the Henvey Inlet First Nation. To prevent their overuse, specific campsites have not been identified in this chapter. The exposed landscape along the northeastern coast is exquisitely barren and its environment especially vulnerable. Wherever you pitch your tent for the night, be sure to practice responsible, low-impact camping to ensure the site's continued viability.

Distance
- Short Loop South (red dots): Byng Inlet to Gereaux Island and McNab Rocks = 10–15 km paddle (1–2 days)
- Short Loop North (orange dots): Byng Inlet to Black Bay and Cunninghams Island = 12–18 km paddle (1–2 days)
- Long Loop (red/orange dots plus green dots): Byng Inlet to the Churchills and One Tree Island = 40–55 km paddle (4–7 days)

Access
- Exit Hwy 69 onto Hwy 526 approximately 65 km north of Parry Sound or 85 km south of Sudbury.
- Drive 7.5 km through the village of Britt to the end of the road, where parking, camping and launch facilities are available for a small fee at Georgian Cottages & Camping (for information call 1-877-591-5987 or visit www.georgiancottages.com).
- Other marinas in Britt also offer parking and launch facilities if you are prepared for the longer paddle of 2 to 4 km down the busy boating channel to the mouth of Byng Inlet.

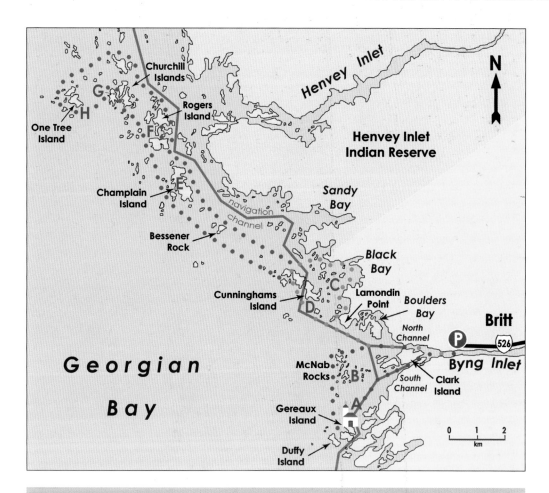

Route Description

1st Segment: Britt to Gereaux Island Lighthouse (5 km paddle)

Passing through the community of Britt on your way to the launch site and seeing its tiny neighbour to the south across Byng Inlet — their combined full-time population about 25 people — you will have no inkling that a century ago this was one of Georgian Bay's largest and busiest industrial ports, boasting three lumber mills, a massive coal dock and more than 4,000 residents.

Henry Bayfield surveyed and named the inlet (in honour of the British admiral John Byng) in the early 1820s during the epic journey that produced Georgian Bay's first marine charts. Possessing a deep natural harbour and access to an extensive interior wilderness via the Magnetawan and Still rivers, Byng Inlet became a major lumbering centre when timber leases were issued in the late 1860s, sparking a flurry of logging activity in the nearby forests. A trio of sawmills — the first on Mill Island in 1866, the second on the south shore of Byng Inlet in 1871 and the third on its north shore in 1880 — provided employment for settlers who flocked to the area. Many had emigrated from fading mill towns like Trois-Rivières in Quebec; their legacy survives in the French names of local landscape features like Gereaux Island and Lamondin Point.

The supply of timber dwindled during the 1920s, and the mill in Byng Inlet South closed in 1927. Byng Inlet North flourished for several more decades, as an active fishery and a fuel distribution terminal bolstered its industrial base. When the Canadian Pacific Railway extended its line north from Parry Sound to Sudbury in 1908, the track passed close to Byng Inlet's northern shore. The railway's coal-powered steam locomotives were voracious in their demand for fuel, so supply depots had to be constructed around the Upper Great Lakes to receive the shiploads of coal brought by freighter from the big American mines. Byng Inlet's harbour earmarked it as a suitable terminal, and in 1911 a vast dock and coal storage sheds were built at the confluence of the Magnetawan and Still rivers. Conversion of the railway's locomotives to diesel during the 1940s made the coal port obsolete, but residents were granted a reprieve in 1952 when Texaco erected storage tanks and established an oil distribution centre there. By then the town's name had been changed to Britt — after Thomas Britt, a prominent CPR fuel superintendent.

Launch your canoe or kayak from one of the town's marinas, and paddle west towards Georgian Bay. At Clark Island, near the mouth of Byng Inlet, you must choose between the North and South channels. If you are planning a day paddle to Black Bay or have only a few days for your excursion to the Churchill Islands, take the North Channel for 3.5 km to Lamondin Point and skip ahead to the 3rd segment of this route description. Otherwise, take the South Channel for 3.5 km to Gereaux Island, whose charming old lighthouse **A** will guide your approach. You may wish to land and explore the site on foot for an hour or two, giving yourself a chance to stretch your legs and absorb some of the island's human history.

Gereaux Island's first light, built in 1870, was a lantern mounted on a wooden skeleton tower that marked the entrance to Byng Inlet for steamships collecting timber from the sawmill at Mill Island. Due to an increase in shipping traffic after two more mills opened in Byng Inlet during the next decade, the original tower was replaced in 1880 with a

Gereaux Island lighthouse.

conventional lighthouse manned by a full-time keeper, and the navigation system was further augmented in 1890 with two range lights on the shore of the South Channel. The Gereaux Island light station was maintained for more than half a century by members of the Lamondin family. Louis Lamondin, its longest serving keeper (1925–1946), did double duty as a tugboat captain and pilot for the coal freighters entering the busy port. Eventually, as part of the coast guard's downsizing scheme for all the Great Lakes lighthouses, the Gereaux Island light was automated and the station destaffed in 1989. The original building with its square tower remains, however, its beacon flashing at ten-second intervals for the few small ships, mostly pleasure craft, that visit the inlet today.

2nd Segment: Gereaux Island to Lamondin Point (4 km paddle)

Back in your canoe or kayak, paddle north from Gereaux Island. The bustling human heritage of Byng Inlet is quickly forgotten as you weave through the wild landscape of islands and shoals that lie across its mouth. These are McNab Rocks B, and in rough weather they can feel like the ragged ends of the Earth. If your trip is limited to a day paddle, turn right from McNab Rocks and follow the North Channel for 4 km up Byng Inlet and back to the launch in Britt. Otherwise, continue north for 800 m to Lamondin Point.

3rd Segment: Lamondin Point Around Black Bay to Cunninghams Island (4 km paddle)

Black Bay opens invitingly beyond Lamondin Point. Sheltered by a phalanx of islands, the bay provides tranquil paddling and some beautiful sites for camping or a picnic lunch. The north side of Black Bay marks the southern boundary of the Henvey Inlet First Nation's reserve, so turn away from the mainland here and paddle out to explore Cunninghams Island D and its neighbours. You will find some cottages on these islands, and the main boating channel cuts between them, but the prevailing atmosphere is still one of wilderness.

For day paddlers it is a 7.5 km return journey from Cunninghams Island, around Lamondin Point and up the North Channel to the launch in Britt. If you are continuing north for an extended trip, be aware that the next opportunity for camping is more than 4 km away.

4th Segment: Cunninghams Island to Champlain Island (4 km paddle)

Between Cunninghams Island and the next significant member of the archipelago, Champlain Island E, lies an open-water crossing of 4 km where you are vulnerable to buffeting by wind and waves. Only Bessener Rock breaks the passage, offering limited shelter about two-thirds of the distance across. On a calm day, however, steaming through the deep water outside the shoals makes a pleasant change from dodging the rocks that lurk beneath the surface closer to shore.

Upon reaching the southern tip of Champlain Island, you will notice that the character of the terrain has changed: rough, fractured rock replaces the smooth, weathered whalebacks, and elegant pines are supplanted by a scruffier mix of cedar and shrubs. This fascinating pattern — smooth rocks and pine alternating with rough rocks and cedar — occurs all along Georgian Bay's northeastern shore in response to subtle variations in its geological underpinnings. The smooth rocks return just a kilometre or two farther north.

Looking across a windy channel toward One Tree Island. PHOTO BY RICK CHUCHRA

Champlain Island was for many years an outpost of the Gauthier fishery. From their base near the mouth of the French River, the Gauthier family operated one of the largest fishing businesses on Georgian Bay, starting in the early 1890s and lasting until collapse of the bay's fish stocks forced its closure in 1969. Today a group of cottages stands at the site on the island's southeast corner.

5th Segment: Champlain Island to Churchill Islands (5 km paddle)

The boating channel runs along Champlain Island's eastern side and then weaves through the cluster of islands surrounding Rogers Island **F**, where channel names like Free Drinks Passage and Rogers Gut evoke unappetizing images if you are prone to seasickness. To minimize navigational challenges, you may wish to follow this route, or if you are confident with your map-and-compass skills, you may prefer to tackle the maze of tiny islands that lie to the west and north of Champlain Island. Be prepared for twists, turns and dead-end passages here and for many occasions when your map fails to match reality; even the most up-to-date marine charts lag behind Georgian Bay's fluctuating water levels.

The Churchill Islands are less than 3 km (as the crow flies) from the northern tip of Champlain Island, but you might paddle more than twice that distance before you reach them in your canoe or kayak. Once there, be sure to allow at least a day to explore the shoreline thoroughly — on foot to admire its twisted rocks and varied vegetation, and by boat along the deep V-shaped channel that cuts between the islands. Near the northwestern edge of the V, some crumbling pilings at the water's edge and rusting metal debris along the shore suggest the site was once used as a fishing camp **G**. Now it makes a sheltered place to enjoy a picnic lunch.

6th Segment: Churchills to One Tree Island (1 km paddle)

Surveying the western horizon from a vantage point on the northern Churchills, your attention will be drawn to One Tree Island, its single deciduous tree, a surprising elm, standing above the ubiquitous cedars and pines. On a windy day, the channel that separates the Churchills from One Tree Island will seem impossibly wide, but in calm weather the crossing is easy and the paddle is rewarded with the chance to poke among a collection of even more remote and beautiful satellite islands.

7th Segment: Homeward (17-20 km paddle)

A purposeful crow will speedily cover the distance from One Tree Island back to Britt, but in your canoe or kayak, with so many fascinating distractions and obstructions along the way, it may take a day or more to complete the return journey. The homeward route will depend on wind and waves, and even if you try, there is little chance you will retrace more than a few metres of the outward route. In any case you will enjoy the fresh perspective on this glorious landscape when you are facing south!

Possible Extensions

- ***To the North***: Dead Island lies less than 4 km north of the Churchill Islands, and beyond that are the French River delta and the Bustard Islands, places rich in both human and natural history. In order to extend your trip into this area, you will require a minimum of ten days and a camping permit from the French River Provincial Park. See Chapter 6 for details.
- ***To the South***: From Gereaux Island you may wish to extend your route in a 16 to 20 km loop around Foster Island and Norgate Inlet, where you will find some pleasant cottages, an old lodge and, perched on the rocky shore of Bourchier Island, a bizarrely out-of-place automobile dating from the 1950s.

Maps & Information

- NTS maps 41 H/15: Key Harbour (northern area) and 41 H/10: Naiscoot River (southern extension).
- Nautical charts 224401: Alexander Passage to Beaverstone Bay (overview), 2204A01: Byng Inlet to Key Harbour (detail), 229301: Byng Inlet and Approaches (greater detail for southern day paddle) and 2203C01: Isle of Pines to Byng Inlet (southern extension to Foster Island).

One Tree Island's solitary elm, slightly forlorn in early spring without its season's foliage.

CHAPTER 8

Dillon to the McCoys ...and Beyond

OVERVIEW

As outdoor enthusiasts we delight in self-propelled activities — hiking and paddling through magnificent wilderness landscapes by day and resting overnight at primitive backcountry campsites. Northeastern Georgian Bay is our utopia, its myriad isolated islands and sheltered channels providing plenty of scope for adventure. The McCoys — Big McCoy, Little McCoy and a small cluster of islands and shoals around them — are a favourite destination for paddlers. Lying 5 km offshore from the mainland, about 35 km northwest of Parry Sound, they offer many popular wilderness paddling routes, ranging from a short circuit around the McCoys to longer trips that combine a visit to the McCoys with a journey south through the Minks (see Chapter 9).

(Above) Xanthoria adds a cheerful splash of orange to Birnie Island's pink shoreline rocks.

The McCoy Islands are named, reputedly, after a man who set up a trading post on Big McCoy Island and prospered by cheating his patrons, mostly local Native people. When Mr. McCoy was murdered — by the light of a full moon one September night — no one mourned his passing and little effort was ever made to find his assailant. Rumour has it that McCoy's ghost lets out a terrible scream once a year on the night of the September full moon, perhaps something to consider if you are planning an autumn trip to these islands! Though the McCoys have been used as a base for trading and fishing, scant evidence of human habitation remains here today. The landscape is an exquisite wilderness of barren rocks and windblown pines.

Northeast of the McCoys lie two large islands — Hertzberg Island and Shawanaga Island — and a vast, disorganized archipelago of smaller ones, separated from the mainland by Shawanaga Inlet in the east and Pointe au Baril Channel to the north. Outdoor enthusiasts generally avoid the northern part of this area, the fashionable cottage district of Pointe au Baril. Its waterways hum with motorboats (and often, alarmingly, with float planes!), and its shores are lined with cottage properties. Yet, amid this modern chaos await some unexpected delights. Armed with a healthy spirit of adventure, you will discover fascinating fragments of history and surprising patches of wilderness, and you will enjoy a paddling holiday that is decidedly out of the ordinary, with at least one bizarre experience that guarantees an entertaining story.

Route planning can be a challenge here, in part because the many islands, channels and features of interest provide an overwhelming number of options. These options, already numerous on your maps, become infinitely more convoluted in reality, because Georgian Bay's fluctuating water levels have altered the shoreline greatly in places, requiring impromptu route changes during your journey. The challenge is further compounded

Boulder ridge on Big McCoy Island's southeastern shore.

by the dearth of backcountry campsites in the northern area of the route, where cottages occupy most of the islands and mainland shore. Naturally, the weather, the time available, and the interests and skill level of individual paddlers will also influence your plans.

Between Dillon and the McCoys, the route is quite straightforward, and a pleasant long-weekend or leisurely week-long trip can be had poking through the cluster of offshore islands and returning by way of Hertzberg Island (the short and medium loops, and features A to H described below). However, if you wish to venture farther north to explore Shawanaga Island and Pointe au Baril (the long and extended loops, and features I to X), you must be adaptable to the changing conditions and prepared for long stretches of paddling with few suitable sites for pitching your tent. Camping is not usually such a problem in the southern area, as much of the land is either within conservation reserves or Crown land (where Canadian residents may camp free of charge, and visitors from abroad may camp with a permit from the local office of the Ontario Ministry of Natural Resources). There are many excellent sites around Big McCoy Island, Hertzberg Island and on the mainland shore of Shawanaga Inlet below Shawanaga Landing. Wherever you spend the night, be sure to respect the rights of property owners and the fragility of the environment; low-impact camping is imperative here. To avoid overuse, specific campsites have not been identified in this chapter, though some general recommendations are given to assist in planning your route through this complex landscape.

Distance: 35-40 km, 45-50 km, 60-70 km or 70-80 km paddle

Access
- North of Nobel, exit Hwy 69 west onto County Road 559.
- After 10 km, where County Road 559 turns sharply south, continue straight onto the Dillon Road.
- Follow the Dillon Road for 8.8 km to its end. Here you will find the Dillon Cove Marina & Resort, where parking and launch facilities are available for a modest fee. For information call the marina at (705) 342-5431 or visit www.dilloncove.com.

Route Description

SHORT LOOP: Dillon to McCoys, Southern Hertzberg Island and Turtle Rock
- Distance: 35–40 km paddle
- Minimum time: 2–3 days
- Route on map: red dots
- Features of interest: A-H

MEDIUM LOOP: Dillon to McCoys, Northern Hertzberg Island and Turtle Rock
- Distance: 45–50 km paddle
- Minimum time: 3–4 days
- Route on map: red dots plus orange dots
- Features of interest: A-H

LONG LOOP: Medium Loop Plus Circumnavigation of Shawanaga Island

- Distance: 60–70 km paddle
- Minimum time: 4–6 days
- Route on map: red/orange dots plus green dots
- Features of interest: **A-N**

EXTENDED LOOP: Long Loop Plus Extension to Pointe au Baril Lighthouse

- Distance: 70–80 km paddle
- Minimum time 5–6 days
- Route on map: red/orange/green dots plus purple dots
- Features of interest: **A-X**

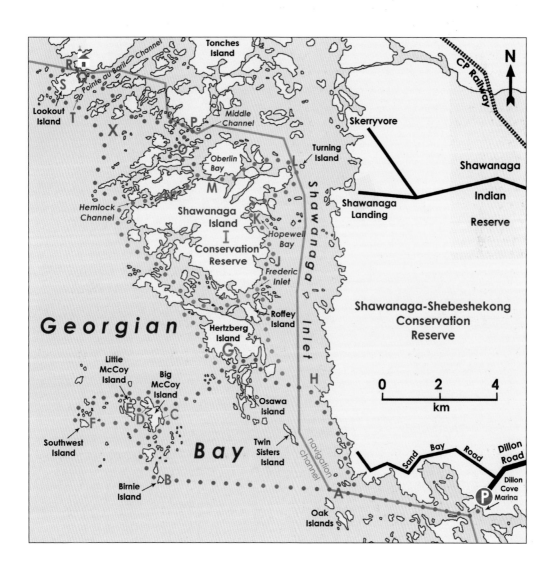

Features of Interest

A Buoy A44

Buoy A44, located at Duett Rock on the northeastern side of the Oak Islands, marks the channel leading to Dillon and the small-craft route southward. Its significance is no greater than that of any other red or green metal cylinder marking the route, but it serves as a handy reference point for your comings and goings in this excursion. Paddlers using a GPS may wish to note the marker's UTM coordinates: 0547785E, 5030815N. The 5 km passage between Dillon Cove Marina and buoy A44 is usually busy with boating traffic, and cottages line the shores on both sides. Amid this congestion an osprey nesting platform (on a rock about two-thirds of the way along the channel west from Dillon) seems oddly out of place. Ospreys are surprisingly tolerant of human presence, however, and you may be fortunate enough to see a family of these fish hawks in residence here if you are paddling between early May and mid-July.

B Birnie Island

After an open-water crossing of 6.3 km westward from buoy A44, you will arrive at Birnie Island, one of the many exposed slabs of rock that make up the chain of Minks and McCoys. Birne Island's shoreline rocks are encrusted with bright orange lichens in starburst patterns — xanthoria, one of Canada's most common and widely distributed lichens. Xanthoria thrives on open rock in nutrient-rich environments like that found on Birnie Island, where nesting birds provide a plentiful supply of fertilizer.

C Big McCoy Island's Boulder Ridge and Pukaskwa Pits

At the edge of a sheltered cove on Big McCoy Island's southeastern shore, an enormous ridge of boulders rises steeply about 5 m above the waterline and extends 10 m back from the shore. Geologically speaking, the ridge is a fine example of the boulder concentrations produced by significant subglacial flood events. Large rocks were commonly trapped in glacial ice as it advanced across Ontario and then disgorged in the meltwater when the ice began to thaw. In the turbulent environment beneath the ice, the boulders were jostled and abraded. As the flow of meltwater slowed, the boulders sank and accumulated in piles on the underlying bedrock. The pile on Big McCoy Island looks incongruous — man-made almost — beside the sloping rock tables that characterize the rest of the island's shoreline.

There is more to the ridge than its geology, however. The presence of Pukaskwa (pronounced "PUCK-a-saw") pits in the boulders indicates that the Ojibwe people used the site in centuries past. Pukaskwa pits are circular depressions, often ringed with low walls of rock, found commonly on the cobble beaches of Lake Superior and less frequently along Georgian Bay. Their purpose is the subject of much speculation. They may have been utilitarian structures (food caches or hunting blinds, for instance) or ceremonial sites for Native vision quests. Today the pits are of spiritual significance to people of the Shawanaga First Nation, who request that visiting paddlers treat the site with respect.

D Land Bridge Joining Big McCoy, Agassiz and Langridge Islands

During your circumnavigation of Big McCoy, you may become confused as you approach the island's northern tip, where Agassiz Island and Langridge Island — shown as separate, adjacent islands on many maps — are nowhere to be seen. In fact, they no longer exist, except as names on a map. The falling water level in Georgian Bay has gradually obliterated the shallow channels that used to run between them, so that Big McCoy, Agassiz and Langridge islands are now joined into one even bigger McCoy. Indeed, the land bridges are so substantial they support pioneer species of trees. The smooth rocks revealed above the island's receding waterline are streaked with bands of pink, white and grey — a petrified palette left behind by some ancient artist. Many happy hours can be spent exploring this shoreline on foot.

E Little McCoy Island

Little McCoy Island is privately owned, but the property is managed by the Georgian Bay Land Trust. The trust, formed in 1991, works in partnership with the Nature Conservancy of Canada to protect areas of natural significance along Georgian Bay's eastern shore and to promote environmentally responsible human activities in those areas. It acquires properties by conservation easement, donation, outright purchase or, as in the case of Little McCoy Island, lease of private property. The land trust designation safeguards Little McCoy's unique and fragile environment — a barren tableland along the perimeter and a leatherleaf bog community running through the island's interior. The tableland was once a gathering place for travellers and traders, but camping is no longer permitted on Little McCoy Island.

F Southwest Island

Reaching Southwest Island through the maze of nameless islands and shoals that surrounds it is a considerable challenge, especially if the weather is breezy, as this remote group of rocks bears the brunt of the prevailing westerlies blowing off Georgian Bay. Magnificently bleak, except for a few sheltered pockets of shrubs where cormorants and gulls like to nest, Southwest Island provides an interesting day paddle from your base at Big McCoy Island, and the humps of rock in the centre of the island afford splendid views across the chain of Minks and McCoys.

G Hertzberg Island and Its Satellites

Hertzberg Island, lying 2 km west of the mainland and 2.5 km east of Big McCoy Island, makes an excellent stopover during your paddling excursion to the McCoys. Most of Hertzberg Island and the smaller islands around it are Crown land. The few private cottage properties are concentrated mostly on Osawa, Roffey and Twin Sisters islands. Along the eastern side of the island group, the flat rocks offer some lovely sites for camping. The terrain on the western side, by contrast, is too rough and angular to comfortably pitch a tent. If your trip is limited to a short loop, follow one of the many channels between Hertzberg Island and its southern satellites. Frederic Inlet provides a pleasant, though longer, alternate route along Hertzberg Island's north shore.

H Turtle Rock

According to Native legend, a young Ojibwe boy paddling on Georgian Bay was caught one day in a violent storm. Frightened and exhausted, his canoe about to smash into the rocks, the boy scanned the shoreline and saw a giant turtle peering back at him. Turtle is important to this region's Native people as the chief messenger between Earth and the spirit world of the manitous, so the youth appealed to him for help through the waves and spray. Suddenly the storm ended and the canoe floated safely ashore, but when the boy turned to thank the turtle, he saw only a turtle-shaped rock. Leaving an offering there, he paddled home to his village.

Turtle Rock is a spiritual site for the Shawanaga First Nation. Visiting paddlers are welcome, but must treat the turtle with respect. To find this remarkable rock (*without* the benefit of GPS coordinates, as that would make the search less significant!) paddle 2.5 km due east from the northern end of Osawa Island or north along the mainland shore for 2 km beyond the last cottage at the end of the Sand Bay Road. The turtle can be seen on the east side of a small cove — a striking rock structure about 6 m long, with two large black humps (the turtle's head and body) separated by a ribbon of banded black-and-white rock (the fluted edges of the turtle's shell). The cove is lined with smooth, flat shelves where you may pull your canoe or kayak ashore. After marvelling at the twisted geology of turtle rock, you may wish to climb the hummock behind the cove to admire the lovely views across Shawanaga Inlet. The wild landscape along this coast is part of the Shawanaga-Shebeshekong Conservation Reserve.

I Shawanaga Island

Shawanaga Island, with an area of 10 km², is one of the largest islands on Georgian Bay's eastern shore. Its terrain is wonderfully varied, ranging from treeless barrens and bald headlands to mature stands of pine, deciduous forests, sandy beaches and reedy marshlands. The island's western shore, facing the open water of Georgian Bay, is ragged and windswept. The relative shelter of the eastern shore makes its environment lush by comparison, and many species of flora and fauna make their home here. Indeed, in recognition of the island's exceptional ecological diversity and vulnerability, the Ontario government established the Shawanaga Island Conservation Reserve. This does not mean, however, that the island landscape is entirely wild. Private cottage properties are scattered liberally along the shore, and sites for backcountry camping can be difficult to find in the pockets of wilderness between them.

From the perspective of your canoe or kayak, Shawanaga Island can be a confusion of bays and channels peppered with a multitude of tiny satellite islands. Navigation is especially challenging on the island's western side, where only *some* of the many shoals shown on the maps are still below the waterline. Others, due to lower water levels in Georgian Bay, have surfaced to become small islands. Likewise, some of the islands clearly marked as islands on the maps are now peninsulas connected solidly to Shawanaga Island. With these cautionary notes in mind, however, you can happily spend a day or two circumnavigating the island to see its fascinating natural and human features.

Turtle Rock pokes its nose into a cove along the shore of the Shawanaga-Shebeshekong Conservation Reserve.

J Josephine Rocks

Josephine Rocks is a group of tiny islands that lie off the southwestern side of Shawanaga Island just north of Frederic Inlet. Cutting across them are beautiful, twisted ribbons of black and white rock — gneiss that was metamorphosed beneath the ancient Grenville Mountains a billion years ago and then scraped bare by glaciers. Though vegetation is limited, if you poke along the water's edge, you may find hardy wildflowers and carnivorous sundews growing in damp nooks. A patch of sand on the most westerly of the Josephine Rocks makes a pleasant site to land and stretch your legs.

K Hopewell Bay

Looking at the map, and perhaps recalling other "islands" that weren't, you may be tempted to stay out in the open water of Shawanaga Inlet rather than risk a possible dead-end paddle into Hopewell Bay. If water levels are particularly low, your concern might be justified, as the head of Hopewell Bay is shallow and thick with reeds. However, a small, muddy channel cuts behind the large island that lies in the middle of the bay, and you can usually paddle or pole your way through to the other side. The reward is the chance to enjoy a relatively undisturbed area of shoreline and perhaps spot wildlife in the peaceful shelter of the bay — a foraging bear, a sandhill crane, a turtle sunning itself on a log or a great blue heron fishing in the reeds (or, if you are as fortunate as we were during our last visit here, *all* these creatures within an hour!).

L *Metamora* Wreck

Approaching the wreck of the Metamora, *her old boiler sporting a modern navigation marker.*

At Turning Island, just off the northeastern tip of Shawanaga Island, the main small-craft channel from Shawanaga Inlet squeezes through a narrows and veers west. A navigation marker rises from a white metal fixture in the water 200 m west of Turning Island. Mariners whizzing down the channel aboard their motorboats will miss the significance of the fixture. In your canoe or kayak, however, you might wish to ease alongside for a closer examination. What you will find is an old ship's boiler sticking out above the water and, beneath it, an extensive, well-preserved structure of timbers and metal fittings — the wreck of the *Metamora*. Built in Cleveland, Ohio, in 1864, the *Metamora* served a brief stint as a gunship during the Fenian raids, patrolling the Great Lakes from 1866 to 1871 for Irish-American attackers (Irish loyalists who were attempting, by striking British installations in Canada, to persuade Britain to end its occupation of Ireland). Most of the *Metamora*'s 43 years of service, however, were spent more mundanely as a Georgian Bay freighter and passenger steamer. Then one day in the summer of 1907, on her way up Shawanaga Inlet from Midland to Byng Inlet, the aging ship caught fire. Her crew escaped the blaze, but the *Metamora* burned to the waterline. She came to rest on the rocks near Turning Island, where she remains, her white-painted boiler still serving the maritime interest, if only as a base for a channel marker.

M Shawanaga Island's Northern Passage

The passage along Shawanaga Island's northern shore, like the eastern passage through Hopewell Bay, seems an unlikely prospect amid all the blocked channels and former islands along this coast. Certainly, the northern passage is narrow — so narrow as to be almost invisible until you actually paddle into it! — but it is surprisingly deep. Running between sheer cliff walls, the waterway spills through a fracture in the bedrock that separates Shawanaga Island from the large unnamed island to the north. The passage opens at its eastern end into a quiet rocky bay and at its western end into a wide sandy channel where you may beach your canoe or kayak and enjoy a rest before continuing your paddle around the island.

N Hemlock Channel

Hemlock Channel cuts across the northwestern side of Shawanaga Island. Though it zigzags alarmingly between islands and dodges rocks all the way along its 2.5 km route, the channel provides a convenient connection between the open water of Georgian Bay and the sheltered basin of Oberlin Bay. It can be busy with motorboat traffic, but for paddlers seeking a quick passage around Shawanaga Island, it eliminates more than a kilometre of paddling from the alternate routes to the north.

O Ojibway Hotel

At the turn of the twentieth century, northeastern Georgian Bay was a remote patch of windblown wilderness, far from the urban bustle of southern Ontario and even farther from the vigorous cities of the United States. Without the benefit of roads or even railway service, until the first line pushed north from Parry Sound to Sudbury in 1908, only people of considerable wealth and leisure could visit this shoreline. Yet visit they did — at first by private yacht or passenger steamship from ports like Collingwood and Midland and then by first-class railway ticket from Toronto. Many of these early tourists were affluent Americans, like Hamilton C. Davis from Rochester, New York, who was so taken with the Pointe au Baril landscape that he bought one of its prominent islands and built a hotel there. The Ojibway Hotel opened for business in 1906. It was a luxurious establishment that catered to patrons with lavish expectations, and it grew over the years to include a dance pavilion, tennis courts, shops, a post office and a boat refuelling station

The century Ojibway Hotel, now the not-for-profit Ojibway Club.

and repair facility. However, like so many of the grand hotels constructed about the same time across Muskoka and Georgian Bay, several decades into the century the Ojibway saw its fortunes begin to slide. Local residents and cottagers became concerned that the area would lose an important piece of its heritage, so in 1942 they marshalled their resources under the Pointe au Baril Islanders' Association and purchased the hotel property from the Davis family. The association maintained the hotel until 1962, when it was converted into a not-for-profit community centre — the Ojibway Club. Since then, the Ojibway Club has been a focal point for summer activity in Pointe au Baril, providing supplies and services, offering day camp programs for children and hosting an array of social activities for people of all ages. Paddling in your canoe or kayak today towards the sweeping wharf below the elegant century hotel (recently renovated, thanks to the nearly $3 million that members raised for its restoration!), you will feel dwarfed indeed by the magnificence of the place.

P Champlain Monument

A sombre stone cross stands on a rocky headland overlooking Middle Channel. This historical monument was erected in 1946, a joint project of the Georgian Bay Association and the provincial government, to commemorate Samuel de Champlain's arrival on Georgian Bay in 1615. Champlain, a celebrated explorer and the first governor of New France, is credited with the "discovery" of Georgian Bay. In fact, his emissary Étienne Brûlé was the first European to see the bay, having paddled down the French River five years earlier and settled among the Huron people on Georgian Bay's southern shore. Quoting from Champlain's writings, the inscription on the cross reads: "As for me, I labour always to prepare a way for those willing after me to follow it." His success in this regard was considerable, apparently, as the navigation channel beneath the monument is always abuzz with boats.

Q Belleview Hotel

The Belleview Hotel, like the Ojibway Hotel just 4 km away, was established at the turn of the twentieth century to accommodate the influx of hunters, fishermen and wealthy tourists seeking wilderness adventure (with every imaginable comfort, mind you!) in the Canadian hinterland. Samuel Oldfield — who also served as Pointe au Baril's lightkeeper and postmaster — opened the Belleview Hotel in 1900. The hotel and its adjacent cottages were located on the northeastern shore of Lookout Island, 200 m across the channel from the Pointe au Baril lighthouse, so that Oldfield and his wife, Elizabeth, could shuttle back and forth, juggling their many duties as lightkeepers and lodgekeepers.

The fate of the Belleview Hotel was less favourable than that of the Ojibway Hotel. The main building was destroyed by fire in 1920, and although it was quickly rebuilt, the hotel's success after that was short-lived. In the wake of declining prosperity, it became rundown and finally closed in the mid-1900s. The abandoned building still stands after decades of neglect, its beautiful stone veranda now overgrown with lilacs and its lawns shaded by enormous willow trees. New windows were installed recently, giving hope that this charming old structure may yet be salvaged. The No Trespassing signs are unmistakable, however, so you must conduct your investigation from the water.

Across the channel from the Pointe au Baril lighthouse, the Belleview Hotel has withstood decades of neglect.

R Pointe au Baril Lighthouse

The story of Pointe au Baril — whether truth or fairy tale, no one can quite remember — begins with a troupe of voyageurs paddling their canoe through the (yet to be named) Pointe au Baril Channel. Near the channel mouth, they came across wreckage from a boat that had been dashed on the rocks some time before. The voyageurs discovered, bobbing in the debris, a miraculous barrel of whisky. After stopping to enjoy its contents and sleep off the effects, they stuck the empty barrel atop a pole to mark the channel's treacherous entrance for travellers who followed. "Point of the barrel" became Pointe au Baril, and in time Pointe au Baril Channel became a bustling thoroughfare.

Local fishermen modernized the channel marker a century later, cutting a hole in the barrel and placing a lantern inside every evening to guide fishing boats returning with the day's catch. The improvised beacon proved inadequate by the late 1800s, however, when the fishery's expansion and the advent of logging brought larger vessels into Pointe au Baril. So in 1889 the Department of Marine and Fisheries replaced the barrel with a conventional lighthouse manned by a full-time lightkeeper and built a range light tower on nearby Macklin Island. When an approaching ship correctly aligned the two beacons (the lighthouse beacon in front and the range tower beacon behind), the heading would lead along a safe passage between the rocks.

The lighthouse — and Samuel Oldfield's Belleview Hotel across the channel — became the social hub of Pointe au Baril, a gathering place for the area's many scattered residents and cottagers. Samuel and Elizabeth Oldfield were Point au Baril's first lightkeepers, but the longest-serving were its last, Carl and Emmaline Madigan. Carl filled the post from 1949, and Emmaline continued her husband's duties after his death

97

in 1977. The beacons were automated the following year, but Emmaline stayed on as caretaker and guide for summer tourists visiting the lighthouse. You may wish to tie your canoe or kayak to the wharf and enjoy a walk around the grounds. Be sure to note the legendary barrel (not the original, perhaps, but a passable modern replica) on the point overlooking the channel.

S Lookout Island

The Georgian Bay Land Trust acquired two parcels of land on Lookout Island from the Nature Conservancy of Canada: MacKenzie Point at the island's western tip in 2002 and an adjacent property in 2005, both generously donated to the Nature Conservancy by private landowners. Together they form a protected patch of wilderness in a landscape that has been largely eclipsed by cottage development. You will find rock barrens and coastal wetland communities on Lookout Island that sustain a surprising variety of plants and animals, hardy creatures that have learned to weather the fierce blasts from Georgian Bay. It is a scenic place to come ashore for a picnic and a brief exploration on foot, but, for the shoreline's preservation, the Georgian Bay Land Trust does not permit camping here.

T Shipwrecks of Brooker and Other Islands

Pointe au Baril Channel runs 11 km from the Pointe au Baril lighthouse to the tiny town (once a vital railway terminal, now a busy marina centre) of Pointe au Baril Station and gives access to the sheltered navigation route down Shawanaga Inlet. Pointe au Baril Channel has afforded safe passage for countless vessels — the canoes of Native travellers and of voyageurs, the working boats of fishermen and loggers, the passenger steamers and cargo freighters in the heyday of Great Lakes shipping, and the sleek pleasure craft of today. Others, however, have come to grief here, miscalculating the narrowness of the channel or missing its entrance altogether through the shoals. Their wrecks lie scattered along the channel shores and among the many islands (a splendid example is wedged between the Brooker Islands). As we paddle, we come across the timber hulls and rusting boilers, and we wonder about their stories.

X Landscape Between Pointe au Baril and Shawanaga Island

X is for extraordinary. X is for exquisite. X is for extravagant. Perhaps X is even for excessive! Paddlers like us, poking along in our scratched canoes and kayaks with our battered dry bags, our soggy tents, our filthy clothes and our packages of dubious dehydrated cuisine, may find these X words popping to mind as we journey through the cottage landscape between Pointe au Baril and Shawanaga Island. To be sure, there are modest cabins and rustic old lodges on some of the islands, but the "cottages" that will catch your eye are the multi-million dollar spreads, lavishly landscaped and decked out with satellite dishes, float plane hangers and fleets of personal watercraft.

It was the wilderness that attracted people to Pointe au Baril in the early 1900s — those first tourists who could afford the time and money to travel to such a remote place and to holiday at hotels like the well-appointed Belleview or the luxurious Ojibway. During the first decades of the twentieth century, some of these visitors, including many from the United States, began to buy up the slands near Pointe au Baril and build summer residences there. The area soon became, and remains today, one of Georgian Bay's busiest and most affluent cottage communities, its year-round population of 500 swelling to more than 8,000 in summertime. Whether you emerge from this human landscape envious or appalled, awed or amused, or merely suffering culture shock from the whole experience, you will undoubtedly feel relieved as you paddle south, back into the relative wilderness of Hertzberg Island and the McCoys.

Pointe au Baril's namesake, a wooden barrel, still marks the treacherous channel entrance.

Alternative Routes and Extensions

- *Combine the McCoys with the Minks*: This popular paddling route follows the 13 km Minks and McCoys island chain all the way from Red Rock in the south to Big McCoy and Little McCoy islands in the north, starting either from Dillon or from Snug Harbour (see Chapter 9). Total trip distance is 50 to 75 km.
- *A Day Trip to the Pointe au Baril Lighthouse*: This route involves a strenuous day's paddle down the busy Pointe au Baril Channel to visit the lighthouse, and the option of looping back around Lookout Island to take in several of this chapter's other features of interest (Q to T and X). Access is from one of the marinas at Pointe au Baril Station (minimum 12 km each way) or from the campground at Sturgeon Bay Provincial Park (minimum 14 km each way).

Maps & Information

- NTS maps 41 H/8: Parry Sound (southern area of this excursion), 41 H/9: Pointe au Baril Station (northeastern area) and 41 H/10: Naiscoot River (northwestern area).
- Nautical charts 224301: Bateau Island to Byng Inlet (overview), 228401: Parry Sound and Approaches (south), 2203A01: Carling Rock to Twin Sisters Island (southeast), 2203B01: Twin Sisters Island to Raspberry Island and Tonches Island (central east) and 2203B02: Raspberry Island to Isle of Pines (northwest).
- Chrismar Mapping Services (www.chrismar.com) has published, as part of its Adventure Map series, an excellent waterproof 1:30,000 map, Franklin, Minks & McCoys, showing detailed topographic and marine features in the southern area covered by this excursion.
- Georgian Bay Land Trust: www.gblt.org.
- Pointe au Baril Chamber of Commerce and tourism information: www.pointeaubarilchamber.com.
- Pointe au Baril Islanders' Association: www.pabia.on.ca.
- The Ojibway Club: www.ojibwayclub.com.
- Sturgeon Bay Provincial Park: www.ontarioparks.com.

CHAPTER 9

Snug Harbour to the Minks

OVERVIEW

A band of isolated islands, a maze of shoals, some jagged underwater shelves, knobs of smooth, pink granite, windswept pines, billowing clouds, occasional crumbling fragments of human history among the rocks — this is the magnificent landscape of the Mink Islands. Located 25 km northwest of Parry Sound, the Minks and neighbouring Franklin Island make a splendid long-weekend or week-long paddle, depending on the weather and your preferred pace of travel. The natural highlights along the route include the extraordinary twisted rocks at Henrietta Point and the wave-battered islands in the Minks chain. Historical highlights are the wreck of the *Seattle* off Green Island, the remains of the old fishing station at Stalker Island, and the desolate Red Rock lighthouse.

On the Minks you are guaranteed a glorious view and a refreshing breeze.

Camping on these exposed slabs of rock can be idyllic. There are many excellent places to set up your tent where you will be guaranteed a glorious view, a panoramic sunset and a refreshing breeze. Franklin Island, Green Island and several other Minks in the northwestern part of the chain are Crown land (where Canadian residents may camp free of charge and visitors from abroad must obtain a permit from the local office of the Ontario Ministry of Natural Resources). Most of the southern Minks are cottage properties whose privacy should be respected. View them from the water, but do not land or attempt to camp. The increasing popularity of the area around the Minks, their small size, and the absence (as yet) of a formal system of campsite allocation or maintenance has put great pressure on the fragile environment, so responsible, low-impact camping is more important than ever here.

Your exact route from Snug Harbour to Franklin Island and the Minks and your direction of travel (clockwise or counter-clockwise) are not important. The route described in this chapter is just one of many possibilities. With all the fascinating twists and turns in the landscape, you will likely be distracted from it in any case! What is important is a reliable navigation system. Along this eastern shore of Georgian Bay, where thirty thousand islands can feel like thirty million when you are lost, a compass and a detailed map (and the knowledge to use them correctly!) are critical, and a GPS can be very helpful indeed.

Distance: **30-40 km loop paddle (2-4 days)**

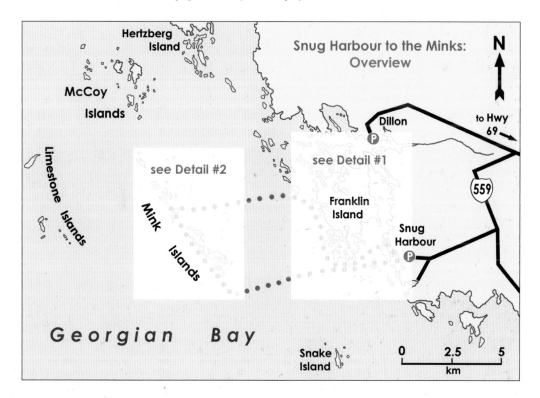

Access

- North of Nobel, exit Hwy 69 west onto County Road 559 and drive 14.8 km (be careful not to miss the sharp left turn 9.8 km along the road).
- Turn right onto the Snug Harbour Road and follow it 4.8 km to its end.
- Here you have two options: You can pay a small fee at Gilly's Snug Harbour Restaurant & Marine to use their launch and parking facilities. Or you can launch from the government dock and park in the small public lot about 500 m back up the road. (Note that the regulations and proposed fees for public access at this location are under review, so be sure to follow any instructions posted at the site.)

Route Description (see map Snug Harbour to the Minks: Overview)

1st Segment: Snug Harbour and Snug Island to Franklin Island (4 km paddle) (see Detail #1 map)

From the launch in Snug Harbour, paddle west towards open water. If time is tight, head directly out past the Snug Island lighthouse **A** and across Shebeshekong Channel to Franklin Island. A more interesting route, however, is to curve to the right into the sheltered bay less than a kilometre from the launch and make your way northwest. At the top of the bay, a very narrow channel with steep rock walls **B** and a sharp jog to the left will bring you around the top of Snug Island into Shebeshekong Channel. Paddle 1.5 km across the channel to Phoebe Point **C** at the southeast corner of Franklin Island.

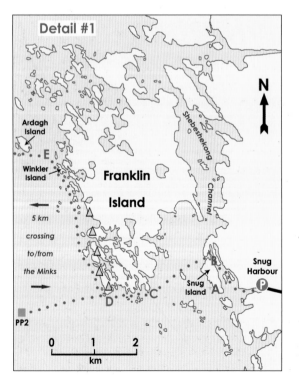

2nd Segment: Franklin Island's Southwest Coast (5 km paddle)

Franklin Island, with a circumference of about 15 km, is the largest of the many islands that lie offshore from Snug Harbour. Its topography is punctuated with interesting bays and channels, a splattering of tiny satellite islands and several inland lakes that can be accessed either by paddling or lift-over. The island makes a pleasant weekend paddle by itself if time or weather precludes the longer journey to the Minks. Franklin Island has been designated a provincial conservation reserve, so it is protected from commercial use and, unlike the mainland and many adjacent islands, has no cottages. On a busy summer weekend, however, the shore is dotted with colourful tents, and canoes and kayaks (and even small powerboats) skim across the surface of every bay.

Franklin Island's southwestern shore is its most rugged and exposed and, therefore, usually the least crowded. It makes an excellent place to camp on the first night of your trip. Although the entire shore deserves thorough exploration, the southwestern extremity at Henrietta Point **D** has spectacularly twisted rocks that will catch the eye of the most geologically challenged traveller. Rounding Henrietta Point, make your way up the western side of Franklin Island for about 4 km. Then, conditions permitting, strike out into open water just north of Winkler Island **E**, and begin the crossing to the Minks.

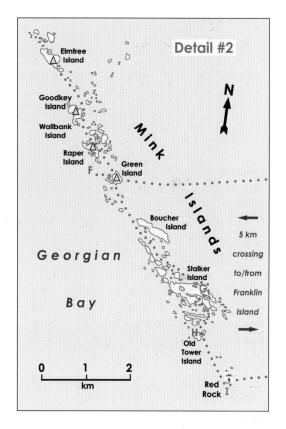

3rd Segment: Franklin Island to Green Island (6.5 km paddle)

Paddle west at a compass bearing of about 275° for 6.5 km across the channel. At first it will be difficult to identify distinct islands in the chain of Minks, but as you draw closer, you will notice that one island towards the northern end presents a raised, symmetrical shape topped with trees. This is Green Island, whose rocky headlands provide some excellent sites for camping.

4th Segment: Exploration of Minks and Red Rock (5-10 km paddle) (see Detail #2 map)

Of the dozens of small islands and rocks in the 8 km chain that makes up the Minks, some lie just above the waterline and others form shoals beneath the surface — sizzling frying pans in rough weather. From Green Island to Elmtree Island at the northwestern tip of the chain, the islands are exposed to the full force of wind and waves blowing off Georgian Bay and able to support only a few hardy trees and grasses tucked into sheltered nooks. Paddling among the channels between these islands is fascinating, and as they are Crown land, you are permitted to pull your canoe or kayak ashore and investigate more closely on foot. Tread gently, however, as the islands' small size and limited vegetation make the environment here more vulnerable to overuse.

When you have finished your exploration of the northwestern Minks, backtrack to Green Island and continue in a southeasterly direction. The islands in this part of the chain are generally larger and more protected, yielding stands of pine and cedar and a greater variety of shrubs and wildflowers. These islands have been the focus of most of the human activity in the Minks — an enviable collection of private cottages today and a thriving fishing station a century ago.

The first human relic you will find, lurking beneath the surface about 300 m west of Green Island and 300 m south of Raper Island, is the wreck of the *Seattle* **F**. The steamer was carrying a load of timber from Parry Sound to Detroit on November 11, 1903, when her engines failed during a vicious storm and she was battered on the shoals until she sank.

Crumbling pilings and rusting metal mark the site of the Mink Islands fishing station, which once supported a community of more than 100 people.

Enterprising locals salvaged her cargo the following spring, and it is said that many of the old cottages on the Minks are constructed of *Seattle* lumber. The wreck is 48 m long and lies about 6 m deep, oriented northeast to southwest. It can be challenging to find unless the water is very calm or you have some guidance from a GPS (the hull is centred on UTM coordinates 0542820E, 5027140N).

Farther south, rounding a headland on the southeastern side of Stalker Island, you will see some of the crumbling pilings and dilapidated buildings of the former fishing station G (UTM coordinates 0545550E, 5024910N). From the 1880s to the 1930s, the Minks station was among the busiest on the bay, and as many as 150 fishermen and their families lived here for the three summer months, working almost around the clock throughout the week to catch, pack and transport trout and whitefish to market in Parry Sound. In addition to the net houses, ice houses, warehouses and piers that formed the fishing station infrastructure on the islands, there were cabins, a small church and even a floating grocery store that visited the community twice a week. With collapse of the fishery during the 1940s and 1950s, the summer community gradually dwindled. Some of the buildings were restored and converted into cottages, while others rotted away. Remember that Stalker Island and most of the adjacent islands are privately owned, so please confine your exploration to the water.

Old Tower Island is the most southerly in the Mink Islands chain. It was the site of the Minks' first lighthouse H, a wooden structure built in 1870 and swept away in a storm just a few years later. Today, looking up from the water across the brilliant orange lichens and towards the bare rock summit, you may shiver to imagine how big those waves must have been!

Across the channel on Red Rock, 1 km southeast of Old Tower Island, lies the lighthouse's modern incarnation I. It was built in 1911, a flattened cylindrical structure whose metal base is anchored to the rock with concrete, its predecessor (which replaced the Old Tower Island lighthouse in 1881) having also been destroyed by storms off Georgian Bay. The island is almost inaccessible, utterly bare and less than 100 m across, yet the lighthouse was manned until its automation in 1977. A more desolate posting can hardly be imagined! Perhaps that is why the names of the lightkeepers and their families are carved so resolutely into the rock face beside the tower. Approach Red Rock with caution, as its steep shore is unforgiving. Only if the water is perfectly calm should you attempt to tie up briefly at the eastern side of the island and explore the rock on foot.

5th Segment: Red Rock to Henrietta Point (5 km paddle)

Turn east from Red Rock at a compass bearing of 84° for the return crossing to Franklin Island at Henrietta Point **D**. Navigation buoy PP2 (UTM coordinates 0549050E, 5024160N) lies almost directly along your route, giving encouragement just past the halfway point across the channel.

6th Segment: Henrietta Point to Snug Harbour (3.5 km paddle)

After a last evening or at least a rest stop on Franklin Island, continue across busy Shebeshekong Channel towards the cheerful red-and-white Snug Island lighthouse **A** and back into Snug Harbour to finish your journey.

Alternative Routes and Extensions

- *Combine the Minks and the McCoys*: This is a popular extension of the Franklin–Minks route, starting either from Snug Harbour or from Dillon (see Chapter 8). The extension adds at least another 15 to 20 km and several more days to the journey, depending on how much zigzagging you do among the islands.
- *Add Snake Island*: Snake Island and its several smaller satellite islands lie 4 km directly south of Franklin Island. They make a pleasant 8 km extension of the return paddle from Red Rock to Snug Harbour, adding another day or two to your trip, though the crossing is very exposed both to wind and to boating traffic.
- *Limestone Islands*: This small group of islands, lying 5 km west of the Minks, is a nature reserve whose white limestone rocks, fossils and colonies of birds are protected by provincial law. Camping is not permitted here, and access is prohibited altogether during the nesting season. Still, the paddle out to the Limestones is possible as a day trip from your camp on the Minks, as long as you exercise extreme caution with the weather in such exposed conditions.

Maps, Publications & Information

- NTS map 41 H/8: Parry Sound.
- Nautical chart 228401: Parry Sound and Approaches.
- Chrismar Mapping Services (www.chrismar.com) has published, as part of its Adventure Map series, an excellent waterproof 1:30,000 map, Franklin, Minks & McCoys, showing detailed topographic and marine features. The map's reverse side contains information about the natural and human history of the area, and lots of practical advice about trip planning.

CHAPTER 10

Killbear's Hiking Trails

OVERVIEW

Killbear Provincial Park, located northwest of Parry Sound, is one of the province's busiest, boasting seven campgrounds with 881 campsites, a fine new visitor centre, 3 km of sandy beaches, a popular "jumping rock," a 6 km recreational trail for cyclists, and three short hiking trails. The Twin Points, Lookout Point and Lighthouse Point trails, as their names suggest, lead to headlands with splendid views, but their routes pass many other features of interest and introduce hikers to the diverse landscape of the park.

Distances: **2 km, 3.5 km and 800 m hikes**

(Above) Along the Twin Points Trail, a bench gives a pleasant view over Kilcoursie Bay.

Access

- North of Nobel, exit Hwy 69 west onto County Road 559 and drive 19 km to the Killbear Provincial Park boundary (be careful not to miss the sharp left turn 9.8 km along the road).
- Buy a permit from the gatehouse inside the park entrance or, if the gatehouse is closed, from the park office 500 m farther down the road.
- For the Twin Points hike, turn right just past the park office and drive 1.5 km to the trailhead at the day-use parking lot.
- For the Lookout Point hike, continue 1 km past the park office and pull into the parking area on the left-hand side of the road.
- For the Lighthouse Point hike, continue 5 km past the park office to the trailhead on the west side of the large parking lot at the end of the road.

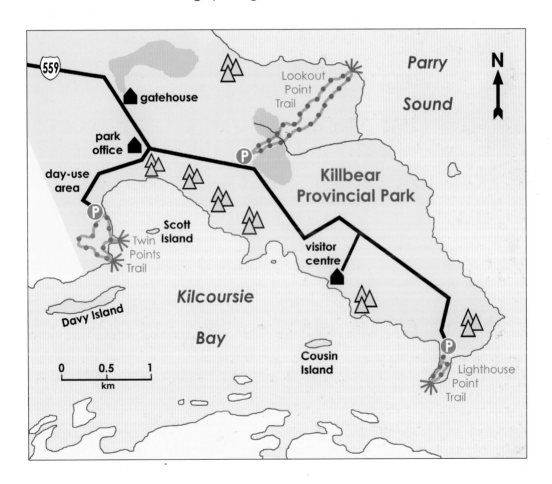

The dramatic rocky shore of Killbear Provincial Park.

Route Description

Twin Points Trail (2 km loop hike)

Leaving the parking lot, the Twin Points Trail passes briefly through a deciduous woodland and then crosses a series of smooth rock outcrops to Kilcoursie Bay before looping back along the shoreline to the day-use beach. The route is short, but it covers millions of years of Killbear's fascinating geological history. Numbered posts correspond to entries in the trail's interpretive booklet, introducing the hiker to prominent glacial landforms.

Killbear was sculpted by ice and water. As glaciers advanced across the landscape, they scraped it clean, removing overlying layers of soil and leaving scratches in the bedrock. When the last glacier began to recede about 14,000 years ago, a massive release of meltwater surged beneath the ice at tremendous pressure, carving shapes in the bedrock surface and polishing them smooth. The retreating ice left behind debris that it had plucked from the terrain farther north — glacial till (a gravelly mix of rocks of assorted sizes) and erratics (larger rocks, typically very different in appearance and chemical composition from the surrounding bedrock). Glacial rivers dumped sand, too, to form Killbear's luxurious beaches. And the landscape was further moulded between 10,000 and 5,000 years ago by the ebbing and flooding of glacial Lake Algonquin, the large precursor of the Upper Great Lakes.

Evidence of this glacial activity can be found all along the Twin Points Trail, but you may find it tempting to put the trail guide in your pocket for a few minutes and just sit on a bench and admire the glorious scenery that the glaciers have created!

Lookout Point Trail (3.5 km loop hike)

The highlight of the Lookout Point Trail is the expansive view over Parry Sound from the headland at the midpoint of the hike. In getting to and from the lookout, however, the trail winds through a variety of ecosystems, the important features of which the trail's interpretive booklet describes, its entries corresponding to numbered posts along the route.

Deeper soil in the lowlands near the start of the trail permits the growth of deciduous trees, predominantly birch and maple, and a proliferation of wildflowers every spring. The low-lying terrain also supports a lush marshland where a boardwalk keeps your feet dry as you seek out the many examples of wetland plants and animals (in springtime you may prefer to scurry through this stretch to avoid the insect inhabitants!). The trail then climbs to higher ground, and the landscape becomes drier and more exposed, revealing lichen-encrusted outcrops of rock and sun-loving trees like pine and oak. On the headland the vegetation becomes a sparser mix of shrubs and wildflowers. A couple of convenient picnic tables perched on the rocks here give you an impressive view to enjoy with your lunch. You may also wish to scramble down the hill to the right of the picnic area to dabble at the water's edge before continuing the hike.

The return trail loops back through terrain similar to the outward journey, only in reverse, from highland to lowland. By the time you return to the trailhead, you will have seen examples of all stages of the ecological cycle: lichens creeping across the rocks and breaking them down to make soil; increasingly large and sophisticated plants taking over the terrain until a mature forest develops; changes in ecosystems caused by flooding, fire and wind; and the death and decay of vegetation to produce organic debris that supports the next generation.

Lighthouse Point Trail (800 m loop hike)

There is no interpretive booklet for this, Killbear's shortest hiking trail, but its features can be enjoyed without explanation. From the parking lot, the trail makes its way to the shore and clambers over the rocks to the peninsula's southwestern tip, overlooking the entrance to Parry Sound. Considering the rich history of this part of Georgian Bay, one would expect to find an elegant old lighthouse perched on this headland, steeped in ghosts and interesting stories. Instead, a red and white metal cylinder — the product of twentieth-century automation — guides ships perfunctorily through the channel.

Lighthouse Point's natural beauty, however, makes it easy to forgive the lighthouse its shortcomings. After taking in the vista and the slabs of twisted rock stretching into the water, the trail turns away from the point and loops through the woods back to the parking lot.

Other Things to Do in the Parry Sound Area

- *West Parry Sound District Museum and Observation Tower*: Located at the top of the hill on George Street in Parry Sound, the museum has three galleries that showcase the human history of the area. The observation tower stands among the gardens outside the museum. The 30 m climb to the top is rewarded by a stellar view of the town and its environs. For information call (705) 746-5365 or 1-888-624-9005, or visit www.themuseumontowerhill.com.
- *The* **Island Queen**: Offering day cruises of the shoreline around Parry Sound, Georgian Bay and the Thirty Thousand Islands, the 550-seat *Island Queen* operates from its wharf on Bay Street in downtown Parry Sound. For information call 1-800-506-2628 or visit www.islandqueencruise.com.

Maps, Publications & Information

- NTS map 41 H/8: Parry Sound.
- *Killbear Provincial Park Information Guide* is published annually and available from the park office.
- Trail guides for the Twin Points and Lookout Point trails are available for a nominal fee at the park office and from a box at the trailheads.
- Killbear Provincial Park: (705) 342-5492, www.ontarioparks.com, www.friendsofkillbear.com.
- Parry Sound Tourism: www.parrysound.net/home, www.townofparrysound.com.

CHAPTER 11

Depot Harbour

OVERVIEW

Parry Island is home to the Wasauksing First Nation. For centuries it was part of the Ojibwe's vast hunting grounds. Then during the mid-1800s as European settlement pushed north along the shore of Georgian Bay, the island was set aside as an Indian reserve. Likely it would have remained a tranquil patch of wilderness amid the increasing bustle of the bay, had its deep, sheltered harbour not attracted the attention of Ottawa business magnate John R. Booth.

Booth had spent the latter half of the 1800s building a lumber empire in the Ottawa Valley and Algonquin Highlands. By clever management of his railway interests in eastern Canada, he forged a transportation network from Ontario to Montreal and the ice-free ports on the Atlantic coast. In 1890 Booth was looking to extend his railway line to Georgian Bay, thereby securing a direct trade route to the Upper Great Lakes and the enormous Prairie grain market beyond. The obvious port and railway terminus would have been the town of Parry Sound, but Booth found the land in Parry Sound too pricey. In addition, the townspeople were dominated by a competitor, the Beatty family, who operated several lumber mills and owned the timber rights to large tracts of forest in the area. So in 1895 the ever-resourceful Booth began to construct his own railway terminus just 7 km away on land expropriated from the Ojibwe of Parry Island. Soon afterwards he acquired an adjacent property along the railway corridor, and there he laid out the new town of Depot Harbour.

Depot Harbour became the busiest port on Georgian Bay. During its heyday in the first three decades of the 1900s, trains and Great Lakes freighters steamed in and out, exchanging cargoes of grain, timber and manufactured goods from all over the world. The port facility included vast warehouses, two enormous grain elevators and a railway roundhouse. The town, home to as many as 1,500 permanent residents and another 1,500 seasonal labourers, contained dozens of company houses and transient lodgings, and a full complement of community amenities. It even boasted luxuries like paved sidewalks, piped water and sewer services, and an electrical generator.

Depot Harbour's success, like that of most company towns, depended on the business that created it, which in turn depended on the town's direct railway link with the Atlantic coast. When that link was severed, Depot Harbour lost its raison d'être. In 1933 unusually heavy spring ice destroyed the Cache Lake trestle (a long wooden bridge that supported the tracks across an isolated lake in the Algonquin Highlands), and the Canadian

(Left) Perhaps a stairway to heaven now, these steps once led to Depot Harbour's Roman Catholic church.

Massive timbers and submerged cribbing are all that remain of Depot Harbour's oldest wharf.

National Railway, which owned the line then, decided not to replace it. Depot Harbour was doomed by an ice floe, but other factors hastened the town's demise. The Great Depression of the 1930s, coinciding with severe drought on the Prairies, left Canadian trade generally, and the grain business in particular, in a state of extreme economic hardship. The financial misfortunes of the nation's railways prompted the amalgamation of many lines and the closing of railway infrastructure, including the station and roundhouse on Parry Island.

Without an economic base for employment, most of Depot Harbour's residents moved away, and by 1940 the town had been largely abandoned. Several attempts were made to revive the port; its silos were used to house such things as coal, iron ore pellets from a Sudbury mine and, most notably, cordite, an ingredient used by the explosives factory in nearby Nobel. Exuberant end-of-war celebrations in 1945 ignited the cordite accidentally, destroying most of Depot Harbour's buildings in a single, fiery blast. The few remaining houses were sold for lumber that was used in the construction of local cottages.

In 1987 the Depot Harbour property was transferred from the CNR to the federal Department of Indian and Northern Affairs and the land was returned to the Ojibwe of Parry Island, who restored its original name, Wasauksing. The once-bustling port lies quiet now. Fishermen cast their lines from the crumbling wharves. The townsite is almost invisible among the trees, its sidewalks overgrown with moss and its foundations mere undulations in the landscape. Only a few structures remain — part of the roundhouse and an adjacent railway building — and the stairs that once led to the doors of the Roman Catholic church now climb merely to a heavenly view over the Parry Sound shoreline.

This paddling excursion approaches Depot Harbour in the tradition of Native canoes and Great Lakes steamers — by water. From Killbear Provincial Park, the route takes you along the spectacular shoreline of Kilcoursie Bay and through the channels leading into Depot Harbour to explore the remains of the port terminal and townsite. The starting point for the excursion, however, is a telephone call to the Wasauksing band office to ask for permission to visit the site. We have always been warmly welcomed, with the caution (especially appropriate in light of the town's history!) that we tread gently and respectfully on Native land.

Distance: 12 km linear paddle (24 km return) or 14 km return paddle (2nd to 4th segments only)

Access
- North of Nobel, exit Hwy 69 west onto County Road 559 and drive 19 km to the Killbear Provincial Park boundary.
- Buy a permit from the gatehouse inside the park entrance or, if the gatehouse is closed, from the park office 500 m farther down the road.
- If you are doing the full version of this paddle, turn right just past the park office, drive 1.5 km to the day-use parking lot and launch from the beach into Kilcoursie Bay.
- If you opt for the shorter alternative, continue 5 km past the park office to the large parking lot at Lighthouse Point at the end of the road, where you can launch directly into the channel between Killbear and Parry Island.

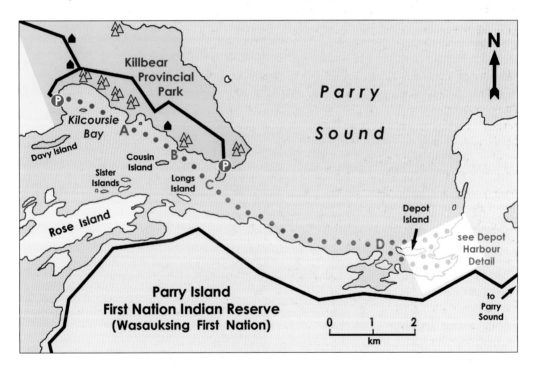

Route Description

1st Segment: Kilcoursie Bay to Lighthouse Point (4.5 km paddle)

From Killbear Park's day-use beach, paddle southeast along the shoreline of Kilcoursie Bay. Fine sandy beaches alternate with dramatic rocky headlands here, and several of the park's campgrounds line the shore, so it can be busy with swimmers and boaters. The first headland, Harold Point **A**, has a popular "jumping rock" where Killbear's more adventurous visitors congregate. Paddle past the beautiful rocks of the second headland, Granite Saddle B, and continue towards Lighthouse Point C at the tip of the Killbear peninsula.

2nd Segment: Lighthouse Point to Cadotte Point (4.5 km paddle)

Those of you taking the abbreviated (though less scenic) version of this paddle join the route here. The channel between Lighthouse Point and Parry Island is the main access for vessels entering Parry Sound from the open water of Georgian Bay, so be alert for traffic as you paddle the 1 km crossing. Then turn left and make your way along the Parry Island shore for 3.5 km to Cadotte Point D. Around the point a channel opens up, separating Parry Island (on the right) from Depot Island (on the left), and you will see a rustic wooden lighthouse E (now a private cabin) on the Depot Island side. Enter the channel and paddle between the islands into Depot Harbour F.

3rd Segment: Depot Harbour (4 km paddle) (see Depot Harbour Detail map)

From the water, the only evidence of the former port town is an array of wharves — crumbling pilings and waterlogged timber along the right-hand shore, and more recent cement and concrete structures ahead and to your left. You may also see netting and other equipment belonging to the salmon trout fish farm that operates from Depot Harbour. If you come ashore at the head of the harbour

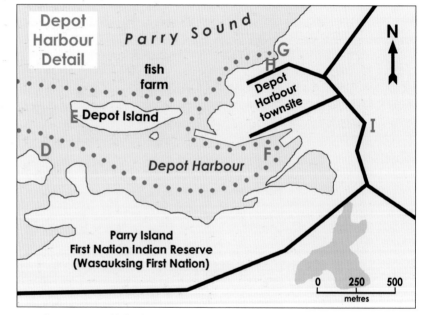

and explore the wharf area on foot, you will find some rusting remains and scattered fragments that will allow your imagination to reconstruct the railway tracks, coal sheds and storage warehouses that once lined the terminal.

After exploring the wharves and harbour, paddle through the channel on the east side of Depot Island and continue along the shore for 1 km, where you will find a large sloping rock at the eastern edge of a small bay G. Pull your canoe or kayak ashore here, and follow the track inland to see the remains of the Depot Harbour townsite — church stairs H on the headland beside the bay, overgrown sidewalks and foundations of houses and, if you walk far enough (about 1 km to the south), the remaining few walls of the railway roundhouse I.

The holding pens of a salmon trout farm are moored off Depot Island, their escapees attracting hungry gulls — and fishermen!

4th Segment: Homeward (12 km paddle)

Paddle around the outer side of Depot Island, where the floating pens of the salmon trout fish farm are moored. Make your way back along the Parry Island shore and across to the Killbear peninsula, where a swim at the day-use beach may be a welcome conclusion to the day. Paddlers following the shorter, alternative route return to the beach at Lighthouse Point.

Maps, Publications & Information

- NTS map 41 H/8: Parry Sound.
- Nautical chart 228401: Parry Sound and Approaches.
- Wasauksing First Nation: (705) 746-2531, www.anishinabek.ca.
- Killbear Provincial Park: (705) 342-5492, www.ontarioparks.com, www.friendsofkillbear.com.
- Parry Sound Tourism: www.parrysound.net/home, www.townofparrysound.com.

CHAPTER 12

The Massasauga's Moon and Wreck Islands

OVERVIEW

Like a straggly prehistoric beast, Moon Island sprawls across the mouth of the Moon River, one of the legendary Thirty Thousand Islands of Georgian Bay's southeastern shore. Moon Island was the first in a labyrinth of islands, shoals and chunks of mainland that were gathered together to form The Massasauga Provincial Park.

Paddling through the park today, you will applaud those far-sighted officials who, in 1969, sought to preserve these dwindling fragments of wilderness from the frenzy of cottage building. The Massasauga safeguards an area of about 130 km² and provides a sanctuary for many endangered species, including its namesake, the massasauga rattlesnake. Instead of luxury waterfront cottages, Moon Island boasts a collection of rustic backcountry campsites and a pleasant hiking trail. The 4 km Moon Island Trail, developed with funding from the provincial Great Lakes Heritage Coast initiative, opened in 2004. It winds across the southern lobe of the island through deciduous woodlands and visits a pretty beaver pond and an extensive marshland.

Several kilometres to the west, along the outer fringes of The Massasauga Park system, lies Wreck Island, battered regularly by the prevailing westerlies that hurtle across Georgian Bay. The rugged 1.5 km Wreck Island Trail loops around the island's western tip, threading its way between windblown pines and over barren rock outcrops and clinging so closely to the shore that it almost dips into the water at times. An interpretive trail guide introduces the visitor to the fascinating geology underfoot. Geology is what gives the Thirty Thousand Islands the distinctive character that draws travellers back to their shores year after year. The islands formed during a particularly turbulent time in Ontario's history. Between 1.5 billion and 1 billion years ago, several small continents collided along what is now Georgian Bay's eastern shore, pushing up the massive Grenville mountain range. The rocks at the base of the mountains, buried 20 to 30 km deep and subjected to extraordinary heat and pressure, were profoundly altered both chemically and structurally. The result was Wreck Island's distinctive rock — gneiss (pronounced "nice") — with its twisted, multicoloured ribbons. Glaciers exposed the rock in more recent millennia, grinding down the mountaintops with ice and washing away the debris with meltwater.

For the geologically challenged, it may be a relief to know that there is more to Wreck Island than its beautiful rocks. There is also the shipwreck that gives the island its name.

(Left) Fascinating geology along the Wreck Island Trail.

The wreck of the Waubuno *nudges the shore of Bradden Island.*

The *Waubuno* ran aground here in 1879 during a November gale, and all souls on board were lost. Built in 1856, the *Waubuno* served the Beatty family. William Beatty and his sons owned extensive timber rights and lumber mills across the Algonquin Highlands and around Georgian Bay, and they developed a network of steamships and railway lines to transport their lumber — and then grain and other cargo — to market. The *Waubuno*, a sleek 41 m steamer with a coal-fired engine and a side-mounted paddlewheel, joined the Beatty transportation business as a carrier for freight and passengers. Her route between Collingwood and Sault Ste. Marie, with stops at ports on Georgian Bay that included Parry Sound, competed directly with that of the *Maganettawan*, owned by rival lumber interests in Byng Inlet.

The autumn of 1879 had been a particularly stormy one, and on the evening of November 21, the *Waubuno* and the *Maganettawan* were both moored in Collingwood, waiting out another squall. When at four the next morning the weather abated slightly, the *Waubuno*'s captain, George Burkett, assembled his crew and passengers and steamed out of port. Several hours later the lightkeeper at Christian Island saw the ship heading briskly northeast towards Parry Sound and into gathering wind and snow. That was the last record of the *Waubuno*, though loggers working near the mouth of the Moon River reported hearing what could have been a steamship's distress signal at about noon that day. When the *Maganettawan* reached Parry Sound on November 24, the *Waubuno* was nowhere to be seen. Piecing the story together from wreckage discovered afterwards, investigators surmised that she sought shelter from the storm among the islands that now form part of the provincial park but was tossed onto the rocks and torn apart. Her deck and superstructure, together with 24 passengers and crew, sank somewhere in deeper waters, never to be recovered. The hull drifted towards the north shore of what is now called Wreck Island and lodged itself in the gap between Wreck Island and neighbouring Bradden Island, where it lies still.

This excursion combines the two hikes on Moon Island and Wreck Island with a visit to the *Waubuno* wreck and a paddle of 25 km or more. It can be done at a leisurely pace as a weekend trip from the Pete's Place access point at Blackstone Harbour, spending one or two nights in backcountry campsites along the route. It is also possible to tackle segments of the excursion as energetic day trips by launching from Woods Bay and paddling directly to Moon Island or Wreck Island.

Conversely, the route may be extended almost indefinitely, either northwest among the windswept islands, shoals and open water of Georgian Bay or northeast over one of the short portages into the sheltered bays and inland lakes of the park's interior. Armed with a map and a little imagination, many holidays can be enjoyed here. Do not underestimate the navigational challenges in this part of Georgian Bay, however. Always carry a detailed, reliable map, and follow your progress across the bay closely, noting landmarks or marking GPS coordinates along the way.

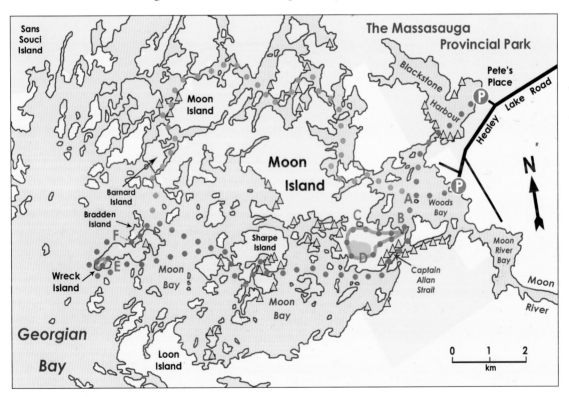

Distance: 25-35 km paddle, plus 4 km and 1.5 km loop hikes
(many shorter or longer versions of the route are also possible)

Access

- Take exit #189 from Hwy 400 onto Hwy 69.
- Follow Hwy 69 for 4 km to MacTier and turn left onto County Road 11.
- Drive 6 km, turn left onto Healey Lake Road and follow it 16 km to the Pete's Place access, which exits on the right.
- If you are planning to spend a few days paddling and hiking at The Massasauga Provincial Park, register and pay your backcountry campsite fee at the Pete's Place office (or at the self-serve station during off-peak times), and launch your canoe or kayak into Blackstone Harbour.
- Day-use parking is not permitted at Pete's Place, so if you wish to do all or part of this excursion as a day trip, continue for 2 km along Healey Lake Road to Woods Bay, where private marinas provide parking and launch facilities for a modest fee.

Route Description

1st Segment: Pete's Place or Woods Bay to Moon Island (2-4 km paddle)

From the launch at Pete's Place, paddle for 2 km across Blackstone Harbour and through the narrow channel into Woods Bay; then set your course southwest across Woods Bay. If you are launching from one of the bay's marinas instead, paddle directly west across Woods Bay. About 700 m outside the entrance to Captain Allan Strait, a navigation marker perched on a rock **A** provides a nesting platform for ospreys.

The osprey is a mid-sized member of the raptor family that has characteristic talons and a hooked beak for seizing and devouring prey. Unlike many of its relatives — hawks, eagles, falcons, vultures and owls — the osprey feeds almost exclusively on fish and has developed some adaptations for this diet, including a flexible outer toe and spiny feet to hold slippery catches while in flight (the fish typically oriented in the same direction as the bird to maintain aerodynamic efficiency!). Human activity virtually eliminated the species from the Great Lakes several decades ago by destroying its shoreline habitat and introducing chemical pollutants into the ecosystem. Crops and forests were sprayed extensively with the pesticide DDT in the 1950s and 1960s, and the chemical drained into the waterways, where it accumulated in fish stocks and became increasingly concentrated in fish-eating predators like the osprey, causing eggshells to thin and break.

Public concern about the declining osprey population led to scientific research and government bans on DDT across North America in the early 1970s, and the species has gradually recovered. The osprey is surprisingly tolerant of human presence and will happily substitute navigation markers, satellite dishes, cottage chimneys and other man-made structures for the dead trees that are its traditional nest sites. Many Georgian Bay cottagers have constructed nesting platforms on poles to attract ospreys to their properties, and success has been remarkable. From a single breeding pair atop a hydro pole in 1973, the number of ospreys grew to 50 breeding pairs in 1993. The Georgian Bay Osprey Society, in an effort to better understand, protect and promote the species, monitors the nesting platforms and maintains an annual census of the ospreys that use them. Census numbers show worrying population fluctuations over the past decade, indicating that ongoing work is needed to ensure their rehabilitation.

Keep a respectful distance from the ospreys' navigation marker and use your binoculars to check activity at the nest (between early May and mid-July, the adult birds will be scrambling to feed and guard the year's brood until they have fledged). Then paddle 700 m from the navigation marker to the southeastern corner of Moon Island, where you may tie your canoe or kayak to the day-use dock **B** for the hike that follows.

2nd Segment: Moon Island Trail (4 km hike)

Pick up the Moon Island Trail from the day-use dock, and follow it across a small marshy area behind the dock. You will likely see sundews here, members of the carnivorous plant family that includes pitcher plants and Venus flytraps. These remarkable plants trap insects in their sticky leaf hairs and use specialized enzymes to digest them, thereby supplementing the meagre supply of nutrients they are able to get from the saturated, acidic soil. From the marsh the trail climbs to drier ground and makes its way west along a gentle track through a deciduous woodland. After 1 km the trail passes a tiny beaver pond **C** and soon afterwards skirts a large wetland. A forest of

This osprey family has built its nest atop a navigation marker along the busy marine channel through Woods Bay.

dead trees, their branches bleached white by the sun, makes an ideal nesting environment for birds like the great blue heron. Elegant and superbly efficient when standing motionless among the marsh grasses waiting to spear a fish, the heron takes on an ungainly and almost comical appearance when perched on its untidy stick nest in the treetops. The trail pauses at a rocky shelf overlooking the wetland **D** and then loops back through the forest to the day-use dock **B**.

3rd Segment: Moon Island to Wreck Island (10.5 km paddle)

Paddle around the corner into Captain Allan Strait and west along the channel for 1.5 km into Moon Bay. On a sunny summer weekend, The Massasauga's wilderness can seem illusive here. Busy campsites line the strait, the waterway throbs with motorboat traffic, and out in Moon Bay, the islands sport cottages of all sorts, from rustic camps to extravagant chalets. Although the distance across Moon Bay northwest from Captain Allan Strait to your destination on Wreck Island is only 7.5 km as the crow flies, your route by canoe or kayak will weave among the bay's many islands, increasing that length considerably. The most direct, though busiest, of the many possible routes is the main boating channel running around Sharpe Island's eastern and northern shores. The most interesting — and most peaceful — is a narrow channel that squeezes along the south side of Sharpe Island. Whichever route you choose, wend your way to the day-use dock on the south side of Wreck Island E. The picnic tables and outhouse here may be welcome after your morning's paddle.

4th Segment: Wreck Island Trail (1.5 km loop hike)

Guided by the Wreck Island Trail interpretive booklet, follow the trail from the picnic area as it loops in a counter-clockwise direction around the western tip of the island. Engraved rocks along the route correspond to entries in the booklet that explain the geological features seen around you. You will hike past "erratics" and "percussion boulders," incongruous rounded rocks abandoned here by the last glacier; you will walk across the multicoloured ribbons of gneiss, quartz, mica and pegmatite formed when this island was buried deep beneath the Grenville Mountains; and you will stop beside sculpted rocks resembling giant clam shells and dinner rolls that were shaped by the erosive force of water. Though the trail is short, the billion years of Earth's history contained in its 1.5 km may slow your hike to the leisurely pace of a geological event. Even if you are not much interested in their geology, you will certainly pause to admire the extraordinary beauty of Wreck Island's rocks.

5th Segment: Wreck Island's Wreck (2.3 km paddle)

Back at the day-use dock E, launch your canoe or kayak and paddle around the western tip of Wreck Island to appreciate the shoreline from the perspective of the water. The route exposes you to the afternoon wind and open water of Georgian Bay, so you may find the paddling more challenging here. As the shore curves back towards the east, you will pass between some tiny rocky islands and into the shelter of a small channel between Wreck Island and Bradden Island. In this channel the hull of the doomed *Waubuno* came to rest; you will find her skeleton F reaching up from the shallows, her nose pressed against the Bradden Island shore (with a GPS the wreck can be located at UTM coordinates 0570880E, 4999090N). This part of the island is privately owned, so you will have to restrict your investigation of the wreck to what you can see from the water.

6th Segment: Homeward (12-18 km paddle)

Between Wreck Island and your take-out at Pete's Place or Woods Bay lies the sprawling expanse of Moon Island. Your homeward journey, therefore, must either retrace your outward route through Captain Allan Strait along the south side of Moon Island, or it must loop around the north side of the island and down the busy boating channel along its eastern shore. The latter alternative adds at least 6 km to the paddling distance but offers interesting new vistas and the opportunity to extend your exploration into The Massasauga Park's northern waters and inland lakes.

A lush wetland along the Moon Island Trail.

Maps, Publications & Information

- NTS maps 31 H/4: Lake Joseph and 41 H/4: Sans Souci.
- Nautical charts 2202e01: Moon Island and Surrounding Areas and 2202c01: Twelve Mile Bay to Rose Island.
- The Massasauga Provincial Park has published an excellent topographic map covering the entire parkland on a single sheet. It includes detailed information about paddling routes, hiking trails, campsite locations and the park's natural and human history, and it is widely available in outdoor stores or from the Pete's Place access.
- The *Wreck Island Trail* interpretive guidebook explains the geological features found along the trail. Copies are usually available from a box at the trailhead, but during busy times or in the off-season the box may be empty. To avoid disappointment pick up a guide from the Pete's Place access before heading out.
- The Massasauga Provincial Park: (705) 378-0685, www.ontarioparks.com.
- Parry Sound Tourism: www.parrysound.net/home.
- The Georgian Bay Osprey Society: www.gbosprey.ca.

CHAPTER 13

Beausoleil Island

OVERVIEW

Beausoleil Island is the largest of the 59 islands and shoals — tiny fragments of protected wilderness — that make up the Georgian Bay Islands National Park. The park is scattered among the Thirty Thousand Islands of southeastern Georgian Bay, in the heart of the bay's cottage country. Beausoleil is wedged among navigation channels leading into Honey Harbour, Midland and the Severn River that buzz with boating traffic throughout the summer months. During the off-season, in early spring or late fall, the waterways become more peaceful, and a visit to the island yields many fascinating discoveries.

Beausoleil Island is only 8 km long and little more than a kilometre wide for much of its length. Yet it has an extraordinary diversity of natural features and inhabitants. This is because it straddles the geographic boundary between southern Ontario and the Canadian Shield.

(Above) Fairy Lake is a peaceful pool nestled in the bedrock of northern Beausoleil Island.

The southern half of the island is covered with glacial till, a thick mixture of soil, sand and rock left behind by the Wisconsin glacier as it retreated from the area 10,000 years ago. Till holds moisture effectively, and its composition is relatively rich and alkaline, so it is able to support southerly species of plants — deciduous forests of maple, birch and beech, stands of hemlock and carpets of spring wildflowers — which demand more nutrients than their northern counterparts.

In stark contrast, the northern half of the island is characterized by extensive outcrops of bedrock, scraped almost bare by the same glacier that left such nourishing deposits of till just a short distance away. The windswept rocks are interspersed with boggy lowlands, and the thin pockets of soil that remain are either coarse and dry or saturated and acidic. Only a few hardy species can tolerate the harsh habitat of the north — white pines and red oaks on the dry uplands, cattails and sphagnum moss in the wetlands, and lichens creeping across the surface of the bedrock.

The animal population of Beausoleil Island is dominated by reptiles and amphibians — 33 species of frogs, salamanders, turtles and snakes in all. More of these herpetiles live in the park than anywhere else in Canada, and they include the rare massasauga rattlesnake, Ontario's only venomous snake. The island's prevailing mammals, appropriately, are aquatic creatures like mink, muskrat and beaver. And it has a large transient population of migratory birds.

Beausoleil Island's human population has also been a transient one. Native cultures used the island as a seasonal base for hunting and trading for at least 2,000 years before the arrival of Europeans on its shores. For the voyageurs it was a rest stop during their travels between the Severn River and northern Georgian Bay. In fact, the name Beausoleil comes from a Metis fur trader who camped on the island in 1819. With increased colonization during the seventeenth and eighteenth centuries, Georgian Bay's Native people were forced into reserves, where Christian teachings and an agricultural lifestyle replaced their traditional beliefs and annual patterns of migration. In 1836 a group of nearly 250 Ojibwe, led by Chief John Assance, established a settlement on the southeastern side of Beausoleil Island. They built a small community and a church and planted fields of corn and potatoes. But their attempts to farm the unyielding land ultimately failed, and in 1856 most of the band moved to Christian Island where their descendants, the Beausoleil First Nation, still live. The few Ojibwe that remained on Beausoleil Island were joined by some hardy immigrant families from Scotland and France. They subsisted by fishing and farming, hunting and trapping, and they worked in the logging and gravel-quarrying industries that flourished during the latter half of the nineteenth century.

Fairy Trail boardwalk.

By 1900, with the extension of railway lines into major towns along Georgian Bay, the shoreline and islands were being snapped up for vacation properties by city dwellers from the south. Beausoleil Island escaped cottage development, ironically, because its forests were protected by the logging company that owned the timber rights to them. Growing concern during the 1920s about the pace at which Georgian Bay was losing its wilderness prompted local residents to petition the federal government to preserve the few islands in the southeastern part of the bay that were not yet in private hands. So, in 1929, Beausoleil Island and 26 other, smaller islands were gathered under the protective banner of the Georgian Bay Islands National Park, and the three families still living there received financial assistance to relocate.

Additional land acquired during subsequent decades has increased the number of the park's islands to 59, ranging from barren rocks along the outer fringes of Georgian Bay, to Beausoleil Island, which boasts 11 campgrounds, two YMCA youth camps, and dozens of docks, picnic shelters and other visitor amenities. Despite its accessibility and popularity, the island's natural habitat has been largely preserved so that the outdoor enthusiast may enjoy exploring the varied landscape. An extensive network of hiking trails criss-crosses the island, giving access to sites of natural and human historical interest. And, being an island, Beausoleil has abundant opportunities for paddling.

The three excursions in this chapter — a hike across the rugged northern Shield, a gentler hike through the glacial terrain of the south, and a paddle around the island's entire shoreline — give a comprehensive introduction to Beausoleil Island. But they are just three of many possibilities. Armed with a park map and a little imagination, other alternatives can be devised, depending on your starting point and the time available.

Access
- Take exit #156 from Hwy 400 and drive west on Muskoka Road 5 for 12 km, into Honey Harbour.
- During the regular season (from mid-May to late October), buy a permit from the Georgian Bay Islands National Park Office, on the left as you reach the waterfront.
- During the off-season, permits are available from self-serve stations at access points on Beausoleil Island.
- Expansion of the park's Honey Harbour facilities is expected to include parking, but as this book goes to press, the parking lot is still in the planning stage. Meanwhile, parking is available for a small fee at several nearby businesses and at the church across the road.
- Launch your canoe or kayak from the beach behind the park office.

Circumnavigation of Beausoleil Island
Distance: **27-35 km paddle**

Route Description

Circumnavigation of Beausoleil Island is possible, theoretically, in a single day from Honey Harbour. But with such variety of landscape, so many bays and inlets to explore

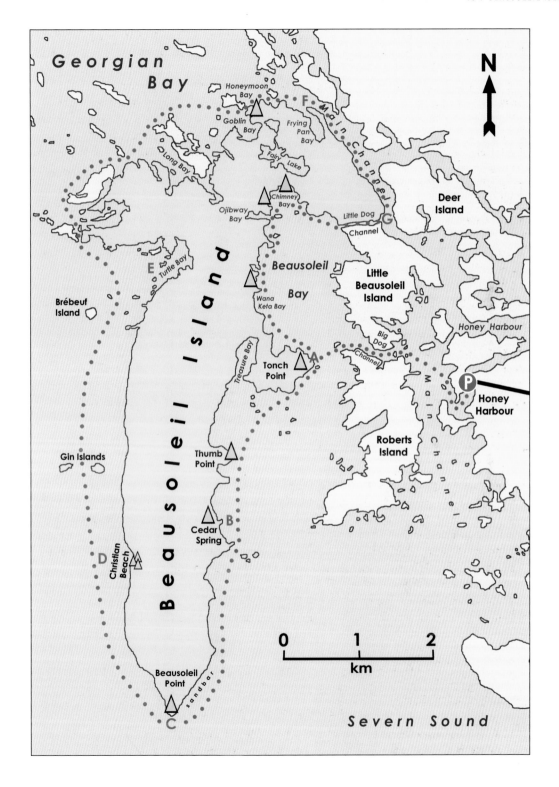

View from the Christian Trail lookout. PHOTO BY RICK CHUCHRA

and interesting places to pull ashore, the paddle around the island is more appropriately done over two or three days. You can pitch your tent overnight in the semi-serviced Cedar Spring campground or in one of the smaller, more primitive campsites along the shore. These sites are all on the eastern half of Beausoleil Island. The western shore is exposed to prevailing winds off Georgian Bay, and its shoreline is rocky and rugged; the only campsites here are in the group campground at Christian Beach (see the park office for camping regulations).

In this chapter we circumnavigate Beausoleil Island in a clockwise direction. The route is organized into eight segments, and the route description contains an overview of the landscape and a list of facilities and points of interest for each section. If you wish to paddle in a counter-clockwise direction or start from a different location, simply shuffle the segment descriptions to match your preferred route.

1st Segment: Honey Harbour to Tonch Point (2.5 km paddle)

From the launch, paddle 500 m out to the Main Channel. Turn right and make your way northwest along the channel for 750 m and then turn left into Big Dog Channel. After another 750 m, Big Dog Channel opens into Beausoleil Bay, and Beausoleil Island appears on the opposite shore. Turn southwest and paddle 500 m across Beausoleil Bay to Tonch Point **A**.

2nd Segment: Tonch Point to Cedar Spring (2.5 km paddle)

This section of shoreline is one of the park's busiest, with beaches, picnic areas, docking and mooring facilities, the park information office, and campgrounds at Tonch Point,

Thumb Point and Cedar Spring. Treasure Bay, tucked into a narrow fold in the shore, still holds a centuries-old secret. It is said that in 1649, when the Huron fled to Christian Island to escape Iroquois attacks on their mainland villages, they stopped on Beausoleil Island en route and buried a fortune in silver coins and priceless relics from the Jesuit mission at Sainte-Marie. This treasure has never been discovered!

3rd Segment: Cedar Spring to Beausoleil Point (3 km paddle)

South of Cedar Spring B, the shoreline is somewhat quieter. The terrain is shallow and sandy, fringed with small lagoons full of aquatic grasses. Sandbars extend far from the shore and can snag your canoe or kayak when water levels are low. Approaching Beausoleil Point at the southern tip of the island C, the sand gives way to rocks, and the water becomes deeper. The Beausoleil Point campground, with half a dozen reservable sites, is the last opportunity for camping until Honeymoon Bay, more than 10 km to the north.

4th Segment: Beausoleil Point to Turtle Bay (6 km paddle)

This section of Beausoleil Island's coast is exposed to weather hurtling across Georgian Bay from the west. Except for a small sandy bay at Christian Beach D, the character of the shoreline is quite rugged, with jumbles of boulders and pebbles, and scrubby, windblown vegetation. Just offshore, the smooth, sculpted rocks of the Gin Islands and Brébeuf Island give a taste of the northern landscape just a short distance up the coast. The transition E between the southern glacial terrain and the Canadian Shield happens as you cross Turtle Bay.

5th Segment: Turtle Bay to Frying Pan Bay (5 km paddle)

The northwestern shore of Beausoleil Island is quintessential Canadian Shield landscape — rocky headlands and deeply indented bays, windswept trees perched on twisted ribbons of rock, and a generous scattering of small islands that can make navigation a challenge. At the base of some of the bays, tempting crescent-shaped beaches, like those in Goblin Bay and Honeymoon Bay, make splendid places to stop for a picnic lunch and a swim. Camping facilities are also available at Honeymoon Bay.

6th Segment: Frying Pan Bay to Little Dog Channel (2.5 km paddle)

Rounding Spero Point F, the route follows the busy Main Channel, which passes along the northeastern side of Beausoleil Island and into Honey Harbour. Keep close to the shore of the island, and turn into the narrow entrance G to Little Dog Channel.

7th Segment: Little Dog Channel to Tonch Point (3 km paddle)

Paddle 400 m through Little Dog Channel, which is shallow and reedy and considerably quieter than the Main Channel. At its western end, the channel passes between rock outcrops into Beausoleil Bay. The bay has a pleasantly varied shoreline, with smooth rocks, marshlands, sandy beaches and several facilities for camping and day use. Paddle around the bay, poking into Chimney Bay and Ojibway Bay at the northern end and into Wana Keta Bay at the southern end. Follow the shoreline as it curves back towards Tonch Point A to complete your circumnavigation.

8th Segment: Tonch Point to Honey Harbour (2.5 km paddle)
Return via the outward route through Big Dog Channel and Main Channel to the launch at the Honey Harbour park office.

Beausoleil's Southern Terrain and Human History
Distance: **6.4 km loop hike**

Route Description

This hike explores the glacial landscape of southern Beausoleil Island and visits the site of the former Ojibwe farming settlement. The route follows sections of the Huron, Georgian and Christian hiking trails. As described here, the hike begins at Cedar Spring, but it can also be accessed from Beausoleil Point or Christian Beach.

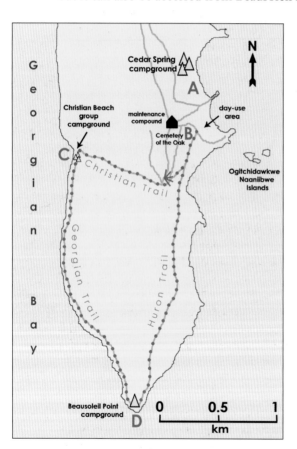

1st Segment: Cedar Spring (500 m hike)

Now the summer headquarters of the Georgian Bay Islands National Park, with an information centre, a popular day-use area and an 87-site campground, Cedar Spring **A** was once a peaceful village — the farming settlement that Chief John Assance and his Ojibwe band established between 1836 and 1956. The only evidence of their labours today is a field, overgrown with meadow grasses and sumac, and a cemetery encircled by oak trees. The carved wooden crosses in the Cemetery of the Oak **B** are poignant reminders of the lives lived and lost in this harsh landscape. Cedar Spring was also the site of an aggregate quarry. During the early 1900s, glacial sand and gravel were dug from several sites on southern Beausoleil Island and transported over a tramway at Cedar Spring onto cargo ships bound for construction sites near Midland.

2nd Segment: Cedar Spring to Christian Beach (1 km hike)

From the hub of hiking trails at Cedar Spring, the Christian Trail leads up the hill to a pleasant lookout over Beausoleil Bay and then across to Christian Beach **C** on the Georgian Bay side of the island. The gently rolling terrain, with its mixture of sand, soil and pebbles is the legacy of the Wisconsin glacier, which left deposits of glacial till

10,000 years ago and provided the foundation for the forest of deciduous trees and hemlock that stretch above us today.

3rd Segment: Christian Beach to Beausoleil Point (2.2 km hike)

Christian Beach is an isolated crescent of sand along the island's otherwise rugged and rocky southwestern shore. From Christian Beach southward to the tip of the island at Beausoleil Point D, the Georgian Trail closely follows this shoreline, providing many glimpses through the windblown cedars and across the jumble of cobbles and shale at the water's edge, out to Georgian Bay. At Beausoleil Point there is a small campground and picnic shelter.

4th Segment: Beausoleil Point to Cedar Spring (2.7 km hike)

Between Beausoleil Point and Cedar Spring, the Huron Trail follows an inland track through the woods. The shoreline along the southeastern side of the island is low and sandy and has many reed-filled lagoons. The trail emerges into the overgrown field at the edge of the old Ojibwe settlement, bringing you back to your starting point at Cedar Spring.

Beausoleil's Northern Terrain
Distance: **3-15 km loop hike**

Route Description

This hike explores the rugged Canadian Shield landscape of northern Beausoleil Island. The route winds over rock outcrops, through pine and oak woodlands, into moss-carpeted valleys, and around small lakes, marshlands and bays — all characteristic features of Shield terrain. The park's network of trails makes possible a choice of several loop hikes of different lengths, depending on your interests, energy and time. For a brief but glorious taste of the northern terrain, you can hike the Fairy Trail (3 km). For a longer hike with greater variety of scenery, you can combine the Fairy Trail with the Cambrian Trail (5.7 km). Or, for a challenging full-day trek, you can add the Massasauga, Huron, Dossyonshing and Rockview trails to the loop (15 km). There are many access points for these hikes — Honeymoon Bay or Frying Pan Bay on the north side of the island, or one of the many campgrounds, docks and day-use areas along the northern shore of Beausoleil Bay and Chimney Bay.

Option 1: Fairy Trail (3 km hike)

The Fairy Trail is a gem of Canadian Shield wilderness. It includes a splendid variety of scenery over a relatively short hike. The terrain can be rough, however, and you will want to stop often to admire the views, so allow several hours for the journey. From the Chimney Bay dock A, take the short access trial north 185 m; then turn left onto the Fairy Trail, and follow its red markers in a clockwise direction.

Much of the route is across bald outcrops of rock, dappled with colourful lichens and fringed with juniper bushes and isolated pine and oak trees. Intermittently the trail drops

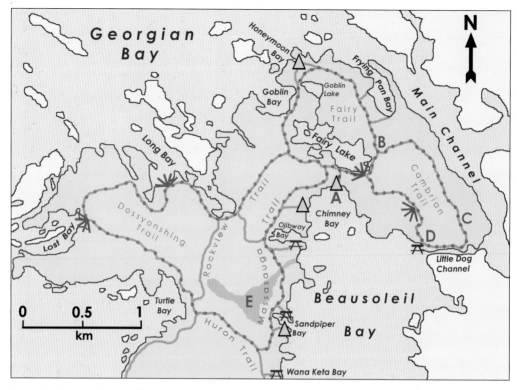

into shallow valleys with softer footing over pine needles and moss. Boardwalks have been constructed along some of the soggier sections of the route.

The trail visits two beautiful small lakes along the way. Fairy Lake is directly ahead of you at the end of the access trail, and its shoreline has several smooth rock ledges that make perfect picnic places. You will see Fairy Lake again towards the end of the hike as the trail loops back to a scenic lookout. Tiny Goblin Lake is tucked into the northwest corner of the island about 1.2 km from the start of the hike. The trail also passes the heads of four bays — Chimney Bay, where the hike begins; Goblin Bay, where a fine crescent of sand will tempt you to swim; Honeymoon Bay, with its beach and campground; and finally, the long, sheltered inlet of Frying Pan Bay.

Option 2: Fairy and Cambrian Trails (5.7 km hike)

Adding the Cambrian Trail (2.9 km) to the Fairy Trail nearly doubles the length of the hike, but it introduces several interesting landscape features to the route. Leaving the Fairy Trail three-quarters of the way around the loop B, turn left onto the Cambrian Trail and follow its yellow markers in a clockwise direction. The trail descends from the rock outcrops into a forest of hemlock and hardwood. After 1.2 km it passes a rock wall C that is home to many ferns, mosses and lichens, including a display of rock tripe, whose large lobes may be brittle and brown in the heat of summer or leathery and green after a rainfall. Just 200 m past the wall, the trail comes to the shore of Little Dog Channel. It follows the channel west to Beausoleil Bay, where there is a day-use dock D (an alternate

Dossyonshing Trail lookout over Long Bay.

access point for this hike). Here the trail climbs back onto the Shield bedrock. Turning north, it crosses a kilometre of open rock with marvellous views towards the bay, rejoining the Fairy Trail at the lookout over the lake.

Option 3: Massasauga, Huron, Dossyonshing and Rockview Trails Extension (up to 15 km hike)

The Fairy Trail hike may be extended south to take in several other trails and an even greater variety of scenery. This route crosses the boundary between the northern landscape of the Canadian Shield and the glacial landscape of the south, and the terrain alternates between bedrock outcrops and valleys forested with hardwoods and hemlocks. Highlights along these trails include the extensive marshland **E** to the west of the boardwalk below Ojibway Bay, and the lookouts over Lost Bay and Long Bay on the Dossyonshing Trail. The brief encounter with the Huron Trail at the south end of the route, as it crosses the island on a wide, gentle track, will seem incongruous after all the bedrock scramblings in the north.

If you elect to hike this extended route, you may prefer to start from one of the campgrounds or day-use facilities along the Beausoleil Bay shore or from Honeymoon Bay, where a swim and a sunset campfire will be a welcome conclusion to a long day on the trail.

Maps, Publications & Information
- NTS map 31 D/13: Penetanguishene.
- Nautical chart 224101: Port Severn to Christian Island.
- Georgian Bay Islands National Park information (including the park's annual *Visitor Guide* and maps) is available from www.pc.gc.ca/pn-np/on/georg, or call (705) 526-9804.
- Honey Harbour tourism information is available from the Southeast Georgian Bay Chamber of Commerce at www.hhpsacofc.ca.

CHAPTER 14

Awenda

OVERVIEW

Awenda Provincial Park is one of south-central Ontario's largest and most comfortable natural environment parks. Formed in 1979 to protect an area of significant ecological diversity at the tip of the Midland peninsula, the park encompasses 18.6 km² of mainland and, lying just 3 km offshore, the monolithic Giants Tomb Island. Park facilities include 333 spacious drive-in campsites, several day-use picnic areas, four sandy beaches along the Georgian Bay shore, seven hiking trails, a nature shop run by the Friends of Awenda Park and a trail/activity centre with a 400-seat amphitheatre. It is a busy place during the summer months and makes an excellent base from which to explore the Midland area.

Awenda straddles two distinct ecological communities, each with its own natural features and unique inhabitants. The larger of the two communities is the upland plateau that covers the park's interior. The uplands are characterized by relatively deep, well-drained soil composed of sand and organic material. They were formed about 12,500 years ago when the Wisconsin glacier withdrew from southern Georgian Bay, releasing a massive quantity of rock debris and depositing it along the retreating edge of the ice. Originally this terrain supported an old-growth forest of white pine, but it was stripped by logging in the late 1800s. Now the land accommodates a mature second-growth deciduous forest, typical of the Great Lakes–St. Lawrence Forest Region, dominated by maple and beech. Many species of spring wildflowers burst forth annually in the brief interval between the melting of the snow and the closing of the leafy canopy over the forest floor.

In the narrow strip of land adjacent to the Georgian Bay shore lies the second of Awenda's two ecological communities: a damp lowland fed by small creeks draining from the uplands. In the thin, acidic soil, the vegetation here is more northerly in character, dominated by coniferous tree species like cedar and hemlock, hardy pioneers like aspen and birch, and moisture-loving mosses and wetland shrubs.

Between the two ecosystems is a drop in elevation of 30 to 60 m — the Algonquin Bluff, which marks the ancient shoreline of glacial Lake Algonquin, precursor of the Upper Great Lakes. Lake Algonquin formed from the meltwater that accumulated along the southern edge of the receding Wisconsin glacier, and for a time it spread across a

(Left) Winter on the beach at Awenda Provincial Park.

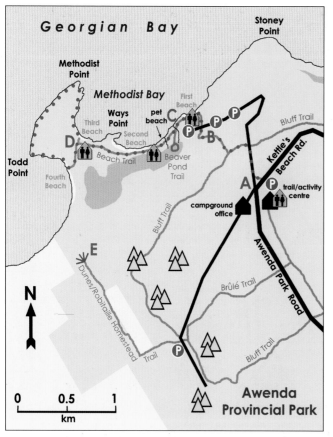

vast area and reached a depth as much as 90 m greater than that of today's Great Lakes. Then, as new outlets became uncovered and the land rebounded from the weight of glacial ice, Lake Algonquin gradually drained away. In its wake it left a steep shoreline and some impressive sand dunes that lie many metres above the present-day lake level.

The excursion in this chapter begins at Awenda's trail/activity centre and makes use of several of the park's hiking trails. It meanders briefly through the upland forest on the Bluff Trail, descends the bluff on the Nipissing Trail, follows the shoreline west along the Beach Trail and then loops back around Methodist Point, scrambling over enormous boulders with spectacular views of Georgian Bay. On the return journey, an optional side trip up the Beaver Pond Trail offers a visit to an abandoned beaver colony and the residual wetland left by their dams.

The trails are accessible year-round, giving good opportunities for snowshoeing and skiing in the winter months. Some lovely hiking can be had here in the "shoulder" seasons during spring and fall, when the park campground is closed, the trails are nearly deserted, and the views from the bluff are less obstructed by deciduous growth. Note that dogs are prohibited on the Beach Trail to the west of the pet beach and on the Beaver Pond Trail.

Distance: **8.4 km hike**

Access
- From Penetanguishene follow the Awenda Park signs that lead you north along County Road 26, east along Concession Road 16 and north again along Awenda Park Road.
- At the junction of Awenda Park Road and Kettle's Beach Road, turn right into the parking lot at the trail/activity centre.
- There is a self-serve station at the west side of the parking lot, where you may buy your day-use permit for the park, and an outhouse, one of several convenient pit stops along the route.

Route Description

1st Segment: Trail Centre to Beach Trail (1.2 km hike)

From the parking lot, follow Awenda Park Road north. There will be car traffic on the road during the summer months, but it is gated A during the off-season when the park campground is closed. After 400 m turn left onto the Bluff Trail, and 300 m later turn right onto the Nipissing Trail. This short trail descends 32 m from the uplands to the base of the bluff, connecting the park's two ecological communities with a wooden staircase B. You will notice the abrupt change in vegetation as you make your way down the steepest section, the airy deciduous forest giving way to a cool, dense and rather scruffy woodland at the bottom. The trail ends where it meets Awenda Park Road, which has descended the bluff on a gentler slope.

2nd Segment: Beach Trail from First Beach to Fourth Beach (1.8 km hike)

Cross the road to pick up the Beach Trail, which will take you 100 m to First Beach. Turn left and follow the trail west along the shore for 200 m to a lookout platform C, pausing there to admire the view across the 3 km channel to Giants Tomb Island and north into the open water of Georgian Bay. Continuing along the flat, wide track, you will cross two small streams and pass the rocky pet beach. Depending on the time of year, you may encounter other hikers, cyclists and swimmers heading for the sandy beaches farther west. The trail cuts briefly inland over Ways Point to Third Beach and then turns left D and crosses the neck of the Methodist Point peninsula to Fourth Beach. You may wish to spend some time here poking along the sand and absorbing the panoramic shoreline view. Immediately to the south is the massive Algonquin Bluff, topped with ancient dunes E, and farther down the shore are the cheerful cottages of Thunder Bay. To the southwest, barely distinguishable from the mainland, lies Christian Island and, north of that, Hope and Beckwith islands. All three islands are part of territory belonging to the Beausoleil First Nation.

3rd Segment: Methodist Point (2.1 km hike)

The Beach Trail ends at Fourth Beach, but the hike continues along the shore to the right. As you make your way towards Todd Point, the sand becomes interspersed with cobbles, and the beach grass with scrubby vegetation. Then the shoreline gives way to increasingly large and colourful boulders. Rounding the peninsula between Todd Point and Methodist Point, your attention will be riveted to the ground, partly because you will be mesmerized by the boulders' beautiful swirling patterns and partly in order to avoid breaking a leg as you scramble over them. Though they make for difficult walking, the boulders provide splendid perches for a rest stop or a picnic lunch away from the crowds and the blowing sand. At Methodist Point the shore curves abruptly south into Methodist Bay, and the terrain becomes gentler underfoot as you approach Third Beach. This small bay was once the site of a logging operation, but now it is the most sheltered and popular of Awenda's beaches.

Glacial Lake Algonquin's ancient sand dunes are now many metres above the waterline, at the top of the Algonquin Bluff.

4th Segment: Homeward (3.3 km hike)

At the trail intersection D above Third Beach, turn left and follow the Beach Trail back along the shore. Just as it reaches the lower-level parking lots, another short trail exits to the right. The Beaver Pond Trail makes an interesting diversion if you have the energy before beginning the final leg of the journey. It leads 500 m inland along a boardwalk, into a wetland area created by beaver dams. The beavers themselves inhabited the area from the early 1970s until the mid-1990s, at which point diminishing food supplies forced them to move on. Without the beavers there to keep the dams repaired, the wetland is gradually draining and plants are re-establishing themselves in a process known as succession — at least until the next generation of beavers and trees begins the cycle again.

Return along the trails to the parking lot using the outward route. The Nipissing Trail's 155 steps may feel steeper on the way up than they did on the way down, but the trail itself is shorter and more comfortable than the trudge up the road along the pavement.

Other Hiking Trails in Awenda Provincial Park

Awenda Provincial Park has other opportunities for hiking and cycling in the summer, or skiing and snowshoeing in the winter. Several trails extend across the upland areas of the park, providing a pleasant variety of excursions. The Dunes/Robitaille Homestead Trail, for instance, is a linear path that leads 1.5 km (each way) across the ancient sand dunes E on the park's western edge and ends with a view over the Algonquin Bluff to Fourth Beach. On its way the trail visits the crumbling foundations, overgrown fields and abandoned orchards of the farming homestead that sustained the sizeable Robitaille family through the early 1900s. On the east side of the park, the 5 km Wendat Trail loops around Kettle's Lake, a water-filled depression that formed when a massive chunk of ice broke off the retreating glacier and lay buried among the glacial debris, gradually melting away. The 13 km Bluff Trail follows the top edge of the Algonquin Bluff, offering fleeting vistas through the trees out to Georgian Bay, and then circles back through the campground and inland forest. Finally, the Brûlé Trail runs 4 km through the centre of the trail system, providing convenient links to the campgrounds and the park's other trails.

Other Places to Visit near Awenda Provincial Park

- *The Wye Marsh Wildlife Centre* protects a provincially significant wetland area and bird sanctuary on the south side of Midland, offers environmental education programs and maintains a network of trails, boardwalks and bird observation platforms for visitors. For information visit www.wyemarsh.com.
- *Discovery Harbour* is a picturesque museum in Penetanguishene that showcases the British naval and military history of the town in the early 1800s. For information visit www.discoveryharbour.on.ca.
- *Huronia Museum* houses an extensive collection of artifacts from the area's Native peoples and Midland's marine history and displays the work of local artists. For information visit www.huroniamuseum.com.
- *Sainte-Marie-Among-the-Hurons* is a reconstruction of the Jesuit mission on the Wye River that served several of the area's Native villages from 1639 to 1649, becoming the first, albeit short-lived, European settlement in Ontario. For information visit www.saintemarieamongthehurons.on.ca.
- *Martyrs' Shrine Church* was constructed in 1926 as a memorial to the missionaries who were martyred during their efforts to bring Christianity to the New World. For information visit www.martyrs-shrine.com.
- The towns of *Penetanguishene* and *Midland* offer accommodation, shopping and a variety of harbourfront attractions. For local tourism information visit www.southerngeorgianbay.on.ca.

Maps & Information

- NTS map 41 A/16: Christian Island.
- Chrismar Mapping Services has published, as part of its Adventure Map series, an excellent waterproof 1:16,000 topographic map of Awenda Provincial Park that shows the campgrounds, hiking trails and points of interest in the parkland, providing a useful reference for visitors.
- Awenda Provincial Park publishes an annual *Information Guide* with maps, news and suggestions to make your visit enjoyable. Contact the park office at (705) 549-2231 or visit www.ontarioparks.com.
- Friends of Awenda Provincial Park: www.awendapark.ca.

CHAPTER 15

Giants Tomb Island

OVERVIEW

From the bluffs and beaches of Awenda Provincial Park, visitors will find themselves drawn to the mysterious profile of Giants Tomb Island looming on the northern horizon. The "tomb" belongs to Kitchikewana, last of the legendary Huron giants. A band of Huron hunters found Kitchikewana as a baby on Manitoulin Island, home of the great spirit Manitou. They brought him back to their village near Penetanguishene and cared for him as he grew up — and *up!* — to become one of the village's strongest and most respected warriors. In time Kitchikewana fell in love with the beautiful Wanakita, but she refused to marry him as her heart already belonged to a warrior from her own tribe. Grief-stricken and enraged, the giant snatched up handfuls of earth and flung them into Georgian Bay. Then, exhausted, he fell asleep on a large island. It is said that the five inlets along the southwestern shore of Severn Sound — Penetanguishene Harbour and Midland, Hog, Sturgeon and Matchedash bays — are the marks left in the ground by his fingers and that the Thirty Thousand Islands are the clods of earth he threw into Georgian Bay. It is also whispered that Kitchikewana will wake one day from his resting place on Giants Tomb Island and throw earth and rocks again until the entire bay is filled and the world comes to an end.

Giants Tomb Island, at least for now, is a peaceful place. An unmanned navigation beacon marks its southern tip, and there are a few private cottages scattered along its northeastern side, but otherwise the island is a wilderness area protected and maintained by Awenda Provincial Park. It is indeed a remarkable wilderness! The island's eastern shore is awash in sand. Beaches stretch for hundreds of metres into the bay, forming sandbars that are sometimes too shallow even for canoes and kayaks to pass, and inland the sand accumulates to form sizable dunes. The unusual terrain along this shore supports a ribbon of oak savannah, one of Ontario's rarest natural habitats, where red oaks vie with juniper bushes, grass and a few white pines for the soil's elusive moisture.

By contrast, barely a speck of sand can be found anywhere on the island's western side. Instead, ragged shoals guard the shore, and boulders the size of small cars lurk just below the surface, polished smooth by waves and ice. Scrubby cedars huddle among the rocks for shelter against the prevailing westerlies. Between the two shores, the island's interior rises 80 m over a series of terraces — beaches left behind as the level of Georgian Bay gradually fell — to a central dome: Kitchikewana's tomb. The terraces and dome are cloaked in a deciduous woodland of maple, beech and birch, punctuated

(Left) A modern navigation tower presides over the ruins of the old lighthouse on Giants Tomb Island.

with occasional stands of hemlock and isolated pines.

This chapter circumnavigates Giants Tomb Island in a day trip from the mainland at Awenda Provincial Park. The paddle must be done in a single day because, in order to protect its unique environment, camping is not permitted on the island. Your direction of travel should be guided by the weather, and the trip should not be undertaken unless the forecast is calm. Because conditions for paddling the western shore are typically best in the morning, and the eastern shore is sheltered from the prevailing wind and waves that tend to build during the afternoon, the trip is described here in a clockwise direction. The exposed crossing between the mainland and the island offers no shelter from any direction, however, and caution must be exercised whatever the time of day. This navigation channel can be very busy with motorboat traffic, as it is one of the main routes between Severn Sound and Nottawasaga Bay.

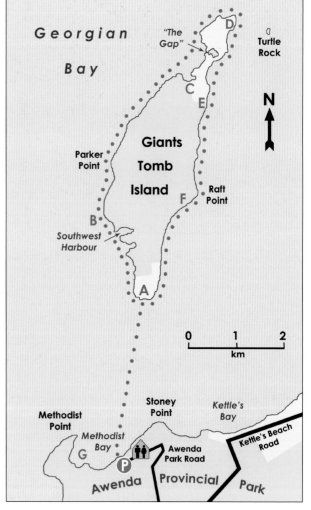

Distance: 23 km paddle

Access

- From Penetanguishene follow the Awenda Park signs that lead north along County Road 26, east along Concession Road 16, and north again along Awenda Park Road.
- At the junction of Awenda Park Road and Kettle's Beach Road, turn left and purchase a permit from the park registration office.
- Follow the road signposted to the beach, which twists down the bluff to a series of parking lots.
- Leave your car in the end lot, and carry your canoe or kayak 100 m to the rocky shore in front of the lookout platform.

Route Description

1st Segment: Awenda to Giants Tomb (3.3 km paddle)

Launch your canoe or kayak into Methodist Bay, and ease your way past the shoreline cobbles into deeper water. Turning towards the southern tip of Giants Tomb Island, you will see a large white navigation marker **A** that makes a clear target for your crossing. As you approach, the marker's modern skeleton tower comes into focus. What you cannot see until you land and explore the site on foot, however, are the crumbling foundations and remnant timber from the old lighthouse, built here in 1892. Manned for almost half a century, the light was replaced by an automated beacon in 1939, and the buildings were destroyed in the late 1960s. Their ruins are now overgrown with saplings and poison ivy. A few lilac bushes still bloom at what was once the corner of the lightkeeper's cottage — a month later than those on the mainland, however, reminding us that conditions are not always favourable here.

2nd Segment: Western Shore (8.7 km paddle)

From the lighthouse, paddle up Giants Tomb Island's western shore which, for the first 1.5 km, seems to be a typical mix of rock and cedar. There are some pleasant views over the bay towards the three large islands — Hope, Beckwith and Christian — barely distinguishable from the mainland, that comprise the Beausoleil First Nation Reserve. Then, past the tiny, sheltered inlet of Southwest Harbour, you will drift into a different, almost surreal world **B**. Feel yourself shrink to Lilliputian proportions as you gaze overboard at the massive boulders sliding beneath your boat. If you have spent any time

The eastern shore of Giants Tomb Island — luxurious sandy beaches and a ribbon of oak savannah.

admiring the twisted patterns and colourful ribbons in the rocks on the northeastern shore of Georgian Bay, you may find yourself reminded of them in the boulders here. They are, in fact, the same — metamorphic rocks that were scrunched into existence a billion years ago beneath the Grenville Mountains, plucked and carried from the northeastern side of Georgian Bay by glaciers more than 20,000 years ago and then left behind when the ice melted away.

Rounding Parker Point, reality gradually returns as you make your way north, the rocks becoming more modest in size and angular in shape as you approach the park boundary C. You may have a moment's doubt when you discover that "The Gap" promised on the marine chart is blocked by shoals, and the shoals at the island's northeastern tip are in reality a cobble plain D and mostly above water. Just remember that geological processes — receding lake levels, for instance — continue today with the same subtle determination that once brought car-sized boulders here from Parry Sound.

Those geological processes were also responsible for the string of islands to the north and east of Giants Tomb Island, including Turtle Rock, which you will notice just offshore. They are the vanguard of the Canadian Shield — that ancient bedrock of the continent, exposed by glacial ice and stunningly visible all across northeastern Georgian Bay but, in the south, buried from view under glacial debris.

3rd Segment: Eastern Shore (7.7 km paddle)

The character of the coast changes dramatically as you begin the journey down Giants Tomb Island's eastern side. Sand replaces the cobbles, and cottages line the shore for 1.5 km up to the park boundary E. South of that boundary, the natural landscape reasserts itself, but it is utterly unlike the natural landscape you have become (almost) accustomed to on the island's western side. Luxurious beaches stretch far out into the water. Above the waterline, wind has shaped the sand into dunes; some particularly large ones can be seen just to the south of Raft Point F. Beach grasses are attempting to stabilize the dunes, and above them an unusual oak savannah community has taken root. The density of vegetation here is limited by the scant moisture and nutrients available in the porous soil, so the red oaks and white pines are widely spaced, and the ground cover is a patchy mix of hardy grasses and junipers. The result is a pleasantly park-like atmosphere that entices you to linger and a beach that invites a swim before pushing on. It is a popular picnic and anchorage site for local cottagers and their motorboats, and may become quite busy on a sunny summer weekend. Paddle, pole and drag your canoe or kayak over the sandbars towards the southern tip of the island, where the shoreline reverts to rock and the water becomes deeper again, bringing you to the skeleton tower A and the end of your circumnavigation.

4th Segment: Homeward (3.3 km paddle)

As you return across the busy channel and approach the mainland at Awenda, the lookout platform that marks your landing site will become obvious. Dodging the boulders one last time, pull yourself ashore to finish the long day's paddle. When you look back, you will find that Giants Tomb Island has become, once again, a mysterious profile on the northern horizon.

Kitchikewana stands in Rotary Park near the bottom of Penetanguishene's Main Street.

A Wreck to Visit in Methodist Bay

On November 9, 1909, the wooden cargo steamship *Reliever G* was taking on a load of lumber from Manley Chew's sawmill on Methodist Point when she caught fire. Cut loose from the dock so that the flames would not spread to the mill, the ship drifted towards Ways Point and ran aground. Only portions of the *Reliever* remain intact today, and every year brings another timber fragment ashore with the spring ice and storms.

Maps & Information

- Nautical chart 224101: Port Severn to Christian Island.
- Awenda Provincial Park's annual *Information Guide* contains park news, regulations and maps for the campgrounds and hiking trails. Contact the park office at (705) 549-2231 or visit www.ontarioparks.com.
- Friends of Awenda Provincial Park: www.awendapark.ca.

CHAPTER 16

Wasaga Beach and the *Nancy*

OVERVIEW

Paddlers and hikers may scoff at the notion of an excursion at Wasaga Beach, as it is better known for bikinis and beach towels than for serious outdoor pursuits. While this may be true during the busy summer months (when, on a typical weekend, the 14 km long beach and its amusement parks attract upwards of 50,000 visitors!), the beach takes on a different character in the off-season. The mist rises on an early spring morning to reveal a panorama of sand, sky and ice. The sand, not yet "groomed" by park maintenance vehicles, lies in drifts like snowbanks, swept into fascinating patterns by wind and waves. A few fishermen and wayward dog walkers are the only people on the shore. It is, in fact, a pleasant place to ease the hiking muscles back into shape at the beginning of the season. Or put your canoe or kayak into the Nottawasaga River, and enjoy a peaceful paddle up this historic waterway without being overrun by powerboats. Even in the summer, the Nancy Island Historic Site, adjacent to the beach, is well worth a visit to learn about the human development of the area and its vital role during the War of 1812.

Its design reminiscent of a sail, this museum on Nancy Island brings to life the story of the British schooner's fate during the War of 1812.

The short hike in this chapter will introduce you to the unexpected delights of Wasaga Beach. It can be done at any time of year, but if you wish to include Nancy Island in your plans, you'll have to visit when the site is open, which is, unfortunately, only between mid-June and Labour Day in early September. Note also that dogs are restricted from all but a very small area near the east end of the beach.

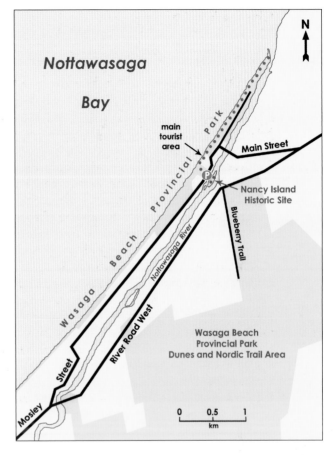

Distance: 4 km hike

Access
- From the southeast, exit Hwy 26 at Sunnidale Corners onto County Road 10 (Sunnidale Road), drive 6.8 km north into Wasaga Beach and turn right onto Mosley Street.
- Drive 1 km to a traffic light where the road forks, Mosley Street continuing to the left and River Road to the right.
- From the west this intersection can be reached by exiting Hwy 26 onto Mosley Street, 8 km east of Collingwood, and driving into Wasaga Beach for 5 km to the traffic light at the fork.
- Take the left-hand fork and drive 4.2 km along Mosley Street (which makes several twists) to the Nancy Island parking lot on the right.
- Buy a day-pass permit from the machine at the edge of the lot.

Route Description

1st Segment: Nancy Island Historic Site
From the parking lot, pass through the entrance to the Nancy Island Historic Site (admission is by donation). The walk across the bridge takes you back almost 200 years in time — to the birth of Nancy Island in the closing days of the War of 1812. Britain and its former colony, the fledgling United States, were embroiled in a conflict over tariffs and trade routes. Upper Canada, still a British territory, bore the brunt of American attacks, most of which occurred in the border areas to the south. A significant American victory in Lake Erie in September 1813 cut off the Great Lakes shipping route and left the important British garrison at Fort Mackinac (on an island at the mouth of Lake Michigan) vulnerable to invasion. To keep supplies running to the fort and other trading

posts in the Upper Great Lakes, the British reverted to an older route, the arduous Toronto Portage from York, as Toronto was then called, to Lake Simcoe and down the Nottawasaga River. Only one ship remained to defend British interests here — the *Nancy*.

The *Nancy* was a 22 m, two-masted schooner built in 1789 as a cargo vessel for the fur trade. She sailed between Fort Mackinac and Sault Ste. Marie with beaver pelts and European trade goods until war broke out in 1812 and she was pressed into naval service as the *HMS Nancy* to transport troops and supplies for the British military on the Great Lakes. The year following the British defeat on Lake Erie, the Americans sent a fleet of three schooners into Georgian Bay to intercept the *Nancy* as she left Nottawasaga Bay. Having received warning of the impending attack, the *Nancy*'s captain, Lieutenant Miller Worsley, took his ship a short distance up the Nottawasaga River to hide her behind the dunes. But on August 14, 1814, the Americans spotted her masts and launched a fierce barrage against her. Vastly outnumbered in personnel and firepower, the outcome for the British forces was inevitable. The *Nancy* was hit and burned to the waterline.

The story did not end there, however. Lieutenant Worsley and his men rowed for two weeks along the 575 km of Georgian Bay coastline between Wasaga and Fort Mackinac, slipping past the American ships en route and arriving in time to lead a successful surprise offensive against them on September 3. This, one of the final battles of the war, was instrumental in preserving British sovereignty over the Upper Great Lakes and her trade routes in the northwest. The boundaries drawn up in the Treaty of Ghent, which ended the war on December 14, became Canada's border with the United States.

Back in the Nottawasaga River, the *Nancy*'s hull came to rest on a sandbar, impeding the flow of water and causing river sediment and sand to accumulate around it. In time this led to the formation of an island. Now named Nancy Island in honour of its origin, the site houses a museum with a fine collection of exhibits and historical artifacts. The museum also puts on an excellent film about the *Nancy* and holds re-enactments of battles from the War of 1812. The highlight of the site, however, is the *Nancy* herself. Unearthed in 1827 by Dr. Frederick Conboy (a Wasaga Beach cottager who was also a dentist, professor and mayor of Toronto!), the charred but still intact hull rests in a climate-controlled glass enclosure beside the museum.

After touring Nancy Island and immersing yourself in the early nineteenth century, make your way back over the bridge to the parking lot, and walk one short block to the beach, where you will be catapulted abruptly into the present.

2nd Segment: Wasaga Beach (2 km hike)

Sand has been both a benefit and a handicap during the human history of Wasaga Beach. In the past century, the beach has attracted increasing numbers of tourists and cottagers, making Wasaga one of the busiest summer destinations in the province. Before it became popular as a getaway for city-weary Torontonians, however, the beach was used for more practical purposes. Stretching many kilometres in both directions, with access from the south via the Nottawasaga River, the beach was an important transportation corridor for Native and early European travellers. First on foot, then by horse and cart, and finally by motor vehicle, people used the hard-packed sand to get from one place to another along southern Georgian Bay. As roads and railways spread across the landscape, the beach

The wreck of the Nancy, *now more than 200 years old, is preserved in a climate-controlled building at the Nancy Island Historic Site.*

became less important — reduced to an automotive showcase where fashionable cars paraded among the sunbathers. Vehicles were banned from the beach in 1974, the year after the shoreline and dunes were taken into the protective custody of Wasaga Beach Provincial Park.

The sandy soil made Wasaga Beach unsuitable for agriculture. And the shallow, shifting sands at the mouth of the Nottawasaga River made access for large vessels unreliable, so the site also failed as a port (neighbouring Collingwood was selected as the area's railway and shipping terminal after a storm destroyed a cargo freighter, the *H. B. Bishop*, on the sandbars off Wasaga Beach in 1852). Consequently, settlement of the beach area was slow, the few settlers during the latter half of the nineteenth century relying on small-scale lumbering and fishing. It was not until the twentieth century that increasing mobility and affluence enabled visitors to travel for recreation, bringing a flourishing tourism industry to Wasaga Beach.

The beach area directly across from the Nancy Island Historic Site is the town's main tourist drag. As you walk east, however, the waterslides, video arcades, fast-food stalls and souvenir shops give way to dunes, beach grass and parkland. Follow the shoreline for 2 km to the sand spit at the mouth of the Nottawasaga River. There, depending on the season, you may see either the ghosts of the *Nancy* and the *Bishop* or a stream of noisy modern motorboats and Jet Skis.

3rd Segment: Homeward (2 km hike)

Return via the outward route along the beach, or if you have had enough sand, you may prefer to walk back on the boardwalk just above the beach or along the park road that runs beside the Nottawasaga River.

Other Things to Do in Wasaga Beach

Wasaga Beach Provincial Park has, in addition to its beach properties, a large tract of land to the south of the Nottawasaga River, a gently rolling landscape of old sand dunes blanketed with forest growth. This Dunes Area has more than 50 km of Nordic trails that are groomed for skiing and snowshoeing in winter and serve as hiking trails in summer, with connections to the long-distance Ganaraska Trail. Access is off Blueberry Trail to the west of the Main Street bridge. The park's *Pine Trail Guidebook* introduces natural features of the area, including the rare pine-oak savannah ecosystem.

Maps, Publications & Information

- NTS map 41 A/9: Nottawasaga Bay.
- Wasaga Beach Provincial Park information and the park's annual printed guide are available from the park office. Call (705) 429-2516 or visit www.ontarioparks.com.
- *HMS Nancy: The Legacy of a War of 1812 Schooner and Her Crew* is a detailed history booklet published by the Friends of Nancy Island & Wasaga Beach Park and available for a small fee at the entrance to Nancy Island.
- The Friends of Nancy Island Historic Site & Wasaga Beach Park (www.wasagabeachpark.com) is an excellent source of information about the history and the current activities in the park.
- The Wasaga Beach Chamber of Commerce (www.wasagainfo.com) has information about the town's attractions and many useful links to services and accommodation.

(Left) Wasaga Beach in winter, when sand, ice and sky dominate the landscape.

CHAPTER 17

Collingwood and Nottawasaga Island

This paddling excursion combines exploration of Collingwood Harbour with circumnavigation of Nottawasaga Island. The island's lighthouse, once a vital beacon for Georgian Bay shipping, is now a seasonal beacon for birds. A fascinating collection of gulls, herons, cormorants and geese colonize the island every spring, their stick nests poking out of dead trees and littering the shingle beaches. In calm weather the paddling route can be extended towards the northwest to take in the many rocks and shoals of the Mary Ward Ledges, graveyard of more than one ill-fated ship!

Distance: **10.5 km paddle**

Access

- In downtown Collingwood, exit Hwy 26 (First Street) north onto Birch Street and drive 300 m to the end of the road at Collingwood Harbour, where there is a parking area, a launch ramp and a portable outhouse.

Route Description

1st Segment: Collingwood Harbour to Nottawasaga Island (4.5 km paddle)

The shape and arrangement of the group of small islands offshore gave Collingwood the name Hen and Chickens when it was first settled by Europeans in the early 1800s. The town's transformation from an isolated outpost to a booming port commenced when the Toronto & Lake Simcoe Railway decided in 1855 to extend its line to Georgian Bay and made Hen and Chickens the line's terminus. The harbour was relatively sheltered and its approaches more reliable than the shallow, shifting sands of Wasaga Beach, the unsuccessful rival for the terminal. Incorporated in 1858 under a more dignified name, Collingwood became a hub of transportation for Georgian Bay, where northern timber, fish and western grain were transferred from Great Lakes freighters to railway cars bound for southern markets. A long wharf was built in the harbour to accommodate the traffic (reinforced to become the man-made peninsula we see today), and massive silos were erected for grain storage. A shipyard appeared soon afterwards, followed by the Queen's

(Left) Nottawasaga Island's lighthouse, one of the six Imperial Towers built in the 1850s, is now as much a beacon for nesting birds as it is for ships.

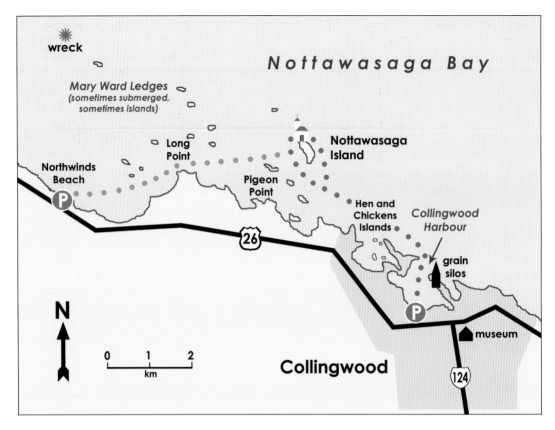

Dry Dock in 1882. By the end of the century, Collingwood's shipbuilding industry employed a thousand people. During its heyday hundreds of boats — commercial freighters, passenger carriers, workaday barges, small fishing skiffs and naval vessels during two world wars — made their maiden voyages from Collingwood Harbour.

The twentieth century brought an increasingly efficient network of roads and railways, which diverted commercial shipping away from the Great Lakes. The opening of the St. Lawrence Seaway in 1959 enabled freighters to bypass Georgian Bay altogether, making ports like Collingwood gradually obsolete. The town's shipbuilding industry declined, and the "Yard" finally closed in 1986. Its infrastructure was dismantled, and the railway tracks were taken up a decade later. Only the empty grain silos remain, their enormous white towers a distinctive landmark for mariners on southern Georgian Bay.

Paddling along the shoreline today, it is encouraging to see that Collingwood Harbour is undergoing another transformation. The town is converting the industrial waterfront, including the man-made peninsula that was once home to the shipyards and port terminal, into parkland. Walking trails and multi-use pathways have been constructed, and marinas and residential properties are replacing the derelict buildings of a bygone era.

With this historical perspective in mind, launch your boat into the harbour, and paddle north past the silos and around the shelter of the breakwater out into Georgian Bay. The Nottawasaga Island lighthouse will then be visible to the northwest — 4 km if you paddle in a more or less straight line, or slightly longer if you hug the shoreline and cross to the island from Pigeon Point.

2nd Segment: Circumnavigation of Nottawasaga Island (1.5 km paddle)

Nottawasaga Island is a sliver of rock that rises only just above the level of the bay. To the north and west lie many other such rocks, some sitting slightly above the waterline and some slightly below, that have long posed a hazard to Collingwood shipping. They are called the Mary Ward Ledges after the luckless steamer that foundered here in a November gale in 1872. The *Mary Ward* was making for Collingwood with a load of cargo and passengers when her captain, according to local legend, mistook the light of a Craigleith boarding house for the Nottawasaga Island lighthouse and ran the ship aground on the shoals. Eight men perished attempting to reach the shore in a lifeboat; local fishermen rescued 24 other frightened passengers and crew the next day. The *Mary Ward*'s battered hull sank off the ledge and lies today in about 6 m of water.

The Nottawasaga Island lighthouse is one of six Imperial Towers erected on strategic islands and headlands during the 1850s to protect the growing fleet of commercial and passenger vessels travelling on Georgian Bay. The lighthouse is an impressive structure — 26 m tall with walls 2 m thick at the base, tapering towards the summit. The rock

We are an eclectic group — with a canoe, a kayak, a rowboat and three dogs — setting out from the launch in Collingwood Harbour.

Shelter is hard to find on this coast, and our canoe lags behind the more wind-efficient boats of our companions.

used in its construction was cut from local dolostone and capped with granite (imported from Scotland!) to support the heavy iron light housing (from France). The light was manned from 1858, when it began operations, until it became automated in 1959. Many of the lightkeepers lived on the island year-round and raised their families in the cottage adjacent to the tower. Captain George Collins was the first and longest-serving keeper, tending the light from 1858 until 1890. Following automation, the uninhabited cottage fell victim to fire and vandalism and was torn down in 1971. The light tower, however, still flashes its signal to guide ships coming and going from Collingwood.

In modern times Nottawasaga Island has become a sanctuary for birds who build their driftwood-and-feather nests in the trees and among the shoreline shingles — entirely appropriate, considering that the lighthouse was built to safeguard the approach to a town called Hen and Chickens! Although the island's status as a bird sanctuary is as yet unofficial, its winged inhabitants should be left in peace, especially during the nesting season.

3rd Segment: Homeward (4.5+ km paddle)

Return to Collingwood Harbour via the outward route, or for a longer paddle, you can explore the many shoals and barren islands that lie northwest of Nottawasaga Island. Just bear in mind the fate of the *Mary Ward* and keep a close eye on the wind and waves across the ledges!

Alternative Approach from Northwinds Beach

An alternative, and just slightly longer, approach to Nottawasaga Island (5 km each way plus the 1.5 km circumnavigation) can be made from Northwinds Beach, about 9 km west of downtown Collingwood. From the beach, where there is a gravel parking area and sandy launch site, paddle northeast along the shoreline for 2.5 km to Long Point. Rounding the point the Nottawasaga Island lighthouse comes into view another 2.5 km to the northeast.

If water conditions are favourable and time permits, an excellent daylong paddle (totalling 21 km) can be had from Northwinds Beach to Collingwood via Nottawasaga Island. In Collingwood Harbour you can tether your boat to the public dock at the marina on the east side of the harbour while you take an hour or two to stretch your legs. From here the Heritage Trail runs north past the grain elevators to Millennium Overlook Park and south to the Collingwood Museum at the old railway station — both places well worth a visit.

Other Things to See on the Collingwood Waterfront

- *Collingwood Museum*: Located in the old railway station at the corner of First Street and St. Paul Street, the Collingwood Museum showcases the town's natural and human history. For information call (705) 445-4811.
- *Heritage Trail and Millennium Overlook Park*: The Heritage Trail leads from First Street down the man-made peninsula (along what used to be the railway line) and past the grain silos to a pleasant lookout over the entrance to Collingwood Harbour and out to Nottawasaga Island. Old pieces of machinery from the Collingwood Shipyards are on display along the trail, and interpretive panels offer a glimpse into the busy history of Collingwood Harbour. The Heritage Trail is just one of many in Collingwood. The town boasts more than 60 km of multi-use trails, some paved, others rough gravel, and many of them through waterfront parks with lovely views out to the bay. For information and a trail map, visit the Collingwood Trails Network on the town's tourism website, www.town.collingwood.on.ca.

Maps

- NTS map 41 A/8: Collingwood.
- Nautical charts 2283A01: Owen Sound to Giants Tomb Island and 2283B03: Collingwood.

CHAPTER 18

Craigleith

OVERVIEW

Craigleith Provincial Park preserves a fascinating shoreline with sedimentary rock formations that contain shale oil, the source of a short-lived petroleum business in the mid-nineteenth century, and an unusual number of fossils.

The rocks of Craigleith formed 450 million years ago when southern Ontario lay at the bottom of a shallow tropical sea called the Michigan Basin. Fine sediments washed down from the Taconic Mountains (today's time-worn Appalachians) in the east, settled in the basin and were compressed into shale. Coral reefs also grew in the saltwater basin, gradually accumulating and consolidating into limestone. These are the two types of rocks in Craigleith — limestone and shale — both rich in organic matter.

Today we see evidence of this organic matter most clearly in the form of fossils. The remains of hard-shelled marine creatures like trilobites (ancient relatives of the modern

(Above) The fossilized remains of hard-shelled marine creatures — brachiopods and trilobites — that lived in a shallow tropical sea here about 400 million years ago.

lobster), cephalopods (cone-shaped ancestors of the squid), crinoids (resembling today's starfish) and brachiopods (a bivalve like the clam or oyster) can be found among Craigleith's rocks, especially after winter storms and ice have shattered the shale along the shoreline to expose fresh samples. It should not be necessary to remind visitors that the fossils are protected and must be left on the beach for others to enjoy.

Less apparent is the organic matter in the form of petroleum contained in Craigleith's shale. In 1859, William Pollard of Collingwood established a shale-oil works at Craigleith and put into practice his patented extraction process, heating the shale in large iron vats with wood-fuelled fires to distill crude oil from the fossilized plant debris in the rock. The crude was then refined to produce oil for lubrication and illumination. It was, after all, the age of the Industrial Revolution, which brought a proliferation of machinery (requiring lubrication) and artificial lighting (requiring, until Thomas Edison invented the electric light bulb in 1879, fuel oil), and the main alternative to petroleum — whale oil — was in short supply. Large amounts of shale were necessary, however, to produce the crude (a single day's operation used an average of 30 to 35 tons of shale quarried at Craigleith to produce 250 gallons of oil), and the extraction process was wasteful, dangerous and very costly. After running only four years, Pollard's shale-oil business folded in 1863, superseded by the less expensive petroleum products from the wells of Petrolia in southwestern Ontario.

The hike in this chapter is really just a gentle stroll along the shore to investigate the rocks and fossils. It can easily be done in a quiet hour while camping at the park. Although the Craigleith campground is close to the highway and sometimes crowded, it provides an excellent base for exploring Georgian Bay's southwestern shore and for tackling some of this book's other hiking and paddling excursions at Wasaga Beach, Collingwood and the Blue Mountains (see Chapters 16 to 19).

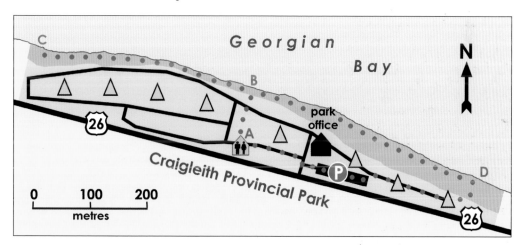

Distance: 1.5 km hike

Access
- Exit Hwy 26 into Craigleith Provincial Park, 12 km west of Collingwood or 10 km east of Thornbury.

- Buy a permit from the park office, and leave the car in the day-use parking lot or at your campsite if you are staying at the park.

Route Description

Follow the campground track west to the park's comfort station **A**, where (besides the obvious benefit of a convenient pit stop) you will find a series of information panels describing some of the features and natural history of the area. Then make your way north to the shore **B**, where you can poke along the slabs of limestone and shale to the park's western boundary at the dog beach **C** and then to the eastern boundary **D**. To finish the walk, cut back through the campground to the parking lot.

Other Things to Do in the Craigleith Area

- *The Bruce Trail*: The Blue Mountains and Beaver Valley sections of the Bruce Trail, containing some of the trail's highest elevations and much lovely scenery, follow the Niagara Escarpment as it approaches Nottawasaga Bay and curves into the Beaver Valley on its way northwest towards the Bruce Peninsula. For information visit www.brucetrail.org.
- *The Georgian Trail*: This 32 km hard-packed trail is built on an abandoned railbed that runs along the flat land at the base of the Blue Mountains, between Collingwood and Meaford. It is maintained by the Georgian Cycle and Ski Trail Association and is restricted to non-motorized use. Closely following Hwy 26 for much of its length, it is perhaps less attractive to hikers than the quieter route of the Bruce Trail along the top of the escarpment, but the Georgian Trail offers some pleasant views of the Collingwood ski hills and the apple orchards of Thornbury and Meaford and gives glimpses north towards Georgian Bay. For information, contact the Georgian Triangle Tourist Information Centre at (705) 445-7722, www.georgiantriangle.com or the Bruce Grey Trail Network at www.brucegreytrails.com.

Maps & Information

- Craigleith Provincial Park information and the park's annual printed guide are available from the park office: (705) 445-4467, www.ontarioparks.com.
- NTS map 41 A/9: Nottawasaga Bay.
- *The Geology and Fossils of the Craigleith Area*, Ontario Geological Survey Guidebook No. 7, written by Harish M. Verma and published by the Ministry of Natural Resources in 1979.

(Right) Layers of shale and limestone form the "beach" at Craigleith Provincial Park.

CHAPTER 19

The Blue Mountains

OVERVIEW

This hike along the Blue Mountains section of the Bruce Trail visits impressive lookouts over the shoreline of Nottawasaga Bay, between Collingwood and Craigleith. Closely following the brow of the Niagara Escarpment, the trail passes delightfully varied scenery — through deciduous woodlands and small river valleys, along farm fields (both active and abandoned) and across the tops of some popular ski hills whose runs provide many glorious views. The route is especially pleasant and airy early in the spring, after most of the snow has melted and the wildflowers are beginning to bloom but before the leafy canopy has grown overhead.

Distance: **14 km or 8 km hike**

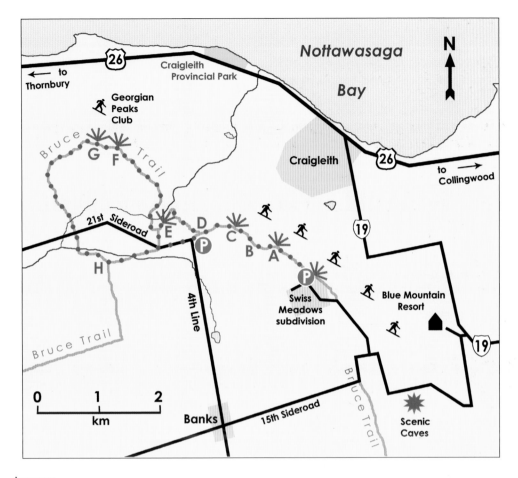

Access

- On the western side of Collingwood, exit Grey Road 19 west onto Mountain Drive and then immediately left onto Scenic Caves Road. Drive 3.5 km to the top of the hill, turn right onto Swiss Meadows Boulevard and follow it to the end. Turn right onto Maple Lane, and park on the north side of the road to avoid blocking residents' driveways. The Dead End sign at the end of Maple Lane marks the start of the hike.
- For a shorter version of the hike, continue along Scenic Caves Road, past Swiss Meadows Boulevard, for 2.9 km. Turn right onto the 4th Line and drive for another 2.9 km to the bend in the road where the 4th Line meets the 21st Sideroad. Park on the northeast side of the curve, and pick up the 150 m Bruce Trail access path to join the 2nd segment of the hike at D. Alternatively, this corner can be reached from Hwy 26 west of Craigleith. Take Grey Road 2 south for 5.5 km to Victoria Corners, turn left onto the 21st Sideroad and drive 5.5 km, arriving at the curve from the opposite direction.

(Left) A delightful rest stop on a knoll overlooking the Loree Forest.

Route Description

1st Segment: Swiss Meadows Subdivision to Road Junction (3 km hike)

At the end of Maple Lane, turn left onto the Bruce Trail and follow the white markers north. The first lookout at the very start of the hike and the second lookout **A** at the top of a ski run, less than a kilometre along the trail, give panoramic views to the east over Collingwood. The historic core of the town stands out prominently — the massive white grain silos that once were the heart of a thriving port. Along the town's rapidly developing outskirts, the ski chalets and waterfront condominiums reveal Collingwood's modern incarnation as a much-loved holiday and retirement destination.

Winding through a deciduous woodland, the trail passes over a spring **B** that trickles from the edge of the cliff about a metre off the path. Soon afterwards the trail emerges into a clearing **C** with another lovely view, this one towards the northeast, where the Mary Ward Ledges and Nottawasaga Island lighthouse can be seen just offshore. Turning away from the cliff edge, the trail heads inland to the junction **D** with the access trail from the intersection of the 21st Sideroad and the 4th Line.

2nd Segment: Loree Forest and Georgian Peaks Ski Hill (4 km)

From this junction the Bruce Trail descends into a small river valley and then scrambles steeply up the other side to a pleasant rest stop — a bench **E** perched on a knoll with a view between two hills. After passing through another valley and crossing another

Mountain bikes replace skiers on the Blue Mountain chairlifts in summertime.

stream, the trail climbs to the top of the dolostone ridge. The footing becomes flatter here as you make your way over a rocky pavement, through the Loree Forest and across an abandoned farm field. From the end of the field **F**, there are pleasant views to the northwest over the Thornbury shoreline, and soon afterwards the trail comes to the top of the Georgian Peaks ski hill with a lookout over Nottawasaga Bay **G**. A large wooden platform with built-in benches, affectionately dubbed Sol's Solace, makes a comfortable place to enjoy a picnic lunch before beginning the homeward trek.

3rd Segment: Homeward (4-7 km)

The trail loops away from the ski hill towards the south, meandering through deciduous woods and stands of pine and fir, skirting farm fields and crossing the 21st Sideroad and several small streams along the way. After climbing over the stile at the end of a field **H**, the main trail heads directly south and the Loree Side Trail exits to the east. Turn left onto the Loree Trail, and follow it along the edge of a stream and up a road allowance to join the 21st Sideroad at the top of the hill. Here the side trail crosses the road and continues back to the main trail near the rest-stop bench **E** (where another rest will be welcome!). Or take a shortcut for 500 m along the 21st Sideroad to the 4th Line where, if you have opted for the shorter loop, your car will be waiting. If you are hiking the longer route, the 150 m access trail from the junction will bring you back to the Bruce Trail **D** for the final 3 km leg of the journey.

Collingwood's Scenic Caves

Near the top of the hill on the road leading to this hike, Collingwood's Scenic Caves Nature Adventures offers a fascinating look into the interior of the escarpment's dolostone cliffs. Admission packages for this privately run site include access to the caves and nature trails, a treetop boardwalk and suspension bridge and, for guests less interested in ecotourism, a miniature golf course and a trout-fishing pond. Information can be found at (705) 446-0256 and www.sceniccaves.com.

Maps & Publications
- NTS map 41 A/8: Collingwood.
- Bruce Trail map #24: Blue Mountain.

CHAPTER 20

Hibou

OVERVIEW

The Hibou Conservation Area was established in 1973 to protect a diverse collection of natural habitats on the eastern shore of Owen Sound and to commemorate a lost ship.

On November 21, 1936, the *Hibou* steamed out of port in fair weather on a routine cargo run from Owen Sound to communities on Manitoulin Island. Within minutes she began to take on water, and shortly afterwards she sank near the site of the conservation area. Survivors swam ashore at Paynter's Bay, but seven of the passengers and crew were trapped aboard and drowned, including the ship's captain, Norman McKay. McKay was an experienced Great Lakes mariner and president of the Owen Sound Transportation Company, which ran the town's vital rail and shipping terminals.

The sand beach at Paynter's Bay is an unusual natural feature on the Owen Sound shore. Most of this coast is a rocky hodgepodge of local dolostone eroded from the nearby Niagara Escarpment cliffs and "erratics" from farther north. The dolostone is light coloured and heavily pitted; the erratics are darker in colour, smoother and considerably older. They were transported here in glacial ice, gouged from the landscape on the northeastern side of Georgian Bay and rounded by abrasion during their travels. The slabs of broken cement and other debris scattered among the rocks remind us of Owen Sound's history as a busy shipping terminal and shipbuilding port. Away from the shore, the terrain is a mixture of deciduous woodland and patchy wetland. Among the trees, however, are scattered bands of cobbles — the ancient shoreline of glacial Lake Algonquin. Five thousand years ago, Lake Algonquin was much deeper and its shoreline higher than that of Georgian Bay today. As the land rebounded, released from the great weight of glacial ice, the water gradually receded to its present level.

The Hibou Conservation Area encompasses examples of these natural ecosystems, and the hike in this chapter, making its way partly along the conservation area's trail system and partly along the shoreline, visits all of them.

Distance: 4.5 km loop hike

(Left) The Hibou shoreline is a rocky hodgepodge — local dolostone interspersed with erratics from the other side of Georgian Bay.

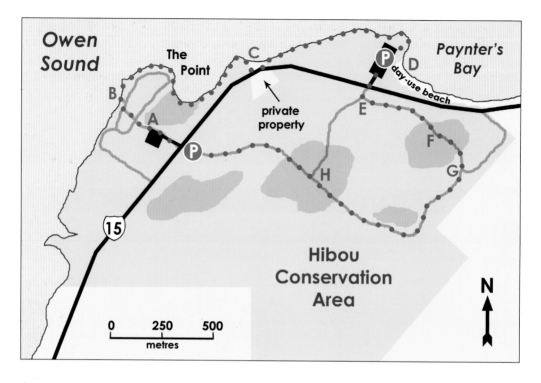

Access

- From Hwy 6 in downtown Owen Sound, turn east onto 3rd Avenue East (which becomes Grey Road 15), and drive for 6 km to the Hibou Conservation Area.
- Parking is available in a gravel lot on the right-hand side of the road, behind a small stone municipal building.

Route Description

From the parking lot, cross Grey Road 15 and walk up the gravel track, past two sets of blue gates to join the trail system **A**. Continue straight for 100 m to the T-junction. Turn right and then immediately left onto a short trail that brings you out to the water **B**. Follow the shoreline to the right for 1.5 km. Rounding the point (once called Squaw Point but now, more acceptably, just The Point), you will come to a reedy bay. Usually the bay is dry enough to walk across, but after a spring thaw or in rough weather, the footing may be soggy. Grey Road 15 comes close to the shore at a small cove **C** soon afterwards. This is private property, so make a short detour for 100 m along the road, and then return to the water's edge. Coming around a small headland, you will reach an unexpected crescent of sand **D** at Paynter's Bay, the Hibou Conservation Area's day-use beach, where you may wish to take advantage of the picnic and toilet facilities.

Across the road from the day-use entrance, pick up the trail into the woods and take the left-hand fork **E**. For the next 1.8 km, the trail winds through alternating patches of deciduous woodland and overgrown wetland. The conservation authority has constructed boardwalks across the wet sections and set up small interpretive panels to explain features of the natural environment. One of these **F**, about 400 m from the start of the trail, draws your attention to a band of smooth cobbles that formed the shoreline of glacial Lake Algonquin. At the next trail intersection **G**, 300 m past the cobbles, take the right-hand fork, and at the final intersection 800 m later **H**, take the left-hand trail, which will bring you out of the woods at the parking area.

Paddling in Owen Sound

You can launch your canoe or kayak from the day-use beach at the Hibou Conservation Area (when the gate is open; expect to pay a small parking fee at the gatehouse) or from the ramp in the rough roadside park 2 km along Grey Road 15 towards Owen Sound.

Opportunities are rather limited, however, as there are few interesting coves or islands to explore in the sound and much of the shoreline is privately owned. Still, on a hot summer's day after a hot hike, some refreshing time on the water may be welcome.

Maps, Publications & Information
- NTS map 41 A/10: Owen Sound.
- The Grey Sauble Conservation Authority has published a booklet containing maps and information about its conservation area properties, available from local tourist offices and on their website, www.greysauble.on.ca.

The Hibou shoreline erupts with summer wildflowers.

CHAPTER 21

West Rocks

OVERVIEW

West Rocks Conservation Area protects a scenic section of the Niagara Escarpment, at the southwestern edge of Owen Sound. The Bruce Trail curves around the clifftop here, past half a dozen lookouts, some with intimate views of the cliff environment and others with panoramic vistas across Owen Sound and out to Georgian Bay.

Owen Sound, the waterway, is an extension of the Sydenham Valley, a "re-entrant" valley that was carved by glacial ice as it advanced along an existing bedrock fracture. Like other such valleys on the Bruce Peninsula — Colpoy's Bay and, farther to the north, Hope Bay — Owen Sound is oriented northeast to southwest, indicating the glaciers' direction of travel. When the last glacier retreated about 12,000 years ago, the valley was scoured by meltwater and flooded by glacial Lake Algonquin, leaving the smooth, rounded contours seen today from the lookouts at West Rocks.

Owen Sound, the town, was incorporated in 1857 and elevated to city status in 1920. Before that, it was known as Sydenham, named (after Canada's governor-in-chief of the time) by British surveyor Charles Rankin when he established the settlement in 1840. Unofficially, it earned the moniker Corkscrew Town, the preponderance of taverns giving it an unfortunate reputation in the latter part of the nineteenth century.

Owen Sound became one of Georgian Bay's major ports and shipbuilding centres, competing with Collingwood, Midland and Depot Harbour. The arrival in 1873 of the narrow-gauge Toronto, Grey & Bruce Railway began the transportation boom. A decade later the Canadian Pacific Railway purchased and upgraded the line and made Owen Sound its transshipping terminal on Georgian Bay. For almost 30 years under the CPR and then under the Owen Sound Transportation Company, trains and freighters steamed in and out, exchanging cargoes of lumber, grain, fish and consumer products. With the development of roads and truck transport around the bay during the mid-1900s, the need for rail and freighter services waned, and the railway and shipbuilding yards were abandoned. The Owen Sound Transportation Company shifted its focus to tourist passenger-and-vehicle transport instead. Today it operates the *Chi-Cheemaun* ferry service between Tobermory and Manitoulin Island. Meanwhile, Owen Sound's economic base has become more diverse, and its population, numbering about 22,000, no longer relies on the shipping business. A few cargo vessels still use the port facility, but from the vantage point of the West Rocks lookouts, the harbour seems a tranquil place more commonly used by pleasure craft than commercial boats.

(Left) This "stack" has broken away from the escarpment face and stands like a sentinel over Owen Sound.

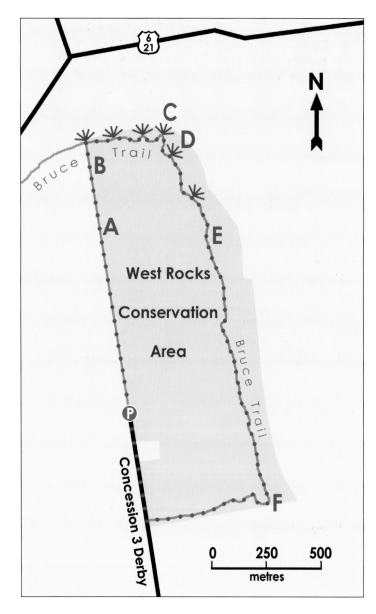

Distance: **5 km loop hike**

Access

- From the Owen Sound bypass (Grey Road 18), turn north onto Concession 3 Derby, and drive for 3.5 km to the end of the road.
- Park on the shoulder of the large turnaround area here, taking care not to block residents' driveways.

Route Description

1st Segment: West Rocks Access Trail (1.3 km hike)

Walk north along the road allowance for 1.3 km to the escarpment edge. The road allowance begins as a gravel track, but when the track swerves into the forest towards the right **A**, continue north on the rocky path that follows the allowance. About 300 m from the edge of the escarpment, you will have to jump across a large cleft in the rock **B**, the first of several such bedrock fractures you will encounter along the trail.

2nd Segment: Escarpment Edge and Lookouts (2.5 km hike)

At the end of the road allowance, the first view is disappointingly urban, overlooking the Grey County Mall. Turn right and follow the white blazes of the Bruce Trail around the escarpment edge, where more rewarding vistas await. The most expansive of these **C**, about 500 m along the trail, is a fine view down the Sydenham Valley and across Owen Sound to Georgian Bay. In the distance Kemble Mountain rises on the left-hand shore, and in the foreground the cliff drops to an impressive dolostone pavement. Another 175 m along the trail, a "stack" **D** has broken away from the cliff face and stands like a sentinel watching over the valley.

A maze of trails runs through the conservation area here, so be sure to follow the white blazes of the Bruce Trail, especially where it jogs to the right, away from a well-travelled path that swings down the hill. From this junction E, the Bruce Trail continues along the top of the escarpment, but the terrain becomes more heavily forested. A canopy of maple and birch closes over the trail, and a phalanx of cedars obscures the view from the cliff, but some massive blocks of fractured rock and several deep chasms will draw your attention instead.

3rd Segment: Homeward (1.1 km hike)

At the southern boundary of West Rocks Conservation Area F, the trail reaches private property and turns right, away from the cliff. After following a fenceline west for 600 m, it emerges onto Concession 3 Derby. Turn right and walk the final 475 m along the road to your car.

Other Things to Do in the Owen Sound Area

- *Grey Roots Museum*: Located on the north side of the Owen Sound bypass (Grey Road 18), this new museum houses a collection of historical archives and artifact displays relating to Grey County and Owen Sound. For information call (519) 376-3690, or visit www.greyroots.com.
- *Owen Sound Waterfront*: At the mouth of the Sydenham River, there is an attractive collection of parks, multi-use trails and historic properties that give opportunities for a pleasant stroll. The town's tourist information centre and the Marine & Rail Museum are located here, in the old railway station on 1st Avenue West. For information call (519) 371-9833 or visit www.city.owen-sound.on.ca.

Maps, Publications & Information

- Bruce Trail map #30: Inglis Falls.
- NTS map 41 A/10: Owen Sound.
- The Grey Sauble Conservation Authority has published a booklet containing maps and information about its conservation area properties that is available from local tourist offices or on their website, www.greysauble.on.ca.

CHAPTER 22

Indian Falls

Indian Falls is an attractive, horseshoe-shaped waterfall — a Niagara Falls in miniature — that plunges 15 m over the Niagara Escarpment near Owen Sound. It is possible to enjoy the short walk to the falls and admire the view from the overhanging ledges without knowing anything about the rocks you are standing on. But your appreciation of the landscape will grow when you pause to consider the fascinating geology that created it.

(Above) Soft layers of colourful shale at the base of Indian Falls have worn away, leaving an overhang of dolostone at the top.

Indian Falls provides an excellent example of the sedimentary rock formations found all along the escarpment and the erosive processes that are gradually wearing them down. Several colourful bands are obvious in the cliff wall beneath the falls. The red and green layers towards the bottom are a fine-grained rock called Queenston shale. This rock formed about 430 million years ago, when southern Ontario was positioned near the equator and covered by a shallow tropical sea, the Michigan Basin. Towering over the eastern edge of the basin were the Taconic Mountains, forerunners of the Appalachians. Rivers tumbled from these mountains, carrying massive loads of sediment. The sediment settled in deltas and shallow waters along the margins of the basin and was compressed over time into shale.

By 400 million years ago, the topography of the Taconic Mountains had been reduced to gently rolling hills, and the flow of sediment petered out. As the waters of the Michigan Basin cleared, coral reefs were able to grow; indeed, they flourished along its shores. The accumulated shells of generations of marine creatures consolidated into a ridge of limestone. As the basin began to dry up about 300 million years ago, magnesium molecules from the seawater infiltrated the limestone, changing it chemically into dolostone. This dense, buff-coloured rock was able to endure the scouring of glaciers in more recent times and has emerged as the caprock of the Niagara Escarpment.

Dolostone is the topmost layer of rock at Indian Falls. Beneath it the Queenston shale, less resistant to the erosive force of water, has receded into the cliff face, undercutting the dolostone, which forms an overhanging ledge. Chunks of the ledge regularly crash to the base of the cliff, collectively creating a jumble of rockfall called talus — an all-too-familiar feature to hikers stumbling along the Bruce Trail! This process of sapping, which wears away the cliff foundation, is gradually moving the escarpment westward, 1 m per year by conservative estimates. Niagara Falls, since its inception about 12,000 years ago at the end of the last glaciation, has retreated more than 10 km up the Niagara Gorge towards Lake Erie — something to think about when you are standing beneath the ledges at Indian Falls, lulled by the sound of water spilling over them into the plunge pool below!

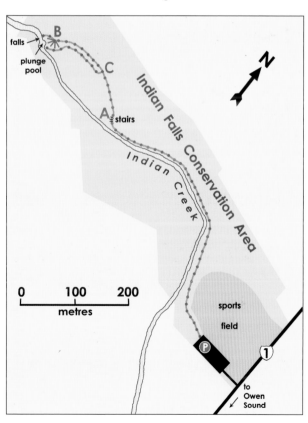

Distance: **0.8 km linear hike plus a short side trail (2 km return)**

Access

- From Hwy 6 (10th Street) in downtown Owen Sound, exit north onto 2nd Avenue West (which becomes Grey Road 1) and drive for 5.7 km to Balmy Beach.
- Turn left into the parking lot at the Indian Falls Conservation Area.

Route Description

Follow the well-worn trail inland from the parking lot. Skirting a sports field (built on a reclaimed gravel pit), the trail makes its way to Indian Creek and follows the creek upstream. The footing here is an uneven and often very slippery tangle of rocks and roots. After 200 m the trail turns away from the water and climbs a series of steps **A** to the top of the cliff. It continues for another 200 m to Indian Falls **B**, where the overhanging rock ledges give impressive views over the waterfall.

On the return, about 75 m back along the trail, an unmarked but obvious side trail **C** leads down the cliff to the plunge pool at the base of the falls, giving a different and often rather misty perspective on the scene.

Another Owen Sound Waterfall

Inglis Falls, located where the Sydenham River descends the escarpment on the south side of Owen Sound (off Inglis Falls Road, 300 m north of Grey Road 18), is a waterfall of a different character. There is no Queenston shale in the cliff face here and no undercutting to create a long drop or a plunge pool at the bottom. Instead Inglis Falls cascades prettily over the escarpment in a series of uneven steps resembling an amphitheatre.

Inglis Falls was named after Peter Inglis, a Scottish immigrant who settled along the Sydenham River in 1843 and established a water-powered gristmill at the falls. Three generations of the Inglis family ran the mill, which served farmers from Dundalk to Lion's Head. In 1932 the 300-acre property and its water rights were purchased by the City of Owen Sound, and in 1960 the conservation authority acquired the property around the falls. Today the

Inglis Falls.

Bruce Trail crosses the river at the top of the falls on its way through the Sydenham Valley, providing another hiking opportunity in the area.

Maps, Publications & Information

- NTS map 41 A/10: Owen Sound.
- The Grey Sauble Conservation Authority has published a booklet containing maps and information about its conservation area properties that is available from local tourist offices or on their website, www.greysauble.on.ca/ca-indianfalls.html.
- *Geology and Landforms of Grey & Bruce Counties*, written by the Bruce-Grey Geology Committee and published by the Owen Sound Field Naturalists in 2004.

CHAPTER 23

Skinner's Bluff

OVERVIEW

Skinner's Bluff is a picturesque wedge of the Niagara Escarpment on the southeastern shore of Colpoy's Bay, located about 15 km from Wiarton. The bluff has many fine lookouts over the bay and the three islands — White Cloud, Griffith and Hay — that guard its entrance. A ribbon of farmland runs along the base of the bluff, dotted here and there with marshland, and to the north, across Colpoy's Bay, the cliffs of the escarpment stretch invitingly up the Bruce Peninsula.

It is possible to visit Skinner's Bluff briefly to admire the views or to spend a whole day hiking along the escarpment edge and through the fields and forests of the Skinner's Bluff Conservation Area. Either way the outlook from the bluff is an excellent introduction to the landscape of Colpoy's Bay.

(Above) Skinner's Bluff lookout over an autumn landscape.

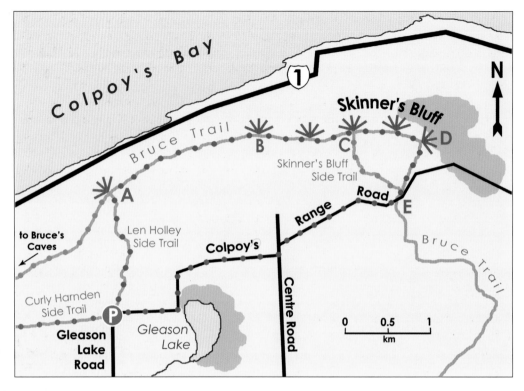

Distance: 10 km loop hike or 5.5 km linear hike (11 km return)

Access

- From Hwy 6 near the top of the hill on the south side of Wiarton, take Elm Street (Concession 21) east for 7.9 km.
- Turn left onto Sideroad 20 (Gleason Lake Road) and drive 4 km to the end, where it curves to the right onto Colpoy's Range Road.
- Park along the curve in the road. (Caution: there is no winter maintenance on some sections of these roads, so be prepared to improvise according to conditions.)

Route Description

From the parking area, take the blue-blazed Len Holley Side Trail (red dots on accompanying map) north for 1.7 km through a pleasant deciduous woodland. The side trail meets the white-blazed Bruce Trail at the edge of the escarpment **A**, where a lookout has been cut through the trees. Turn right and follow the main trail eastward. At first only tantalizing hints of a vista can be seen through the phalanx of cedars that line the bluff. But after 2 km **B**, the forest gives way to farmland and the cedars give way to cedar-rail fences, and for the next 1.2 km, the trail crosses open terrain beside fields and abandoned orchards. There are many wonderful views to the north across Colpoy's Bay, where the escarpment cliffs can be seen snaking along Malcolm Bluff and up the Bruce Peninsula.

At the eastern edge of the farmland **C**, opposite the Skinner's Bluff Side Trail, which exits to the right, an overhanging clifftop ledge gives a sweeping vista over Colpoy's Bay — a good place to stop for a picnic lunch. Then continue along the main, white-blazed trail for 600 m as it curves around Skinner's Bluff to the final lookout **D** on an exposed slab of rock that juts out from the cliff.

You have two choices for the homeward trek: You can retrace your steps along the escarpment edge to appreciate the views from a different perspective. Or you can shorten the route by continuing along the Bruce Trail for 400 m to Colpoy's Range Road, turning right at the junction **E** and following the road for 4.2 km to your car. It is a narrow track, without much traffic, that meanders through a pleasantly varied landscape of woodlands and farm fields.

Alternative 1: Shorten the Hike (1.8 km loop hike)

Park at the edge of Colpoy's Range Road where it crosses the Bruce Trail **E**. Hike north along the Bruce Trail to visit the lookouts between **D** and **C** and then loop back through the woods on the blue-blazed Skinner's Bluff Side Trail (orange dots on accompanying map).

Alternative 2: Lengthen the Hike (16.5 km loop hike or 8 km linear hike — 16 km return)

Park at the Bruce's Caves Conservation Area (see Chapter 24, under Access). After exploring the caves take the Bruce's Caves access trail to the main Bruce Trail at the top of the escarpment. Turn left and follow the main trail east for 3.6 km (green dots on accompanying map) to meet the Skinner's Bluff hike at the junction with the Len Holley Side Trail **A**. For a linear hike, continue along the main trail to visit the lookouts (**B** to **D**) and return by the same route. For a loop hike, follow the escarpment edge all the way around Skinner's Bluff to Colpoy's Range Road **E**, walk along the road for 4.2 km and then take the Curly Harnden Side Trail (purple dots on accompanying map) for 2.3 km to rejoin the main trail 1.2 km from your car.

Maps
- Bruce Trail maps # 32 and # 33.
- NTS map 41 A/14: Cape Croker.

The winter panorama at Skinner's Bluff.

CHAPTER 24

Bruce's Caves

OVERVIEW

Bruce's Caves are a collection of caverns and hollows in the Niagara Escarpment cliffs near Wiarton. They formed between 12,000 and 8,000 years ago when waves, crashing on the shoreline of ancient Lake Algonquin, scoured the rock and eroded any that was weak or soluble. Lake Algonquin covered most of the area encompassed by today's Upper Great Lakes — Superior, Michigan and Huron, including Georgian Bay. It was significantly deeper than the modern lakes, filled with meltwater from the receding Wisconsin glacier. As the glacier moved northward and its meltwater drained away, the land rebounded, released from the weight of millions of tons of glacial ice (a process called isostatic rebound). The old shoreline now lies halfway up the hills, many metres above the present-day lake.

Robert Bruce, after whom the caves are named, was born in the Orkney Islands of Scotland about 1820. At the outbreak of the Crimean War in 1854, he deserted from the Scots Guard and set out for Canada, where he settled on a piece of land near Wiarton. He worked for many summers in railway construction gangs and spent several winters at the county jail (as a paying lodger, not an inmate). But for most of his remaining years, Bruce lived as a recluse in a cabin at the entrance to the caves and charged admission to curious visitors. He died in 1908, leaving 300 acres of land and a sizable bank account, but no known relatives. The property is now protected by the Grey Sauble Conservation Authority.

Distance: 400 m linear hike (0.8 km return)

(Above) The magnitude of Bruce's Caves is awe-inspiring.

Access

- From Hwy 6 in Wiarton, turn east onto Frank Street, which becomes Grey Road 1. Follow it for 5.4 km.
- Turn right onto the Bruce's Caves Conservation Area road and drive 1 km to the end, where there is a parking area and a picnic shelter and toilets.

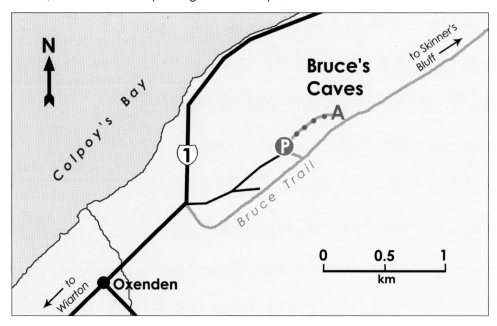

Route Description

Take the well-worn yellow-blazed trail from the east side of the parking lot. The trail makes its way through a deciduous woodland for 400 m and then curves to the right over a jumble of talus to the caves **A**. The enormous main cave has a distinctive double arch with a central column at its entrance. Against the back wall of this cave, a crack in the corner gives a peak into a second cave. Many other caves — some large enough to walk through, others mere crevices in the rock — can be found along the escarpment face on both sides of the main cave. (Note: bring a flashlight or headlamp for a better view.) After exploring the caves, return along the outward trail to the parking lot or, for a longer walk, a visit to Bruce's Caves may be combined with a hike to the lookouts at Skinner's Bluff (see Chapter 23, under Alternative 2).

Maps, Publications & Information

- Bruce Trail map # 33.
- NTS map 41 A/14: Cape Croker.
- The Grey Sauble Conservation Authority has published a booklet containing maps and information about its conservation area properties that is available from local tourist offices and on their website, www.greysauble.on.ca.

CHAPTER 25

Historic Wiarton: Spirit Rock, the Corran and Wiarton Willie

OVERVIEW

Wiarton, with a population today of only 2,300 people, has a long and lively history. Located near the base of the Bruce Peninsula, at the deeply indented head of Colpoy's Bay, Wiarton's sheltered harbour made it an ideal port and base for settlement. The town was established in the 1850s and named after Wiarton Place in southeastern England, the birthplace of Canada's governor general at the time. For centuries before this, Native travellers and fur traders used the site when, to avoid the treacherous waters around the tip of the Bruce Peninsula, they would portage from Colpoy's Bay across the narrow height of land into the Rankin and Sauble rivers flowing west to Lake Huron.

Like most of the towns that sprang up along the Georgian Bay coast during the 1800s, Wiarton, known affectionately as Sawdust Town, was rooted firmly in the logging industry. Sawmills and lumberyards lined the shore of Colpoy's Bay, and Wiarton's business district bustled with factories that supplied the town's population with wood products ranging from building materials and furniture to fence posts and caskets.

(Above) Wiarton Willie presides over the waterfront at Bluewater Park.

At the industry's peak during the 1890s, a dozen boxcars full of timber and finished wood products left Wiarton every day on the Grand Trunk Railway, destined for markets in the south.

The fishery was another early mainstay of the town's economy. With its excellent harbour and access to a transportation network of shipping channels and railway lines, Wiarton became an important centre for packing, freezing and distributing Georgian Bay lake trout and whitefish. The Wiarton Fish House was established in 1883 and prospered for more than 40 years. During its heyday, it was the largest fish processor in Ontario, generating 3 million pounds of fish a year, consuming more than 20 tons of ice every day in the summer months (harvested from Colpoy's Bay during the winter and stored in the plant's four ice houses) and employing 25 people full-time and dozens of others indirectly. The town even boasted a large federal fish hatchery, located at the site of the present-day water filtration plant.

A woollen mill, a sugar-beet factory and a cement works augmented the town's industrial base during the early 1900s. But fortunes changed on many fronts. Depletion of the Bruce Peninsula's forests brought a decline in the timber trade by the 1940s. Overfishing and the sea lamprey's invasion up the St. Lawrence Seaway caused the fishery's collapse during the 1930s. The failure of several other local businesses and the Great Depression of the 1930s compounded the town's economic woes.

Wiarton's recovery — as a glance down the main thoroughfare on a summer day will attest — lay not in industry but in tourism. In 1921 the Wiarton Women's Institute established several bathhouses on the Colpoy's Bay shore. These were followed in 1929 by a collection of one-room cabins. Today, where the mills and woodyards once stood, Bluewater Park extends attractively along the shoreline, home to a campground, a boat launch and a tourist information centre (the old railway station was relocated and restored for this purpose). Colpoy's Bay is now an anchorage for yachts and motorboats instead of barges and cargo steamers. And the town is comfortably furnished with hotels, restaurants and other services for visiting travellers.

As a tourist attraction, a rodent seems an unlikely choice, but Wiarton Willie, the town's famous groundhog, has been drawing visitors since 1956. The tradition of weather prediction by animals has its origin in many winter-weary cultures of the northern hemisphere, and although the details vary from one culture to another, the general theme is the same. In the middle of winter (on Candlemas Day, which falls February 2, halfway between the winter solstice and the spring equinox) a hibernating animal (a hedgehog in Europe and a groundhog, also called woodchuck, in North America) emerges from its burrow. If the day is sunny, the animal will be startled by its shadow and return to the burrow, and winter will continue for another six weeks. If clouds obscure the shadow, then unsettled spring weather has arrived early, and the animal will remain above ground.

North America's Groundhog Day tradition began in Punxsutawney, Pennsylvania, when the editor of the local newspaper published a story about a groundhog hunt and barbecue in the town on Candlemas Day in 1887. The story became embellished in the years that followed, and the spring weather pronouncement by "Punxsutawney Phil" became an annual festival. Years later, in 1956, a Wiarton resident with connections in the Ontario government brought the tradition to his hometown by throwing a party to celebrate Groundhog Day and using his political connections to promote the event. It was covered, unexpectedly, by a *Toronto Star* reporter and picked up by other Canadian media. Wiarton's albino groundhog became an instant legend. Wiarton Willie has had many incarnations in his 50 years of service (the natural lifespan of a groundhog is, after all, a mere five to six years), and he is commemorated by a statue in Bluewater Park — a 4.5 ton groundhog carved from the escarpment's dolomite stone by a local artist.

The hike in this chapter encompasses several of Wiarton's historical features. Beginning at the statue of Wiarton Willie, it follows the Bruce Trail through Bluewater Park and along the shoreline to Spirit Rock, where a Native chieftain and his bride met their deaths long before Europeans arrived in Colpoy's Bay. It then ascends the escarpment to the ruins of a lavish nineteenth-century estate, built by Alexander McNeill, a long-serving Member of Parliament for Wiarton. During its final leg, the hike returns unmistakably to the present, as it makes its way back along Hwy 6 to the lively centre of town.

Distance: **5.8 km loop hike**

Access
- At the traffic lights in Wiarton, exit Hwy 6 east onto William Street.
- Follow the signs to Bluewater Park, where there is a large parking lot, a tourist information centre, a boat launch, picnic tables and toilet facilities.

Route Description

1st Segment: Bluewater Park to Spirit Rock Park (1.5 km hike)

Wiarton Willie presides over Bluewater Park, his statue marking the start of this hike. Follow the white blazes of the Bruce Trail north through Bluewater Park and along Bayview Street beside the busy marina. After 1.5 km the road passes a tiny park **A** at the base of the cliff, where an interpretive panel explains the natural history of the Niagara Escarpment and tells the poignant story of Spirit Rock. During a battle between rival Native tribes, the daughter of one tribe's chief was captured by warriors of the other tribe and held by them in slavery. The young chieftain of the enslaving tribe was so enchanted by the girl's beauty and so moved by her sadness that, without consulting his fellow warriors, he freed her and made her his wife. The warriors were angered by what they considered his betrayal and, during a hunting party, pushed their chieftain over the escarpment edge to his death. The forlorn young woman, rejected as a traitor by her own tribe and an interloper by her husband's, wished only to be reunited with her beloved. When darkness had cloaked the menacing rocks, she walked to the place where he had died and threw herself off the cliff. It is said that the girl's spirit lives on at this site and, when the sun strikes the escarpment at a certain angle, her profile can be seen in the rock face.

2nd Segment: Spirit Rock Park to the Corran (1.6 km hike)

A spiral staircase leads up the escarpment cliff to the Corran.

Continue 400 m along the road to the water treatment plant, where the road becomes a pedestrian trail. The trail follows the shore of Colpoy's Bay, winding over shingles and among cedars for 1 km before turning away from the water. The path then begins to climb, at first up a set of conventional steps to the base of the escarpment and then up a somewhat alarming spiral staircase **B** to the top of the cliff. From the cliff edge, a well-worn trail leads 200 m to the ruins of the Corran **C**.

Alexander McNeill was born in 1842 into a privileged family of the Irish gentry and educated at select schools in Dublin and England. In 1872 he married his cousin Hester, a wealthy widow 12 years his senior. Later that year the couple travelled to Canada to oversee a family property near Paisley, at the base of the Bruce Peninsula. The following decade, in 1881, Alexander left the family property in the care of a manager and purchased 121 hectares of land for himself near Wiarton, where he and Hester settled for their remaining years. They built a luxurious mansion — the Corran — on the cliff overlooking Colpoy's Bay. The place was reminiscent of Alexander's childhood home in Ireland and boasted 17 opulently furnished rooms, with several magnificent stone fireplaces, an extensive library and an impressive collection of artwork. Outside, a veranda spanned the front of the house and the estate stretched across manicured lawns and beautiful gardens to orchards and pasture lands beyond. An enormous barn housed a herd of imported cattle, and more than 500 varieties of roses grew around the house.

For 20 years, from 1881 to 1901, Alexander McNeill was the Member of Parliament for the federal riding of Bruce North, and many of Ontario's social and political dignitaries were guests at the Corran. Hester's early death near the turn of the century and Alexander's in 1932, at the age of 90, left the McNeill estate in the hands of their only

Spirit Rock lookout over Colpoy's Bay.

son, Malcolm. Without his parents' resources, nor an interest in maintaining the place, Malcolm allowed it to decline. Upon his death in 1956, he left the property to his long-time housekeeper, Sally Simmons, who sold it five years later to a Toronto couple. The new owners' plans to restore the manor house were thwarted when the buildings, then vacant, were destroyed by vandalism and fire. In 1976 the Sauble Valley Conservation Authority bought the land and turned it into a park — Spirit Rock Conservation Area — whose fascinating history draws curious visitors like us today.

3rd Segment: The Corran to Spirit Rock Lookout (1.2 km hike)

From the Corran, return towards the staircase, but turn right before reaching it onto the blue-blazed Spirit Rock Side Trail. For 1.2 km this trail makes its way along the edge of the escarpment, offering many splendid views over Colpoy's Bay. The last lookout is at the top of Spirit Rock. The cheerful bustle of boats in the bay on a sunny summer day makes it easy to forget the tragic fate of the young Native woman and her chieftain who fell to their deaths over this cliff.

4th Segment: Homeward (1.5 km hike)

Continue southwest from the lookout, along the blue-blazed Wiarton Side Trail, which emerges suddenly from its historical meanderings in Spirit Rock Conservation Area onto the busy shoulder of Hwy 6, dumping you abruptly into the here and now. After following the highway for 800 m, the trail continues down the hill onto Berford Street in Wiarton. Originally, Berford Street came north through Wiarton to the base of the escarpment and then swung east, away from the cliff towards Colpoy's Bay. With the advent of the automobile in Wiarton in 1912 and increased vehicle traffic during the decades that followed, a direct route through town became necessary, and a road cut **D** was blasted through the cliff in 1927. The new road was opened the following year and subsequently widened and smoothed to become the modern highway that spans the escarpment today. Follow the blue blazes, turning left onto Division Street at the base of the hill, to rejoin the main, white-blazed Bruce Trail at Bluewater Park. Your car is just a short distance to the right through the park.

Maps & Information

- Bruce Trail map #33.
- NTS map 41 A/14: Cape Croker.
- Wiarton tourist information: (877) 844-9884, www.thebrucepeninsula.com/wiarton, www.sbpcc.org.
- Bluewater Park campground information and permits are available from the Town of Wiarton tourist information centre in the old railway building: (519) 534-2592.
- Spirit Rock Conservation Area information is available at www.greysauble.on.ca/ca-spiritrock.html.
- Fascinating old postcards and photographs of Wiarton with accompanying information about the town's history can be found at www.postcard.wiarton.ca.

CHAPTER 26

The Wrecks of Colpoy's Bay

OVERVIEW

In this short paddling excursion, we will peer overboard in search of skeletons. The skeletons along our route — one passenger steamer, two dredging scows and two Great Lakes freighters — were the workhorses of a previous century. All five vessels fell victim not to peaceful demise from antiquity, nor to wreckage in fierce autumn storms, but rather to undignified abandonment in the wake of progress. Their stories will give us a taste of the busy commercial history of Colpoy's Bay.

Colpoy's Bay, the body of water, is a deeply indented inlet near the base of the Bruce Peninsula, whose sheltered harbour made an ideal port and base for settlement. Colpoy's Bay, the village, was the bay's first settlement, established when several families purchased lots and took up residence on the north shore in 1857 and 1858. Nearby Wiarton was not settled until 1866, and its development lagged behind that of Colpoy's Bay for more than a decade. When the Grand Trunk Railway extended its line north through Owen Sound to Wiarton in 1881, however, the economic tables turned and Wiarton quickly became the dominant community.

In their early days, both settlements relied heavily on the timber trade, and a profusion of sawmills and lumberyards sprang up along the shore during the latter half of the 1800s.

Those early years were also the heyday of Great Lakes shipping. Sheltered inlets like Colpoy's Bay became important ports for the passenger steamships that ferried settlers and travellers between coastal communities on Georgian Bay and for the steam freighters that plied the waters with their cargoes of resources, timber chief among them.

For more than half a century, Wiarton and Colpoy's Bay bustled with commerce. Then, during the 1940s, the dwindling supply of Bruce Peninsula timber hit the sawmills hard and adversely affected all the businesses that relied on them. After 1950 the mills around the bay fell silent; many burned. Meanwhile roads penetrated the landscape, blasting through the escarpment face at the north side of Wiarton in 1927 as they moved up the peninsula. By the end of World War II, automobiles had become the preferred method of travel and trucks the more efficient mode of transport, sealing the fate of many small shipping firms. Along the waterfront, shrewd entrepreneurs converted crumbling docks into marinas for the growing fleets of pleasure craft. And the old workhorses of the bay's logging and shipping days — among them the five skeletons we will visit today — were left to disintegrate.

Distance: 3.5 km linear paddle (7 km return)

Access

- In Wiarton, two short blocks north of the traffic light, exit Hwy 6 east onto Division Street. After 100 m Division Street ends at Bayview Street.
- Turn left and follow Bayview Street for 1.4 km, past a series of marinas, to a small waterfront park at the base of Spirit Rock.
- There are picnic tables and a public boat ramp here and roadside parking where you may leave your car when you launch your canoe or kayak into Colpoy's Bay.

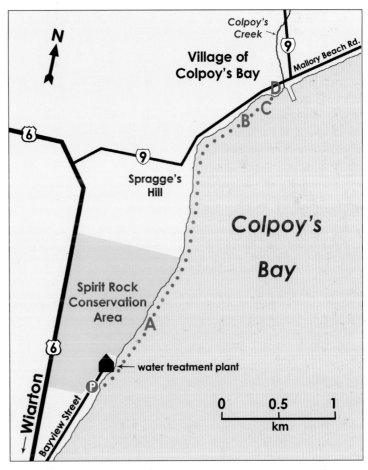

(Left) Drifting over the skeletons of two old cargo steamships, the Lothair *and the* Edward S. Pease.

Route Description

1st Segment: Water Treatment Plant and the *City of Chatham* (0.8 km paddle)

Make your way northeast along the shore from the launch, past the water treatment plant. In 1993 this stark modern structure replaced a charming old building (the federal government fish hatchery) that had graced the site since 1907. Millions of fry from various species were spawned at the hatchery annually and released to boost stocks for the commercial and sport fisheries.

About 500 m past the filtration building, you will find the excursion's first wreck **A**, the *City of Chatham*. Lying about 20 m offshore from a huge boulder, the ruined hull stretches 40 m from stem to stern, roughly parallel to the shore. Paddlers with a GPS will find it centred on UTM coordinates 0489480E, 4956375N. Built in 1888 by Polson Iron Works, of Toronto, the *City of Chatham* was an oak-hulled 627-passenger steamship that operated on Lake Huron and Georgian Bay and for many years ran the busy route between Detroit and Sault Ste. Marie. In 1921 the aging vessel was moved to the Wiarton shipyards for refurbishing. But the improvements were never made and, with the decline in importance of passenger steamships, she was discarded on the shore of Colpoy's Bay.

Wildflowers have cheerfully taken root among the ruins on the Colpoy's Bay shore.

2nd Segment: Scows and Freighters of Colpoy's Bay (2.7 km paddle)

Leaving the *City of Chatham*, continue to follow the shoreline as it curves gradually northward. The land here is part of Spirit Rock Conservation Area, and you may see hikers on the Bruce Trail, which hugs the shingle beach for 200 m near the wreck site before climbing to the brow of the escarpment. Around the headland, past the conservation area boundary, private homes and cottages become visible along the waterfront, and you will likely hear vehicles on Bruce County Road 9 descending Spragge's Hill into the village of Colpoy's Bay.

About 500 m beyond the base of the hill, across the road from a stately old house, you will find an untidy jumble of metal and rotting timbers stretching out into the bay. Further exploration may allow your imagination to untangle the mess and create a vision of a long wharf and two barges, one resting at the end of the wharf and the other slightly to the west. This was the Kalbfleisch marina **B**, a thriving concern during the mid-1900s.

Edwin Kalbfleisch bought the old house (built in 1884) and surrounding property in 1920 and constructed the wharf to accommodate his growing shipbuilding business. With its continued expansion during the 1940s and 1950s under the stewardship of Edwin and his son Frederick, the business came to include boat repairs, mooring, fuelling and tour boat services. Several generations of the Kalbfleisch family were raised in the house, which is still in family hands today.

During the marina's prosperous years, Frederick Kalbfleisch purchased two old flat-bottomed scows that previously had been used for dredging the harbour in Wiarton and scuttled them near the end of his long wharf to form a breakwater that would shelter the marina's patrons. The wreck at the end of the wharf is the *Paul H. M.*, scrapped in 1955. The wreck to the west, with the dreary name *Birmingham Construction Number 3*, followed her sister in 1961. In subsequent decades, the Kalbfleisch business moved down the shore into Wiarton, leaving the original marina infrastructure, including the two old scows, to the mercy of Colpoy's Bay's ice and waves.

Some 200 m to the east of the scows are the remains of two older and larger vessels **C**, the *Lothair* and the *Edward S. Pease*. These wooden-hulled steamships, each with a single propeller and a mast for auxiliary sail power, were built in 1872 and 1873, respectively, and served their early years as cargo freighters on the Great Lakes. Mishaps dogged both ships. The *Lothair* ran aground on Lake Ontario's Amherst Island in 1874 and on a Collingwood breakwater in 1879; she became waterlogged in Tobermory in 1891 and caught fire in a Windsor port in 1893. The *Edward S. Pease* (originally christened the *California*) had a longer litany of disaster, running aground several times, catching fire twice and capsizing once; on more than one occasion, these accidents led to tragic loss of life. Both vessels were acquired by the Crawford Tug Company, of Wiarton, near the turn of the century and spent their declining years doing barge duty in the lumber industry. In about 1907 Charles E. Whicher purchased the barges and had them towed to his sawmill in Colpoy's Bay. There, they were scuttled to form a breakwater so that rafts of logs could be securely stowed in the millpond behind.

A century of battering by Georgian Bay weather has taken its toll on the venerable wrecks, and today only their keels, lower hulls and scattered pieces of hardware remain. The *Lothair* is slightly shorter (just under 40 m) than the *Edward S. Pease* (just over 42 m) and slightly farther east and nearer to shore. Shrinking water levels have brought their remains close to the surface, making them a popular site for divers.

3rd Segment: Whicher's Sawmill

A small point of land **D** juts into the water just beyond the wrecks, where you may wish to pull your canoe or kayak ashore and stretch your legs. Crumbling stone foundations and rusting metal debris, including a massive flywheel, identify this as the location of what was once Whicher's Sawmill. Before Charles Whicher purchased the land in 1901, six other sawmills had operated at the site during the latter half of the 1800s, each in turn either destroyed by fire or dismantled and moved elsewhere. The Whicher mill was a sizable outfit for its time, employing as many as 25 local men, ten hours a day for eight months of the year, and lining the shore with millions of board feet of lumber. The mill's saws were powered, appropriately, by sawdust-fired steam engines. The first mill built by the Whicher family in 1901 was short-lived, consumed in a massive blaze in 1909. Its successor, however, continued production until the failing fortunes of the lumber industry forced its closure in 1953. The following year the abandoned building also burned. With one last puff of smoke, the once-profitable mill, like the industry that had supported it, was extinguished.

4th Segment: Homeward (3.5 km paddle)

Today the character of the shore is decidedly more cheerful. On a sunny summer's day at the mouth of Colpoy's Creek, fishermen cast their lines from the pier, travellers munch picnics in the little park, snorkellers thread their way among the ribs of the old ships, and hikers and cyclists pause to admire the glorious view. It is, after all, the beauty of the escarpment cliffs and the sparkling waters of Colpoy's Bay that draw people here today and tourism that now sustains the town's economy.

Turn your canoe or kayak west, and make your way back along the shore towards Wiarton, leaving the skeletons to rest in peace.

Maps, Publications & Information

- NTS map 41 A/14: Cape Croker.
- The website Postcards from the Bay (www.postcard.wiarton.ca) contains fascinating historical information, including a splendid collection of vintage photographs and postcards of Wiarton and Colpoy's Bay.
- *Days of the "Mud Hen" and Other Memories of Colpoy's Bay Village, Ontario*, compiled and edited by Sheila Gatis, published by Colpoy Creek Books in 1986 and reprinted in 2005.

The old flywheel from Whicher's sawmill.

CHAPTER 27

Hope Bay

OVERVIEW

This scenic hike explores the landscape at the head of Hope Bay — its enticing sandy beach, the cliffs that overlook the bay, two glacial potholes and a cave chiselled into the rock, and the pleasant deciduous woodland at the top of the Niagara Escarpment that forms the Hope Bay Forest Provincial Nature Reserve.

Erosion is a recurring theme along the trail. Hope Bay itself is one of several "re-entrant" valleys on the Bruce Peninsula, carved from the bedrock by glacial ice as it advanced across the region from northeast to southwest. When the last glacier retreated about 12,000 years ago, the land was scoured by meltwater and flooded by glacial Lake Algonquin, leaving the smooth, rounded contours of the valley and the long crescent of sand seen today from the Hope Bay lookouts.

The lookouts themselves, and the cave just past the first lookout, were shaped by another erosive process — sapping. The white rock at the top of the cliffs is dolostone, a relatively dense, durable rock that caps the escarpment. Below it are layers of shale and limestone. These softer rocks erode more easily, leaving the dolostone protruding as overhanging ledges — that is, until the ledges are worked loose by ice and water and come crashing to the base of the cliff!

(Above) Clifftop lookout over Hope Bay.

The large twin potholes along the trail were also formed by erosion, a tremendous downward surge of meltwater beneath the glacial ice. The water, like a high-pressure whirlpool, drilled cavities in the bedrock, leaving cylindrical holes that seem unnaturally smooth and uniform amid the random tangle of rocks and vegetation that surrounds them.

Distance: **9.5 km loop hike**

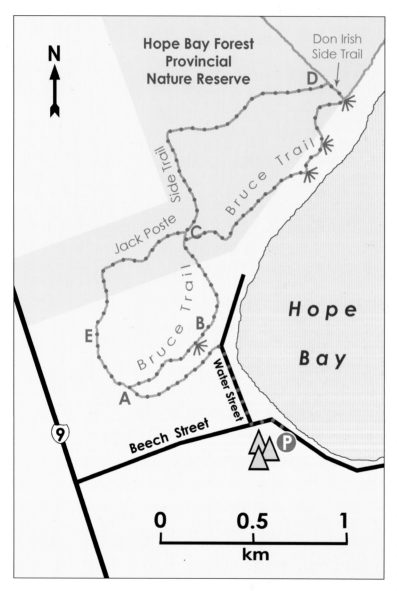

Access

- On the north side of Wiarton, exit Hwy 6 onto Bruce County Road 9, and drive for 16.3 km.
- Turn right onto Beech Street, and drive 1 km down the hill to Hope Bay.
- Parking (with convenient pit toilets adjacent) is available in a public lot on the right-hand side of the road, just past the campground store.

Route Description

1st Segment: Hope Bay to Top of Escarpment (1.5 km hike)

From the parking area, walk back along the road for 200 m and turn right onto Water Street. Follow the Bruce Trail markers, past the rows of cottages and then left along a track leading up the hill to a trail junction **A** near the top. You will return along the blue-blazed Jack Poste Side Trail that continues up the track, but for now keep to the white-blazed, main trail as it exits to the right.

2nd Segment: Hope Bay Lookouts and Glacial Potholes (3 km hike)

The trail scrambles along a rough path to the cliff edge and the first lookout, which has a pleasant view of the beach and cottages at the head of Hope Bay. About 100 m later, the trail skirts a cave **B** formed by an overhanging rock. Continuing inland past another junction with the Jack Poste Side Trail, you will find two large glacial potholes **C** to the left of the main trail. From here the trail makes its way back to the cliff and hugs the escarpment edge for 1 km, passing several splendid lookouts over Hope Bay.

3rd Segment: Homeward via Don Irish and Jack Poste Side Trails (5 km)

At the last of these lookouts, the Don Irish Side Trail leads away from the cliff. Follow it inland for 200 m, and turn left **D** onto the Jack Poste Side Trail. This trail, an old logging track, winds through the gentle terrain of the Hope Bay Forest Provincial Nature Reserve, emerging from the woods after 2.2 km into a pastoral landscape bordering a farm field **E**. The trail hugs the edge of the field, and a stile brings you over a fence at the southern end onto a gravel track. Turn left and follow the track down the hill, rejoining the main trail **A** and retracing your outward journey to Hope Bay, where a swim at the beach or an ice cream from the campground store may be a welcome conclusion to the hike.

Paddling in Hope Bay

From the Hope Bay beach, you may launch your canoe or kayak and paddle along the shoreline to enjoy the escarpment cliffs from the perspective of the water. You might also wish to explore the two small, shallow coves on the northern side of the bay — Shoal Cove (3 km from the launch) and Jackson's Cove (2 km beyond Shoal Cove).

Maps

- Bruce Trail map #35: Hope Bay.
- NTS map 41 A/14: Cape Croker.

Two of Hope Bay's enormous glacial potholes.

195

CHAPTER 28

Cape Dundas

OVERVIEW

The Cape Dundas and Rush Cove trails are recent additions to the Bruce Trail system — the former opened in 2006 when access was secured with the generous permission of the landowner, and the latter in 2007 after a Herculean fundraising campaign enabled the Bruce Trail Association to purchase 1000 m of shoreline that became available in Rush Cove. The Bruce Trail was rerouted to encompass these new sections, which introduce hikers to a superb variety of natural habitats. In this chapter we follow the trail along the shingle beach from Rush Cove to Cape Dundas and across an alvar that straddles the Cape Dundas headland. From the alvar the trail climbs to the top of the Niagara Escarpment, picking its way over a fern-filled talus field and through a mature deciduous forest to the Jackson's Cove lookout. After taking in the view — one of the finest of the Bruce Peninsula's many panoramic vistas — our route returns down the escarpment face and back along the shingle beach.

Distance: 6.1 km loop plus a linear access of 1.1 km and a linear extension of 1 km (10.3 km total)

(Above) Jackson's Cove lookout.

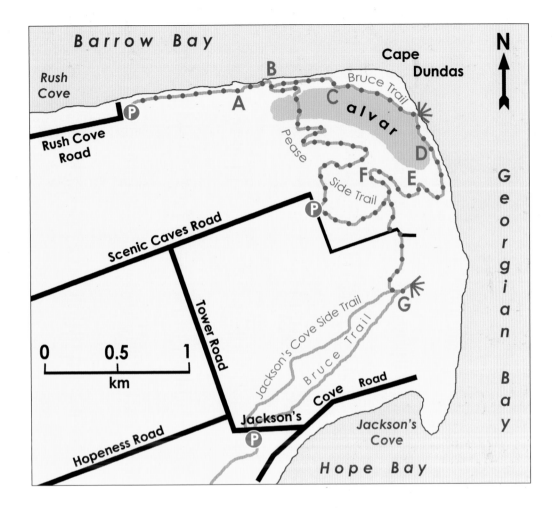

Access
- From the south, exit Hwy 6 on the north side of Wiarton onto Bruce County Road 9, and drive northeast for 21 km. From the north, exit Hwy 6 onto Bruce County Road 9 in Ferndale, and drive southeast for 11 km.
- Turn east onto Scenic Caves Road.
- After 2 km turn left onto Rush Cove Road, and follow it for 3.4 km as it winds down the hill and along the shore.
- Leave your car in the parking area to the right of the road just before it ends.

Route Description

1st Segment: Rush Cove to Cape Dundas (1.1 km hike)

From the parking lot, follow the white blazes of the Bruce Trail for 25 m to an open shingle ridge just above the shore. Continuing east the trail makes its way along the ridge and through a patchy cedar forest. After 900 m it descends the cliff via a wooden

Layers of shale and limestone form the "beach" between Rush Cove and Cape Dundas.

ladder **A** and hugs the water's edge for 175 m. Among the sheets of shale and limestone, you will see occasional colourful rounded boulders — erratics from northeastern Georgian Bay that were brought here by glaciers thousands of years ago and left behind like forgotten beach balls when the ice melted. You will be reluctant to follow the trail when it turns away from the beach and clambers up a steep staircase **B**.

2nd Segment: Cape Dundas Alvar and Lookouts (1.7 km hike)

At the top of the cliff, take the white-blazed trail to the left, through the cedars that line the clifftop ledge. Several breaks in the trees offer views north across Barrow Bay and along the escarpment snaking towards Cabot Head. Some 500 m beyond the staircase, the trail emerges into a meadow **C**. At first it resembles an abandoned farm field, but upon closer inspection you will discover just beneath the surface the telltale bedrock pavement that denotes an alvar.

Alvars are naturally open areas of flat bedrock, either completely barren or covered with a thin layer of soil that supports sparse vegetation. They are rare habitats globally, yet the Bruce Peninsula, with extensive areas of dolostone pavement, has many fine examples. The alvar is an unforgiving environment of extremes: searing sun and blistering heat in summer, bitter cold and desiccating wind in winter, and floods of melting snow and April showers in spring. The alvar's inhabitants, therefore, are an extremely hardy and, paradoxically, extraordinarily vulnerable bunch — lichens and mosses, grasses and juniper, and a proliferation of colourful wildflowers.

To avoid damaging this habitat, the trail skirts the alvar for 700 m and makes its way to a grassy headland overlooking Georgian Bay with views east and south towards Barrier Island and Cape Croker. From this lookout the trail continues to the end of the alvar **D** and along the cedar-lined ledge for another 500 m.

3rd Segment: Ascent to Jackson's Cove Lookout (2.5 km hike)

Turning inland the trail then climbs the escarpment, a set of stone steps **E** helping you up the first steep incline. For 300 m the path picks through the talus at the edge of a cliff, a lush crop of ferns and moss growing among the fallen rock, until a wooden staircase **F** brings you panting to the top. The footing becomes more even here, and the trail meanders through an airy woodland dominated by maple and beech. Soon the Pease Side Trail (named so in honour of the landowner) exits to the right. You will return to this junction later, but for now, continue on the main trail for 1 km along a sometimes confusing collection of tracks and paths. Keep to the white blazes of the main Bruce Trail until it reaches the cliff edge and turns right **G**. Turn left instead and follow the short, blue-blazed side trail to the Jackson's Cove lookout.

The view here is one of the escarpment's most expansive — west across Jackson's Cove and Hope Bay, east over Barrier Island and Georgian Bay, and south along Sydney Bay and Jones bluffs and the Cape Croker peninsula. On a clear day, you may even see the waters of Colpoy's Bay twinkling in the distance and the dark shape of Hay Island on the southeastern horizon. The panoramic vista and the comfortable stone ledge make this the perfect place to rest and enjoy a picnic lunch — fortification for the return journey.

4th Segment: Homeward (5 km hike)

Backtrack along the Bruce Trail for 1 km to the junction with the Pease Side Trail. Turn left and follow it through the woods towards the northwest. After 600 m you will pass an alternate parking area on the left. As the trail gradually descends to lower elevations, birch trees begin to appear among the maples. About 2 km from the alternate parking area, the trail makes a hairpin bend to the right and swings down the hill to rougher ground where the vegetation becomes a jumble of cedar and fir. Then it crosses the western edge of the alvar and cuts through the cedars and along an old wooden fence, bringing you to the end of the Pease Side Trail at the top of the wooden staircase B. Retrace your outward route from here for 1.1 km, over the shingle beach and ridge and back to your car.

Shorten the Hike

Park in the gravel lot on Scenic Caves Road, and hike the 6.1 km loop along the Pease Side Trail and main Bruce Trail around Cape Dundas, omitting the linear wings on either side that lead to Rush Cove and the Jackson's Cove lookout. You will be able to access the shore at the eastern staircase B and enjoy the escarpment face with its talus slopes and alvar below and its deciduous forest above, but you will miss the view from the Jackson's Cove lookout. The lookout can be accessed separately, however, as a short (3.7 km loop) hike from the parking area on Jackson's Cove Road. See Bruce Trail map #35 for details.

Another Alvar to Explore

The Bruce Alvar is a striking example of the alvar environment, presenting barren dolostone pavements and wildflower meadows bordered by Jack pine and cedar woodlands. Acquired in 1994 by Ontario Nature (then called the Ontario Federation of Naturalists) with funds from a generous private bequest, this 67-hectare property is a protected nature reserve. A 500 m trail gives access to the alvar from the west side of Hwy 6 about 400 m north of the Dyer's Bay Road, and a boardwalk and viewing platform have been constructed above portions of the pavement to preserve its fragile habitat. For information visit www.ontarionature.org.

The Cape Dundas alvar.

Maps

- Bruce Trail map #35: Hope Bay.
- NTS map 41 A/14: Cape Croker.

CHAPTER 29

Lion's Head

OVERVIEW

This excursion approaches one of the Bruce Peninsula's most popular attractions — Lion's Head — from an unusual direction: by water via McKay's Harbour. The sheer cliffs of the Niagara Escarpment plunging almost 100 m into Georgian Bay and the spectacular views from the many lookouts along the clifftop have made the Lion's Head peninsula a mecca for hikers and rock climbers. A much-loved section of the Bruce Trail traverses the peninsula's perimeter and several inland side trails can make loops of varying lengths for day hikes. The most exciting part of the trail, with the most impressive vistas, is the 5.5 km segment that rounds Gun Point and Lion's Head Point at the tip of the peninsula, a long trudge from the trail access points in Barrow Bay and Lion's Head at the peninsula's base. The excursion described in this chapter eliminates the trudge, substituting instead a scenic paddle and the opportunity to admire the immense cliffs and overhangs from beneath.

The paddling portion of this excursion must not be undertaken casually, however. The boulder garden at McKay's Harbour exposes you to considerable risk in wind and waves, and the peninsula's cliffs offer few places for an emergency landing. Before launching your canoe or kayak into the sheltered waters at Lion's Head Marina, be sure to check the day's weather forecast at the marina office (especially the predicted afternoon wind that you may have to battle on the return journey). If in doubt, leave your boat behind and take the safer, conventional approach by foot along the Bruce Trail.

The Lion's Head peninsula is one of the few sections of Georgian Bay's Bruce Peninsula coastline that has not been divided up into private cottage properties. The peninsula's only settler was Captain John McKay, a fisherman and tugboat captain who, in the early 1900s, built a homestead and raised a family in the dubious shelter of what is now called McKay's Harbour. At about the same time, the forests on the headland gradually fell to extensive logging and to fires that ignited in the timber debris. In subsequent decades, the peninsula was shielded from development by the exposed and rugged character of its shoreline, allowing Nature to restore the original balance. Most of the land is protected now under the banner of the Lion's Head Provincial Nature Reserve, whose expanse of wilderness is broken only by hiking and cross-country ski trails.

Distance: 4 km linear paddle (8 km return) plus a 9.5 km loop hike (or alternative loop of 4.6 km)

(Left) Approaching Lion's Head.

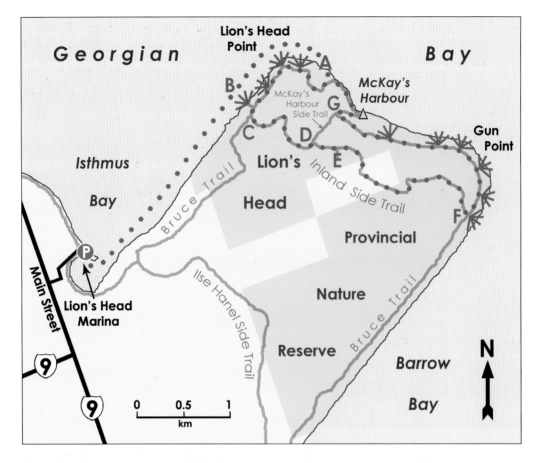

Access

- Exit Hwy 6 in Ferndale onto Bruce County Road 9.
- Drive 2.9 km east to the T-junction at Lion's Head, and turn left onto Main Street.
- Drive to the bottom of the hill, turn right onto Scott Street, left onto Helen Street, right onto McNeill Street, and then right again onto Dock Street, which brings you to Lion's Head Marina.
- Check in at the marina office for the latest weather report and for permission to use their launch and parking facilities.

Route Description

1st Segment: Lion's Head Marina to McKay's Harbour (4 km paddle)

Launch your canoe or kayak into Lion's Head Harbour, and paddle through the channel, past the lighthouse and into Isthmus Bay. Follow the right-hand shore along the base of the escarpment cliffs. Their sheer walls will loom large beside you, and enormous angular chunks of fallen rock may make you wary of the overhanging ledges towering far above. Rounding Lion's Head Point, the shoreline becomes less forbidding, and you will see a small shale beach **A** where you can pull your boat ashore in relative safety (if you are using a GPS, the beach is identified by UTM coordinates 0483250E, 4983480N). An alternative site is McKay's Harbour itself, 500 m farther along the shore, but the shallow boulder-strewn approach makes landings and launches more difficult here. Wherever you land, be sure to haul your boat well above the waterline and tie it securely before setting out on foot.

2nd Segment: McKay's Harbour to Lion's Head Lookout (2.3 km hike)

Walk south along the shale and cobble beach for 215 m, and turn right to join the Bruce Trail as it heads inland on the north side of McKay's Harbour. Crossing a terraced area — cobble shorelines left behind as the lake level receded — the trail climbs steeply, skirting a huge boulder and passing beneath an impressive ledge on its way up the hill. Towards the top you may wish to stop and catch your breath at the first lookout. Many other lookouts follow as the trail continues to climb around Lion's Head Point. A kilometre of scrambling over the rough rocks at the escarpment edge will bring you to a 20 m side trail that leads to the ultimate lookout atop the Lion's Head **B** (a flat-topped outlier jutting away from the cliff wall), with breathtaking views across the turquoise waters and up the escarpment to Cabot Head.

3rd Segment: Lion's Head Lookout to Barrow Bay (4 km hike)

After taking in the panorama, return to the main trail and continue for 50 m past the lookout **C**, where the blue-blazed Inland Side Trail exits to the left, providing a relatively gentle route across the peninsula. Follow this trail as it winds through an airy forest of maple and birch. After 1.6 km it meets a side trail that provides a shortcut (700 m) back to McKay's Harbour **D**. If you are tired, you may wish to return this way (cutting the length of the hike in half). Otherwise, continue along the Inland Side Trail.

Some 400 m past the McKay's Harbour shortcut, another side trail leads 100 m to the right and up a small rise to a cement block **E**. Though not, perhaps, as exciting an objective as others along the trail, the geodetic survey disc embedded in the block marks the 45th parallel, the midpoint between the equator and the North Pole. Markers like this were installed across the Ontario landscape during the early 1900s, providing surveyors and map-makers with a network of precisely plotted points that they used to chart the Earth before the advent of high-tech satellite systems.

Back at the Inland Side Trail, continue south for another 2 km. This section of the trail is less well travelled, so watch for blue blazes to guide you along its twists and turns. As you approach the cliff on the other side of the peninsula, the footing becomes rougher and the deciduous woodland gives way to cedars. The trail ends at a lookout over Barrow Bay **F**.

4th Segment: Gun Point to McKay's Harbour (3.2 km hike)

Turn left onto the main Bruce Trail, and follow it across the rugged, sparsely wooded landscape of Gun Point. There are many rocky promontories around the headland that offer wonderful views across Barrow Bay towards Cape Dundas and Cape Croker. The trail seems perilously close to the cliff edge, at times mere millimetres from certain doom, so be sure to keep your canine companion (and any absent-minded relatives) on

a short leash here! As the path rounds the point and curves northward, you will begin to see McKay's Harbour from the lookouts. Soon the cliff begins to break up, and the trail descends into a glacier-carved valley, turning sharply right **G** onto an old logging road leading to the water.

Loggers brought timber harvested atop the peninsula down this track to the shore, where it was gathered into booms and towed by tugboats to nearby mills. Captain John McKay, who once made this harbour his home and base for fishing, dug a channel and built a protective breakwater here. All his labours were erased in 1913, however, by one of the bay's notorious November gales, which restored the pleasing natural disorder that we see today. In addition to the slabs and cobbles of local dolostone, the beach is littered with erratics — rocks of an entirely different character, many of them banded and brightly coloured, that were plucked by glacial ice from northeastern Georgian Bay and dumped here when the ice melted.

The trail passes a wilderness campsite tucked among the trees at the base of the hill and crosses the beach, picking through the poison ivy that flourishes along the border of the cobble terraces. When the trail veers left towards the escarpment, continue up the shore instead, where your canoe or kayak will be waiting on the shale beach around the corner **A**.

5th Segment: Homeward (4 km paddle)
This is where you will regret your decision if you have ignored the weather forecast, as the shallow, rocky shoreline around McKay's Harbour can make for a wet, if not impossible, launch in rough conditions. Once afloat, make your way northwest around Lion's Head Point, where the afternoon sun will throw a golden glow on the brilliant white cliffs. Enjoy the scenery while you paddle back along the coast to the marina at Lion's Head Harbour.

Alternative Approach if Conditions are Too Rough for Paddling (16 km loop hike)
Starting from designated parking areas on Moore Street on the south side of Lion's Head or from the Cemetery Road parking lot on the north side of Barrow Bay, you can hike the Bruce Trail around the peninsula (11 km), returning across its base via the Ilse Hanel Side Trail (5 km). This route misses the cement block with the geodetic marker along the Inland Side Trail, but you will more than make up for this loss with visits to the glacial potholes located just off the trail, 1 km to the west of the Lion's Head lookout.

Maps
- Bruce Trail map #36: Lion's Head.
- NTS maps 41 A/14: Cape Croker and 41 H/3: Dyer's Bay.

(Left) A trio of kayaks explores the Lion's Head shore.

CHAPTER 30

White Bluff and Reed's Dump

OVERVIEW

This loop hike between White Bluff and Reed's Dump visits almost every kind of landscape that the Bruce Peninsula has to offer, all protected within the Smokey Head–White Bluff Provincial Nature Reserve. The route passes through cedar woods and deciduous forests, crosses the open terrain of alvars and old farm fields, skirts marshlands, scrambles along dolostone clifftops and stops to rest on a beach of smooth, worn cobbles. While the environmental history of the landscape is fascinating, the hike can be enjoyed simply for its stellar views of the Niagara Escarpment's shoreline and for the pastoral charm of its wildflower meadows.

Distance: 9.5 km loop hike

Access

- Exit Hwy 6 onto Caudle Sideroad and drive east for 2 km to the end of the road.
- Turn right onto Forty Hills Road and drive 1 km.
- Pull into the small parking area to the left, just before the left-hand bend in the road.

Route Description

1st Segment: Across Alvar and Fields to Bluff (2 km hike)

The first natural feature of the landscape that you will notice when you get out of the car is the dolostone pavement beneath your feet. Open areas of flat bedrock like this are called alvars. Their thin-to-non-existent soil cover and their exposure

(Left) White Bluff.

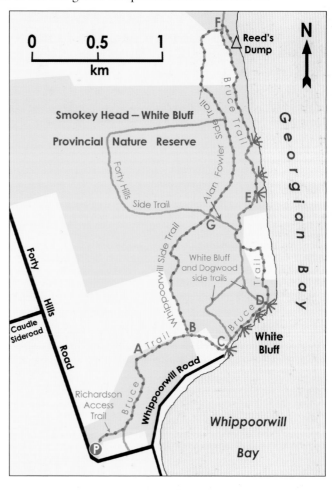

207

White Bluff's wildflower meadows.

to extremes of weather permit the growth of only sparse vegetation, and the vertical cracks that criss-cross the pavement's surface make the footing rough and unyielding to the hiker. (For more information about alvars, see Chapter 28.) Pick up the blue-blazed Richardson Access Trail as it cuts across the alvar and through a cedar woodland for 350 m to join the main Bruce Trail.

Turn left and follow the white blazes of the Bruce Trail, which continues through the cedars and emerges after 1 km into a large meadow **A**. After travelling over a fractured bedrock outcrop that runs up the middle of the meadow (be cautious of poison ivy at the edges of the outcrop!), the trail crosses a gravel track that brings the Whippoorwill Side Trail in from the left **B**. You will return this way, but for now continue along the main trail, past an old barn and across a small field. Soon afterwards the trail reaches the escarpment edge **C**, where underfoot you will see light shining through a deep crevice that connects with the cliff face.

2nd Segment: White Bluff Lookouts to Reed's Dump (3 km hike)

The first lookout is a disappointing view into a cottage yard at the end of Whippoorwill Road. The vistas improve as the trail curves to the left and climbs for 500 m along the edge of the cliff to the summit of White Bluff **D**. Just past the uppermost lookout, the

Dogwood and White Bluff side trails provide an optional return loop for anyone wishing to cut the hike short. Otherwise, keep to the main trail, which descends steeply through the cedars and jogs inland for 1 km. After passing a junction with the Alan Fowler Side Trail and crossing a gravel track, the trail returns to the escarpment edge E and continues north. There are more fine views along the way, at first to the south and then northward towards Cape Chin and Cabot Head. After 1.5 km the trail meets the Alan Fowler Side Trail again F. Just 10 m past this junction, another side trail exits to the right, leading 200 m down the hill to Reed's Dump.

The "dump" is a scenic beach of wave-battered cobbles, littered with slabs of limestone. At one time, however, the beach was a jumble of logs. In the lumbering days at the turn of the twentieth century, timber harvested from the forests behind White Bluff and Smokey Head was brought down the trail to the shore here, destined for towing to one of the many mills along the Bruce Peninsula coast.

Today the beach makes an excellent rest stop, and the limestone slabs, convenient tables for your picnic lunch. Bruce Trail through-hikers also use it as a primitive campsite. Be cautious of the exuberant patches of poison ivy along the fringe of cobbles between the beach and the trees.

3rd Segment: Homeward Along Interior Side Trails (4.5 km hike)

Your picnic and beach explorations finished, return up the hill along the Reed's Dump access trail. Turn left onto the main trail and immediately right onto the Alan Fowler Side Trail F. At first the path winds through a deciduous forest along an old logging road, and then it meets and roughly follows a gravel track (with several short detours into the woods). Running along the border between the forest and the edge of several fields and wildflower meadows, the track gradually makes its way south. At the corner of the field where the Alan Fowler Trail intersects the Forty Hills and Whippoorwill side trails G, take the Whippoorwill Trail, which continues for another kilometre to join the main trail B. Turn right and retrace your steps across the field and through the cedars to the alvar parking lot.

Maps
- Bruce Trail map #37: Cape Chin.
- NTS map 41 H/3: Dyer's Bay.

CHAPTER 31

Smokey Head

OVERVIEW

This hike passes through a pleasant variety of landscapes along the Niagara Escarpment's edge at the northern end of the Smokey Head–White Bluff Provincial Nature Reserve. It includes a walk through cedar and deciduous woodlands, a stroll along a stretch of cobble beach, and a climb to two fine clifftop lookouts. Compared with many of the other Bruce Peninsula hiking routes described in this book, this excursion is relatively short and gentle, giving ample time to poke along the beach or enjoy a leisurely picnic-with-a-view at one of the lookouts. It also makes a suitable winter hike, as the access road is plowed regularly and the trail is easily manageable on snowshoes.

Distance: 2.6 km linear hike (5.2 km return) or 5.1 km loop

Access
- Exit Hwy 6 onto Lindsay Road 5.
- Drive east for 3 km and turn left onto East Road.
- After 2 km the road curves to the right and then jogs immediately left. Instead of taking the left-hand jog, continue straight onto Cape Chin South Road and follow its twists and turns for 7.2 km.
- At Cape Chin South, turn right onto Carter Road and drive 500 m, where you may park in the large turnaround area at the end of the road.

(Left) Cape Chin's terraced cobble beaches, seen from the Fred Binding Lookout.

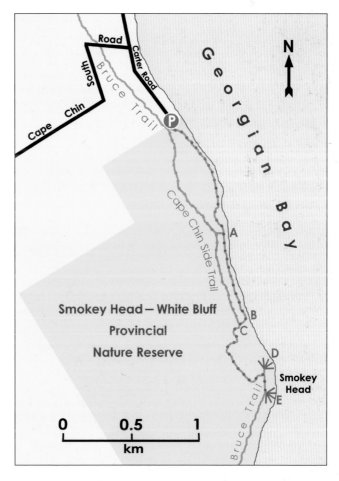

211

Smokey Head in winter.

Route Description

1st Segment: Through Woods and Along Beach (1.6 km hike)

Walk past the iron gate on the west side of the parking area, and follow the track 25 m up the hill. Turn sharply left and follow the white blazes of the Bruce Trail towards the south (the blue-blazed Cape Chin Side Trail is an optional route for the return journey). The main trail passes through a cedar woodland and makes its way along a bluff for 1 km, offering several glimpses out to Georgian Bay. It then descends to a cobble terrace where the trees become sparse and scruffy and poison ivy flourishes underfoot. The terrace is part of an ancient shoreline left behind when the water in the bay declined from historically higher levels. The modern-day cobble beach is several metres farther down the trail, at a junction with a short access trail **A**. The main trail continues along a ridge of cobbles just above the beach or, if you prefer, you may walk along the beach itself for 650 m to enjoy the water (and avoid the poison ivy).

2nd Segment: Climb to Lookouts (1 km hike)

A clearly marked exit **B** takes you away from the beach, and the trail climbs steeply past a junction with the Cape Chin Side Trail **C**. It continues for another 600 m across more level ground at the top of the hill, curving towards the escarpment edge. A 20 m side trail leads to Fred Binding Lookout **D** (so named in honour of a founding member of the Peninsula Bruce Trail Club), which has a splendid view north to Cape Chin, Dyer's Bay and Cabot Head. Back at the main trail, turn left and walk 150 m farther along the trail to the Smokey Head lookout **E**, which gives a view south to the Lion's Head peninsula.

3rd Segment: Homeward (2.5 km hike)

Retrace your steps through the woods to the junction with the Cape Chin Side Trail **C**. Here you have a choice of returning along the beach the way you came (1.6 km) or taking the side trail (1.5 km), which makes its way along a quicker but less interesting route, following a track through the woods.

Possible Extension

A more ambitious hike can be had by continuing south along the Bruce Trail from Smokey Head for 4 km to Reed's Dump (see Chapter 30). This extension adds several cliff-edge views to the hike and almost triples its distance (7 km each way, for a total of 14 km).

Maps
- Bruce Trail map #37: Cape Chin.
- NTS map 41 H/3: Dyer's Bay.

CHAPTER 32

Devil's Monument

OVERVIEW

The Devil's Monument is the highlight of this hike, but in summertime you may find it a somewhat disappointing pile of rocks partially obscured by trees. The monument was once a small headland sticking out from the Niagara Escarpment (like many other clifftop headlands you have stood on to admire views along the Bruce Trail). About 6,000 years ago, when the water level of glacial Lake Algonquin was much higher than that of Georgian Bay today, waves crashed on the shoreline here, eroding away the base of the headland to form an arch. Eventually the arch was undermined to such an extent that it collapsed, leaving the outer supporting column standing as a solitary "sea stack." Subsequent drops in the lake level, to below the sea stack's base, have allowed trees and shrubs to take root among the fallen jumble of rocks. This fringe of vegetation around the monument makes it less visually striking, perhaps, than some of its relatives — the "flowerpots" of Fathom Five National Marine Park, for instance, that stand out starkly from the surrounding rock. Nevertheless, at 14 m high, it is the tallest stack on the Bruce Peninsula and, unlike the flowerpots, is entirely self-supporting (the flowerpots at Fathom Five have been reinforced with concrete).

If you are unimpressed with the Devil's Monument shrouded in summer foliage, you may find this hike's two glacial potholes more interesting. The larger is nearly 4 m in both depth and diameter; the smaller, about half that size. They were sculpted into the bedrock by meltwater as the last glacier began to retreat. Recent geological opinion is that the potholes formed very quickly, following a catastrophic release of water beneath the ice that drilled into weak areas of the bedrock in a matter of weeks or even days! The meltwater formed a downward-spiralling vortex under very high pressure, which, aided by rocks and other debris, scoured out the smooth cylinders we see today.

In addition to fascinating erosional formations like sea stacks and glacial potholes, the trail's many splendid clifftop lookouts and a beautiful cobble beach give plenty of scenic variety along the route. The trail is especially stunning if you hike it on snowshoes in winter. Then there are no leaves to obscure the Devil's Monument, and the lookouts reveal a dazzling landscape of ice and snow. You will also likely have the trail to yourself, a pleasure that is rare at this popular place in summertime. Just take care not to fall into one of the potholes hidden beneath a snowdrift!

Distance: **4.5 km loop hike**

(Left) Devil's Monument in winter.

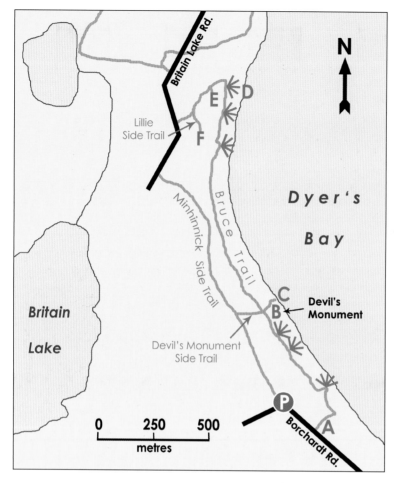

Access
- Exit Hwy 6 onto Lindsay Road 5 and drive east for 3 km.
- Turn left onto East Road and drive north for 4 km (note the right-left jog in the road halfway along).
- Then turn right onto Cape Chin North Road, and follow its twists for 5.6 km.
- Turn left onto Borchardt Road and drive 1.5 km to a gravel parking area 100 m past the Bruce Trail exit **A**.
- Leave your car here and walk back to join the Bruce Trail **A**. Note that during the winter months Borchardt Road may be closed by snow, so you will have to park on Cape Chin North Road and walk the 1.4 km to the start of the trail instead.

Route Description

1st Segment: Along Cliff to Devil's Monument (0.75 km hike)
From Borchardt Road **A**, the Bruce Trail makes its way to the escarpment edge and then north along the cliffs, past several lookouts over Dyer's Bay. After 500 m the trail comes to a fenced ledge overlooking the Devil's Monument **B**, where you will find an interpretive panel explaining the origin of this geological feature.

2nd Segment: Side Trip to Beach (100 m hike)
A staircase takes you to the rocks at the base of the Devil's Monument. Follow the blue-blazed side trail from here as it continues steeply down the hill. The trail passes a spring that emerges surprisingly, midway up the cliff, fed by water that has sunk through cracks in the rock at the top of the escarpment and flowed along an underground channel. The spring forms a stream that tumbles over a series of tiny moss-covered shelves, a favourite haunt of frogs. At the bottom of the hill, you will find a beautiful cobble beach **C** littered

with large slabs of dolostone (or in winter, huge chunks of ice, tossed ashore by waves). The slabs make excellent benches where you may wish to rest and admire the view.

3rd Segment: Devil's Monument to Potholes (1.5 km hike)
With exploration of the beach complete, retrace your steps to the top of the hill. The 140 m Devil's Monument Side Trail exits west here, giving a shortcut back to the car. You may wish to return this way if you are hiking the trail in winter. Otherwise, turn right and follow the main Bruce Trail north. It hugs the escarpment edge for 1 km, climbing to a particularly fine view **D** south over Dyer's Bay and Cape Chin, before turning inland. About 120 m later **E**, a short side trail on the left takes you across rock outcrops to the smaller of the two glacial potholes; 160 m beyond that **F**, also on the left, the Lillie Side Trail provides access to the larger pothole.

4th Segment: Homeward (2.2 km hike)
Back on the main trail, continue 200 m from the Lillie Side Trail and turn left onto the Minhinnick Side Trail. This trail follows Britain Lake Road for 200 m and then an old logging track for 1.8 km through a deciduous woodland and back to the parking area.

The smaller of the two potholes on the Devil's Monument Trail.

Maps & Publications
- Bruce Trail map #38: Dyer's Bay.
- NTS map 41 H/3: Dyer's Bay.
- *Geology and Landforms of Grey & Bruce Counties*, written by the Bruce-Grey Geology Committee and published by the Owen Sound Field Naturalists in 2004.

The wreck of the Gargantua.

CHAPTER 33

Cabot Head and Wingfield Basin

OVERVIEW

The windswept promontory of Cabot Head is one of the Bruce Peninsula's most exposed and dangerous stretches of coastline, and the tiny haven of Wingfield Basin one of its most welcome sanctuaries in stormy weather. The human history of the area is littered with wrecks — shipwrecks like those of the *Gargantua* and the *Kincardine*, as well as the wrecks of buildings and docks that once supported thriving local industries. The Cabot Head lighthouse still stands, beautifully restored as a museum and open to visitors during the summer months. From the lighthouse tower, you will enjoy a stunning view that takes in Cabot Head's quartet of massive bluffs, the snaking curve of the Niagara Escarpment winding west towards Tobermory, and the sweeping expanse of northern Georgian Bay, dotted with lonely islands.

This excursion explores Cabot Head and Wingfield Basin from the water, though it includes a brief leg stretch to visit the lighthouse grounds on foot. Before setting out, however, be sure to check the day's weather forecast, paying special attention to the predicted afternoon winds that might make your homeward paddle miserable. The litany of shipwrecks along this coast speaks for itself!

Distance: **5.2 linear paddle (10.4 km return) and 1.5 km loop paddle around Wingfield Basin, plus 400 m linear hike (0.8 km return)**

Access
- Exit Hwy 6 onto Dyer's Bay Road.
- Drive 8 km east to the T-junction, and jog right and then left into the village of Dyer's Bay.
- At the north end of the village, turn right onto Forbes Drive and immediately right again onto the Cabot Head Road. The road hugs the shoreline along the base of the cliffs and around South Bluff, giving you a last chance to assess conditions before committing yourself to a day in your canoe or kayak.
- After 5 km the road passes between areas of open terrain (approximate UTM coordinates 0477550E, 5007738N) where you may pull your car aside on a patch of grass or rocks.
- Access to the water is via a steep shingle beach and slippery shelves of limestone — manageable in calm weather but impossible in wind and waves.
- If in doubt, save the paddling for another day, and continue along the road for 2.5 km to visit the Cabot Head lighthouse and Wingfield Basin on foot instead.

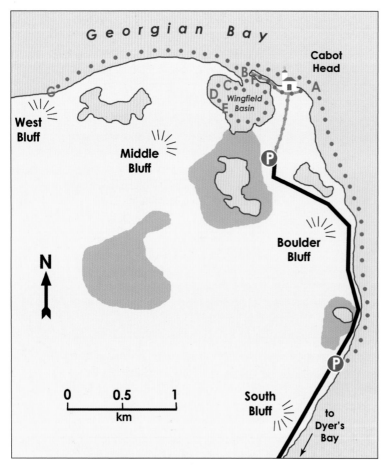

Route Description

1st Segment: Cabot Head to Wingfield Basin (3.2 km paddle)

Once you have slithered off the limestone shelves, set your course north. As you make your way along the shore, you will be impressed by the bulk of Boulder Bluff rising behind the foreshore flats and cobble beaches, the rock that is its namesake perched casually at the top. Rounding Cabot Head **A**, the lighthouse comes into view, a functional, modern steel structure overshadowing the comforting red and white tower of the older wooden building. A narrow channel **B** opens between the cobbles 500 m past the lighthouse, bringing you into the shelter of Wingfield Basin.

2nd Segment: Exploration of Wingfield Basin (1.5 km paddle)

Wingfield Basin is the only refuge of any significance along the 65 km of shoreline between Lion's Head and Tobermory. It was named in honour of Lieutenant David Wingfield, who discovered the basin in 1815 during a survey of the Bruce Peninsula coast with Captain William Fitzwilliam Owen. The basin was at that time partially obstructed by a shallow cobble bar, making it accessible only by canoe or other small craft. In 1893 a channel was dredged through the bar to accommodate the larger vessels used in the fishing and logging industries that had sprung up around the basin.

Although there had been some small-scale fishing off Cabot Head since the 1860s, it was not until 1900, following dredging of the channel, that a fishing station was established at Wingfield Basin. Captain Pankhurst Menery ran a thriving family business there and built an infrastructure of fish houses, net sheds, docks and cabins on the basin's western point. Menery's five sons and four daughters continued the business after their father's death in 1938, until the general decline of the Georgian Bay fish stocks forced its closure in the mid-1950s. The ribs of an old fishing tug can still be seen in the water on the basin's western shore; a private cottage now stands at the site of the fishing station.

The first timber license for Cabot Head was issued in 1870, and cutting and hauling lumber began soon afterwards. Until the channel was dredged, the logs were rafted offshore and towed to larger centres for processing, but in 1908 a sawmill was established in Wingfield Basin. The industry was short-lived, as the area's timber resources petered out during the 1920s. Only the ruined foundations of the shingle mill remain today, a rocky hump overgrown with weeds on the southwestern side of the basin.

The most obvious wreck in Wingfield Basin is the *Gargantua*, tucked behind the cobble finger at its western entrance. The *Gargantua* was built at the end of World War I but was not completed in time to see active service. She was fitted instead as a log-rafting tug and used for many years in that capacity. In December 1952, after refurbishment at the Collingwood Shipyards, she was under tow to her home port of Thessalon when a fierce storm forced her into the shelter of Wingfield Basin. The filthy weather persisted, so she was left to overwinter there. Springtime found her resting comfortably on the bottom, her hull partially submerged in the shallow water; her tenure in the basin has continued to this day. The dry timber of her superstructure caught fire and burned in 1971, but her rusting hull has become a wildflower garden and her beams a nursery for nesting swallows.

Passing through the channel **B** into Wingfield Basin, turn right to visit the *Gargantua* **C**, then continue counter-clockwise around the basin to see the ribs of the fishing tug **D** (easily found by GPS at UTM coordinates 04761319E, 5010162N) and the ruins of the shingle mill **E** (at 0476430E, 5010081N). Beyond the navigation markers, the shoreline curves back towards the cobble beach at the eastern side of the entrance channel. Pull your canoe or kayak ashore here **F** to stretch your legs, and continue the historical tour on foot.

Cabot Head lighthouse.

The alluring view along the secluded shore beyond West Bluff.

3rd Segment: Cabot Head Lighthouse (0.8 km return hike)

A path and a crumbling cement walkway (fringed with an enthusiastic crop of poison ivy!) lead east from the channel for 400 m to the Cabot Head lighthouse. The stretch of coastline along the upper Bruce Peninsula has always been perilous, but it was especially so during the latter half of the 1800s as commercial shipping between southern Georgian Bay and the Upper Great Lakes proliferated with the arrival of the railway into ports like Collingwood and Owen Sound. From the Griffith Island light at the mouth of Colpoy's Bay to the Cove Island light off Tobermory, no significant aids to navigation existed, and nothing marked the Bruce Peninsula's northeastern cape, where ships typically made a major change in course. Eventually the volume of traffic (and the frequency of shipwrecks!) prompted construction of the light station at Cabot Head in 1895. In its early days, the station was a busy seasonal posting for the lightkeeper, who tended the oil lamp and steam-powered foghorn. He was also charged with maintaining the state-of-the-art clockwork mechanism that rotated the light's reflectors so they would flash on a precise schedule and distinguish the Cabot Head beacon from others in the area. The lightkeeper lived in the dwelling connected to the tower until a separate residence was built in the 1950s. The 1960s brought significant changes as first a hydro line and then a road wound around the coast to Cabot Head.

Today the light performs its function automatically atop a modern metal tower. The old lighthouse has been restored as a museum, and the lightkeeper's residence now houses a gift shop and lodgings for volunteers from the Friends of Cabot Head who tend the property during the summer tourist season. Be sure to climb to the observation deck in the light tower to enjoy the stellar view from the top. On the landward side are the four impressive bluffs that make up Cabot Head and the remote and rugged shoreline along the escarpment ridge to the west. On the seaward side, you will be dazzled by the vast expanse of northern Georgian Bay, its sparkling waters dotted with isolated windswept islands, stretching towards Killarney's La Cloche Mountains along the distant horizon.

Your tour of the lighthouse complete, make your way back along the path to your canoe or kayak at Wingfield Basin.

4th Segment: Wingfield Basin to West Bluff (2 km paddle)

Paddle from the shelter of the basin through the channel **B** and into the open water of Georgian Bay where, if the wind has risen during your exploration of Cabot Head, you may feel it prudent to begin your homeward journey. If conditions permit, however, turn left and continue along the shore for 2 km to the base of West Bluff. If you pull your boat onto the steep, rocky beach here, you will find the final resting place of the *Kincardine* **G**. Built in 1871, this steamer ferried cargo across the Upper Great Lakes until, in early June 1892, with a full load of salt, she ran aground in fog just outside Wingfield Basin. Several days later, after much of her cargo and rigging had been salvaged, her superstructure burned (raising more than one suspicious eyebrow, as she was insured only against fire damage). After more than a century of storms, only the *Kincardine's* boiler and some other chunks of rusting metal are left among the cobble slabs.

5th Segment: Homeward (5.2 km paddle)

The alluring view to the west along the secluded shoreline of the Bruce Peninsula National Park will beckon you farther, but unless you have already made arrangements and purchased a backcountry camping permit from the park, you will have to turn back now. Make your way around Cabot Head the way you came, and hope that the wind and waves have not played havoc with your landing site!

Maps & Publications

- NTS map 41 H/3: Dyer's Bay.
- Nautical charts 228202: Wingfield Basin and 223501: Cape Hurd to Lonely Island.
- *Cabot Head: A History of its Lighthouse, Shipwrecks, Fishery and Timber Industry*, by Patrick Folkes, gives an excellent overview of the human history of the area. The booklet is available at the lighthouse gift shop from the Friends of Cabot Head (cabothead@hotmail.com).

CHAPTER 34

Halfway Log Dump and Storm Haven

OVERVIEW

A landscape of superlatives is what you will find when hiking this section of the Bruce Trail, along the coast of the Bruce Peninsula National Park. From the access point at Halfway Log Dump, the trail climbs across the headland at Cave Point and then descends to the relative shelter of Storm Haven. Abundant panoramic vistas and precipitous cliffs line the route, which also visits two beautiful beaches of wave-polished cobbles and limestone ledges. Although the hike is not overly long (less than 4 km each way), the rough terrain and beautiful scenery will slow your progress to a leisurely pace, so pack a picnic lunch and plan to spend the entire day on the trail.

Distance: **3.9 km linear hike (7.8 km return)**

One of many spectacular clifftop lookouts between Halfway Log Dump and Storm Haven.

Access

- Exit Hwy 6 onto Emmett Lake Road and drive 8 km north, following the signs to the Halfway Log Dump access.
- At the end of the road, there is a large parking lot with washrooms and a self-serve fee station where you must purchase a day-use permit for the park.

Route Description

1st Segment: Halfway Log Dump Access (0.9 km hike)

From the parking lot, follow the Halfway Dump Side Trail north on an old logging track. Being the gentlest descent of the escarpment along this stretch of the coast, this was the route used by loggers to haul timber down to the water. In the heyday of logging, at the turn of the twentieth century, trees felled and limbed during the winter in the interior highlands were stockpiled on the shore at the base of the trail, which became known as Halfway Log Dump. When the ice melted in spring, the logs were gathered into booms and towed to one of the many sawmills along the coast.

Today the "dump" is a steep beach of smooth, rounded cobbles; its only logs are those cast ashore by Georgian Bay storms. Walk to the end of the track, 50 m past the junction with the Bruce Trail A, and spend some time exploring the shoreline. The light-coloured cobbles are local limestone and dolostone, while others — the striped and colourful ones — are erratics that were brought by glaciers from their points of origin on the northeastern side of the bay. The character of the beach changes as you work your way towards its western margin, large horizontal slabs of limestone replacing the cobbles and wave-sculpted stacks poking up among the huge blocks of talus that have fallen from the cliffs above.

2nd Segment: Halfway Log Dump to Cave Point (1.7 km hike)

Backtrack from the beach to the trail junction A, turn right and follow the white blazes of the Bruce Trail west. After jogging briefly inland through a cedar woodland, the trail returns to the cliff edge **B**, where a series of ledges offer spectacular views back across the Halfway Log Dump beach and ahead to Cave Point and the islands of Fathom Five National Marine Park. As the trail climbs, the vista becomes almost surreal, the dizzyingly sheer cliffs plunging into the vast turquoise wash of Georgian Bay and waves foaming over the talus chunks that fringe the shoreline. A final scramble brings you to the top of the headland **C** and to the last views east towards Cabot Head. About 200 m farther along the trail, the next view **D**, equally breathtaking, is towards the west.

3rd Segment: Cave Point to Storm Haven (1.3 km hike)

The trail then descends from the headland, at times steeply, to a rock shelf running parallel to and slightly above the shoreline. The view here is largely obscured by cedars, and in any case, you will be busy watching your footing over the rough terrain. Eventually a wooden staircase **E** brings you to the base of the cliff and onto the beach at Storm Haven. Once the location of a hunting camp, Storm Haven is now a popular backcountry campsite for hikers and paddlers at the national park, with tenting platforms, a composting outhouse and bear poles for securing food. (Be sure to purchase a permit from the park office well in advance if you wish to stay overnight here.) The beach, like the one at Halfway Log Dump, is a fascinating mix of rounded cobbles and limestone slabs, with remarkably little shelter to justify the name Storm Haven. The rocks provide a perfect sand-free perch for a picnic lunch while you admire the view. Of particular interest are the massive, wave-carved caves in the cliff face to the east — no question about the appropriateness of the name Cave Point! — reputedly a hiding place for smuggled alcohol during the days of Prohibition that followed the First World War.

4th Segment: Homeward (3.9 km hike)

Having explored Storm Haven, make your way up the wooden staircase and back along the outward route to enjoy the glorious vistas from the opposite direction.

From the terraced limestone beach at Storm Haven, you can see the caverns in the cliffs that give Cave Point its name.

Maps, Publications & Information

- Bruce Trail map #39: Emmett Lake.
- NTS map 41 H/3: Dyer's Bay.
- Jack Wellington's *Guide to the Bruce Peninsula National Park*, published by Parks Canada and the Friends of the Bruce District Parks Association, is available from the park visitor centre and many local stores.
- The Bruce Peninsula National Park information: (519) 596-2233, www.pc.gc.ca/pn-np/on/bruce.

CHAPTER 35

Little Cove to Halfway Rock Point

OVERVIEW

The Georgian Bay coast adjacent to Cyprus Lake contains some of the most extraordinary erosional formations on the Bruce Peninsula — the Grotto, the Natural Arch, Overhanging Point, Lord Hunt's Tunnel, the Indian head at Indian Head Cove, and dozens of other nameless caves and crevices — all tucked into a stretch of shoreline no longer than 2 km! Indeed, the desire to protect these geological treasures motivated the creation of the Bruce Peninsula National Park in 1987, gathering into the federal parks system the former Cyprus Lake Provincial Park and a patchwork of neighbouring properties.

(Above) The full extent of Overhanging Point is visible only when approached by water.
PHOTO BY RICK CHUCHRA

The short loop from Cyprus Lake campground's Head of Trails to Georgian Bay and back via Marr Lake is one of the park's most popular hikes (considered a "must do" if you are camping at Cyprus Lake) and is described in several hiking guidebooks. Preferring a less conventional approach, we will visit the park's celebrated attractions from an unusual direction — the water — before tracing the traditional overland route along the coastal trail to see them again from a terrestrial perspective.

This excursion comes with a stern cautionary note about wind and waves, as the coastline here is utterly unforgiving, with little shelter or opportunity for retreat. Before setting out be sure to listen to the local weather forecast (available on the park's radio frequency), and if there is any doubt, opt for the traditional approach on foot from the Head of Trails instead.

Distance: 8.5 km linear paddle (17 km return) plus 2 km linear hike (4 km return)

Access
- Exit Hwy 6 onto Little Cove Road and drive 2.3 km north to the end of the road. There is space for only two or three cars at the bottom of the hill, and the steep, rocky descent can become severely eroded in wet weather.
- A less alarming alternative is the parking lot at the top of the hill on the east side of the road, from which it is only a 300 m carry down the hill to the beach at Little Cove.

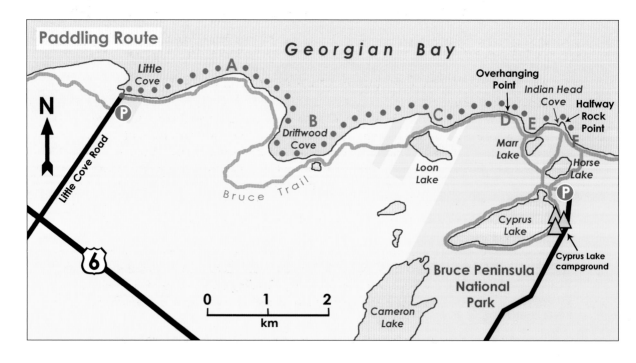

Route Description

1st Segment: Little Cove to Halfway Rock Point (9 km paddle)
(see Paddling Route map)

Little Cove's relatively sheltered waters and curiously eroded shoreline are favourite haunts of novice divers, and it is common to find neoprene-clad groups huddled with their scuba tanks and flippers on the beach in the early morning. Make your way to the shore, and launch your canoe or kayak from the cobbles. Paddling along Little Cove's shoreline towards the east, you will soon see the reason for its popularity — the dramatic troughs and pillars sculpted into the rock by centuries of pounding waves. Unfortunately, only a portion of these features is visible above the waterline; the underwater portion is the divers' domain.

At the mouth of Little Cove, the sheer cliffs of the headland finally curve away to reveal the ridge of the Niagara Escarpment snaking towards Cabot Head many kilometres to the east. Intervening headlands punctuate the shoreline, including Overhanging Point, which is clearly visible just 5 km ahead. Paddle past a tiny cobble beach **A**, around Dufferin

(Above) Light filters through the Grotto's underwater entrance, filling the pool with an eeire blue glow.

229

Point (named after a barge, the *Lady Dufferin*, which sank in deep water off the point in 1886) and into Driftwood Cove. The cove's beautiful cobble beaches and spectacular cliffs are privately owned, but even though you cannot land, the view from the water is worth the longer paddle close to shore. You may also see evidence of divers here, exploring the wreck of a three-masted schooner, the *Caroline Rose* **B**. Built in 1940 in Lunenburg, Nova Scotia, by the same shipbuilding company that launched the famous *Bluenose*, the *Caroline Rose* saw service as a fishing boat on the Grand Banks and then briefly as a cruise ship in Owen Sound before being towed to Driftwood Cove and deliberately sunk in 1990 for use as a dive site.

Beyond Driftwood Cove you will find another cobble beach flanked with limestone slabs **C**, its steep terraces serving as a retaining wall for tiny Loon Lake. Continuing east, you will likely begin to see the familiar shapes of hikers above the cliffs at Overhanging Point **D** and around the corner on the cobbles of Boulder Beach **E**. You are now just a short distance from the hub of park activity at Indian Head Cove, where you will find the Grotto, the Natural Arch and many smaller caves gaping from the cliffs at Halfway Rock Point.

If you ever have the opportunity to see this shoreline during an autumn storm, you will appreciate why these hollows are called "wave-cut" caves. Exploiting natural areas of weakness, waves crashing against the rock have eroded cavities in the escarpment face, sometimes sculpting a traditional cave formation with a single entrance, sometimes chiselling right through the rock to create caves with access from both ends. The Natural Arch is of the latter type, with both of its entrances now above lake level. The Grotto's second entrance is smaller and lies below the water's surface, allowing sunlight to filter eerily into the cave from beneath! You may see divers here, swimming through the tunnel between the Grotto and the bay outside. Slightly farther to the east, at Halfway Rock Point, the entrance to one large cave straddles the waterline, allowing you to paddle into the cave if conditions are calm.

Rounding Halfway Rock Point (so called because it is halfway between Tobermory and Cabot Head), you will find a rough cobble beach **F**. Pull your canoe or kayak ashore here, and secure it well above the water before continuing your explorations on foot.

The expansive raised terraces of Boulder Beach.

2nd Segment: Halfway Rock to Marr Lake (1.5 km hike) (see Hiking Route map)

A maze of trails weaves among the rocks and cedars on Halfway Rock Point, including the white-blazed Bruce Trail. Keep close to the cliff edge and make your way west to Indian Head Cove, where you will likely see visitors from the Cyprus Lake

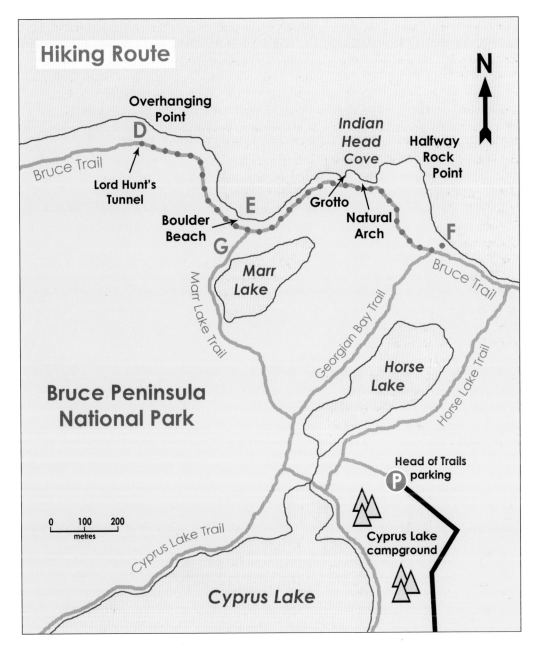

Hiking Route

Overhanging Point

Indian Head Cove

Halfway Rock Point

D

Bruce Trail

Lord Hunt's Tunnel

E

Grotto

Natural Arch

F

Boulder Beach

G

Marr Lake

Bruce Trail

Marr Lake Trail

Georgian Bay Trail

Horse Lake

Horse Lake Trail

Bruce Peninsula National Park

Head of Trails parking

P

Cyprus Lake campground

0   100   200
metres

Cyprus Lake Trail

Cyprus Lake

N

campground, swimming and sunning themselves on the limestone shelves that fringe the tiny cobble beach. Looking back at the cliff face, you may also see the profile of the Indian head that gives the cove its name.

Beyond the beach you will find the Natural Arch and the Grotto, looking quite different from above than they did from the water. Soon afterwards the trail descends over slabs of limestone onto Boulder Beach **E**, whose terraces mark the ancient shorelines of a deeper Georgian Bay and whose rock-walled pits were built to conceal birdwatchers and their binoculars. The beach stretches 120 m inland from the bay, rising to form a dam-like ridge. Behind the ridge, tiny Marr Lake is drained not by a river outlet but by water percolating beneath the cobbles into the bay. At the northwest corner of Marr Lake, you will find the crumbling foundations of a cabin **G** that once belonged to a summer resident named John Howard, before the land was acquired by the national park.

3rd Segment: Marr Lake to Overhanging Point (0.5 km hike)

Do not follow the trail beside the lake, as it leads inland to the park's Head of Trails. Instead, return over the cobbles to the western side of the beach and pick up the white blazes of the Bruce Trail as it clambers up the hill. The slabs of rock at the top are rough underfoot, full of small holes and resembling Swiss cheese. These "pit karren" are common along the Niagara Escarpment, eroded into the dolostone bedrock by mild acids from the resident plants and lichens.

After winding through the Swiss cheese and scrub cedars for several hundred metres, the trail emerges onto a flat ledge. The reason for the ledge's name — Overhanging Point **D** — will become obvious as you inch your way towards the brink. The protruding rock is dolostone (limestone fortified by magnesium, which infiltrated the rock from the shrinking saltwater sea that covered the area millennia ago). Being relatively dense and durable, the dolostone was better able to withstand the force of Georgian Bay's waves than were the softer layers of limestone and shale beneath it. These have eroded away, severely undercutting the ledge. Eventually (one hopes not today!) the overhang will succumb to gravity and join the jumble of talus at the base of the cliff, a process known as sapping.

A small crevice, easily missed, to the left of the trail cuts through the dolostone ledge (for hikers with a GPS, the entrance can be found at UTM coordinates 0458018E, 5010509N). This is Lord Hunt's Tunnel, less elegantly known as Hillary's Hole. It is named after Lord John Hunt, the British climber and military officer who led Sir Edmund Hillary's Mount Everest expedition in 1953 and later participated in the Commonwealth Expedition that hiked a portion of the Bruce Trail in August 1967 in honour of its opening. If you have not eaten too much lunch, you may squeeze through the crevice and descend to the base of the overhang, dropping onto a walkway scattered with pieces of fallen shale. Here you will marvel at the size of the rock shelf that looms overhead (and mutter a few supplicatory words for its continued longevity!). After exploring the long curve of the cliff, hoist yourself back up the crevice. The smooth, worn rocks and cedar roots will reassure you that you are not the first to use this route; the alternative is an even more difficult crevice on the western side of the overhang.

4th Segment: Homeward (2 km hike, 8 km paddle)

As this is a linear excursion, you must return along the trail to your canoe or kayak and paddle back from Halfway Rock Point to Little Cove (cutting across the mouth of the small bays to reduce the distance slightly). Though you have already seen the fascinating caves, cliffs and overhang from both the water and the trail, admiration will not diminish with repetition. Overhanging Point, in particular, is an awe-inspiring sight in the glow of the afternoon light, its full extent visible only from the water.

Alternative 1: Omit the Paddle (5.7 km loop hike)

The exposed nature of the coast between Little Cove and Halfway Rock Point (indeed between Tobermory and Cabot Head!) will often make the paddling portion of this excursion impractical, if not utterly foolhardy. The advantage of the approach by water will be lost if wind and waves prevent you from sliding your canoe or kayak close to shore, so don't waste your time or risk your safety unless conditions are flat calm.

Instead, drive 4.5 km from Hwy 6 to the park office at the entrance to the Cyprus Lake campground, buy a day-use permit and continue 1.5 km to the Head of Trails parking lot at the end of the road. Follow the well-posted trails along the traditional overland route, taking the groomed Georgian Bay Trail or Horse Lake Trail to the Georgian Bay shore and, after following the excursion to Overhanging Point, return via the rougher Marr Lake Trail.

Alternative 2: On Snowshoes

In wintertime, when the cliffs are coated with frozen spray and icicles drip from every cave, the hike on snowshoes from Cyprus Lake to the Georgian Bay shore is glorious, and you will encounter few people along the route. Winter access to the Head of Trails parking lot may be restricted, so turn left at the park office and leave your car at the day-use area at the bottom of the hill instead. You can then snowshoe along the Cyprus Lake Trail or across frozen Cyprus Lake itself, to join the Georgian Bay Trail at the north end of the lake. This will add almost 1.5 km each way to the hike described in alternative 1. The terrain between Halfway Rock Point and Overhanging Point is rugged in summer; when January snowdrifts hide the trail, and the rocks are slick with ice, the 8.5 km (return) trip will be a strenuous full-day expedition. You may wish simply to explore the area around Halfway Rock Point and Indian Head Cove and admire Overhanging Point from a distance. The cliffs above the Grotto give a fine view west towards the overhang.

Maps, Publications and Information

- Bruce Trail map #40: Tobermory.
- NTS maps 41 H/4: Dorcas Bay and 41 H/5: Flowerpot Island.
- Nautical chart 223501: Cape Hurd to Lonely Island.
- *Geology and Landforms of Grey & Bruce Counties*, written by the Bruce-Grey Geology Committee and published by the Owen Sound Field Naturalists in 2004.
- Jack Wellington's *Guide to the Bruce Peninsula National Park*, published by Parks Canada and the Friends of the Bruce District Parks Association, is available from the park visitor centre and many local stores.
- The *Cyprus Lake Hiking Trails* pamphlet and other information are available from the Bruce Peninsula National Park Office: (519) 596-2233, www.pc.gc.ca/pn-np/on/bruce.

CHAPTER 36

Burnt Point and the Parks Canada Visitor Centre

OVERVIEW

Burnt Point is the mainland portion of Fathom Five National Marine Park, one of two national parks established in 1987 when Parks Canada took over a collection of former provincial and private properties at the tip of the Bruce Peninsula. The Bruce Peninsula National Park is responsible for the land-based ecosystems — such as the escarpment's fragile cliff face and alvar pavements, a population of ancient cedars, 43 species of orchids, more than 20 species of ferns, and Ontario's only venomous snake, the endangered massasauga rattlesnake. Fathom Five National Marine Park safeguards the aquatic realm — the ridge of the escarpment that rests below lake level, the 22 islands that lie just offshore, and the wrecks of the many ships that have foundered in the waters around those islands. In 1990 UNESCO designated the Niagara Escarpment as a World Biosphere Reserve. The two national parks have become key components of the biosphere reserve, striving to balance environmental conservation and responsible human enjoyment along the escarpment's northern fringes.

The Parks Canada Visitor Centre opened its doors in June 2006, bringing to life the natural and human history of the Fathom Five and Bruce Peninsula national parks with its excellent interpretive displays. The panoramic vista from the adjacent lookout tower offers a modern perspective on the parkland. Serving also as Fathom Five's administrative and information headquarters, the visitor centre issues diving, boating and day-use permits for the park.

The hike in this chapter will introduce you to the treasures of the northern Bruce Peninsula, beginning with a tour of the visitor centre and lookout tower and then following the Bruce Trail and Burnt Point Side Trail along the rocky shoreline of Dunks Point. The excursion is especially lovely in winter, when billowing snow brightens the normally shadowy cedar forest and the lookout points around the headland become exquisitely windswept and varnished with icy spray. The route's 5 km stretch into a full-day trek on snowshoes, rewarded by sparkling views and peaceful solitude in what feels, in January, like the ends of the Earth.

Distance: **5 km loop hike**

(Left) The Parks Canada Visitor Centre.

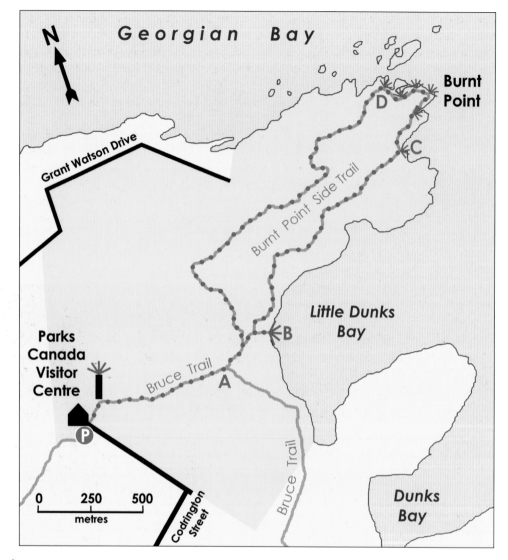

Access
- Exit Hwy 6 on the south side of Tobermory onto Codrington Street, and follow the Parks Canada signs to the visitor centre parking lot, 1 km to the north.

Route Description

1st Segment: Visitor Centre and Lookout Tower
Your first stop on this hike is at the Parks Canada Visitor Centre to pay your admission fee (which is also a day-use permit for other Fathom Five Park facilities) and to spend an hour or two exploring the exhibits and watching the fascinating high-tech film. Then make your way to the lookout tower, where the 20 m clamber up the staircase is

rewarded with a stellar view. The bird's-eye perspective makes it easy to imagine the entire layout of the northern Niagara Escarpment. On a clear day, you can see the white cliffs rounding Cabot Head, snaking west towards you and then curving north across the scattered islands of Fathom Five Marine Park to Fitzwilliam Island and Manitoulin Island on the distant horizon. Only some of this ridge is visible, but it doesn't require much effort to mentally "connect the dots" from island to island and visualize the submerged portion of the escarpment.

Another small stretch of the imagination will enable you to envisage other shoreline landscapes that existed here at other times in history. In the 14,000 years since Georgian Bay began to emerge from the last glacial ice sheet, there have been many ups and downs in water level. These fluctuations have been caused, in part, by changes in the lakes' drainage patterns as the glacier retreated, revealing new outlets at ever-more-northerly locations. As the tremendous weight of ice released the land beneath it, the shore was also gradually uplifted.

At its highest level, 12,000 to 10,000 years ago, glacial Lake Algonquin (the predecessor of the Upper Great Lakes) was so deep that it covered the entire Bruce Peninsula north of Owen Sound, leaving only a few promontories, like West Bluff at Cabot Head, exposed as islands in a vastly larger lake. At the other extreme, about 6,000 years ago, you could have *hiked* along the escarpment from Tobermory to Manitoulin Island. Indeed, Native legends speak of just such a land bridge, and recent scientific discoveries in the Georgian Bay basin confirm its existence. A forest of ancient cedar stumps, carbon-dated to 7,500 years, was found off Cove Island in Fathom Five Park at a depth of 43 m, firmly rooted in the lake bed. As cedars are not aquatic trees, we can conclude that 7,500 years ago this area was dry land — part of the land bridge that separated Lake Huron and Georgian Bay into two distinct lakes. A massive river emptied the water from Lake Huron into Georgian Bay on its way *east*, where it flowed into another massive river running parallel to and slightly south of today's French–Mattawa–Ottawa river route, bound for the Champlain Sea and the Atlantic Ocean. The river between

The visitor centre's lookout tower.

A cozy nook for a winter picnic on the Burnt Point Trail.

Lake Huron and Georgian Bay poured over the escarpment near Middle Island (halfway from Tobermory to Flowerpot Island) with, it is speculated, even more volume than that of the Niagara River over Niagara Falls today. By about 5,000 years ago, the northern lands had begun to rebound and the direction of flow reversed, opening the present channel into the St. Clair River at the southern end of Lake Huron. The remains of the ancient riverbed and waterfall off Tobermory became submerged. They were discovered in 1994 by a research team of geologists and marine heritage scientists who were surveying the lake bed by submersible.

2nd Segment: Lookout to Little Dunks Bay (0.8 km hike)

Having contemplated the panorama — past, present, and future (who knows, the Bruce Trail terminus cairn at Tobermory may have to be moved one day to Manitoulin!) — make your way down the staircase and turn left onto the Bruce Trail, which feels comfortably permanent underfoot. Follow the white blazes of the main trail for 600 m along a groomed gravel walkway. (Note: in winter this part of the trail is used by snowmobiles, and an alternate route for snowshoers runs parallel to the trail, on its north side.) When the main trail curves right **A**, take the left-hand fork and continue for 200 m to a wooden platform **B** with a pleasant view across Little Dunks Bay.

3rd Segment: Burnt Point Loop (3.5km hike)

Backtrack 25 m from the platform and turn right onto the blue-blazed Burnt Point Side Trail. Added to the Bruce Trail system in 2006, this trail does not yet have the well-worn feel that comes with the passage of many pairs of hiking boots. It winds through a cedar woodland for 900 m and then emerges onto a small rocky beach **C**. Half a dozen shoreline lookouts follow in quick succession, some at the end of short access trails. As the trail curves around Burnt Point, the views of Little Dunks Bay give way to views of the Fathom Five islands — the impressive bulk of Bears Rump to the east, Flowerpot Island with one of its namesake stacks visible directly to the north, and Cove Island, the largest of the group, stretching away towards the northwest. In the immediate foreground, the wave-battered rocks along the shore make splendid perches where you may sit and enjoy the view while you eat your picnic lunch. In winter there are many cozy nooks along the south-facing sides of the point's rocky fingers, where you may shelter from the blasts of northwest wind.

From the last lookout, the trail turns inland **D** and makes its way through the forest for 1.5 km, looping back to the gravel walkway.

4th Segment: Homeward (0.7 km hike)

Turn right and follow the walkway to the visitor centre. If you have any energy left for the climb, the lookout tower gives you a final opportunity to admire the view at the end of your hike.

Maps, Publications & Information

- Bruce Trail map #40: Tobermory.
- NTS maps 41 H/4: Dorcas Bay and 41 H/5: Flowerpot Island.
- Information is available from the Bruce Peninsula National Park at www.pc.gc.ca/pn-np/on/bruce and from Fathom Five National Marine Park at www.pc.gc.ca/amnc-nmca/on/fathomfive or by calling (519) 596-2233.
- Information about the UNESCO Niagara Escarpment World Biosphere Reserve is available at www.escarpment.org.

CHAPTER 37

Flowerpot Island

OVERVIEW

Flowerpot Island is famous for the pillars of rock perched on the island's northeastern shore. The pillars were once part of the Niagara Escarpment bluff, but centuries of wave action eroded them into free-standing "stacks." The waves then chiselled flowerpot shapes into the stacks, carving away the softer layers of limestone near the base more quickly than the denser dolostone layers at the top. The structures were cemented — literally! — into place during the 1930s, when the fledgling Parks Service capped and reinforced the flowerpots with mortar to prevent further erosion.

Native legend imbues the flowerpots with a more romantic history. They are said to be the petrified remains of Bounding Deer and Shining Rainbow, young lovers from enemy tribes who attempted to elope by canoe one starry June evening. Paddling north from the Saugeen shore, the couple soon spotted three canoes closing the gap behind them — Shining Rainbow's father and a band of angry warriors. Bounding Deer turned his canoe towards a sacred island just off the tip of the Bruce Peninsula, hoping to hide there. But the spirits that lived on the island did not welcome trespassers, so when the canoe touched the shore, a great wave rose up and the lovers were turned to stone. They stand there together still.

Apparently time has softened the spirits' curse, for thousands of people now visit Flowerpot Island every summer, and few remain behind as pillars of stone! Indeed, the island was occupied for many years, from 1897 to 1987, by the families of the lightkeepers who tended the Castle Bluff light. Today's tourists flock here to hike the trails, visit the remains of the light station and explore the island's geological treasures. In addition to the flowerpots, the island boasts four jagged bluffs, a massive sea cave, some mucky marl beds and, for divers, a magnificent underwater cliff.

This excursion approaches Flowerpot Island by canoe or kayak from Little Tub Harbour in Tobermory. However, it comes with a stern caution about paddling the exposed and unpredictable waters outside the shelter of the harbour. The trip should be undertaken only when the day's wind and wave forecast is completely benign. If in doubt, avail yourself of the services of one of the tour boat companies that operate from Tobermory, and spare yourself an exhausting paddle at the end of the day back from Flowerpot Island into the prevailing westerlies.

Distance: 16 km paddle, 5 km hike (alternatives: 12.5 km paddle, 3.6 km hike)

(Left) The larger of Flowerpot Island's two pillars is perched precariously at the water's edge.

Access

- Exit Hwy 6 onto Bay Street at the bottom of the hill in Tobermory, and drive 100 m to the public boat launch at the end of the road.
- Parking here is for short periods only and extremely limited, so after you have unloaded your canoe or kayak and your day's gear, move your car to one of the free day-use lots in town. The closest is at the community centre 250 m south, on the left side of Hwy 6 near the top of the hill.
- Permits for Flowerpot Island may be purchased in advance at the Parks Canada Visitor Centre or when you land at Beachy Cove, at the island's self-serve station.

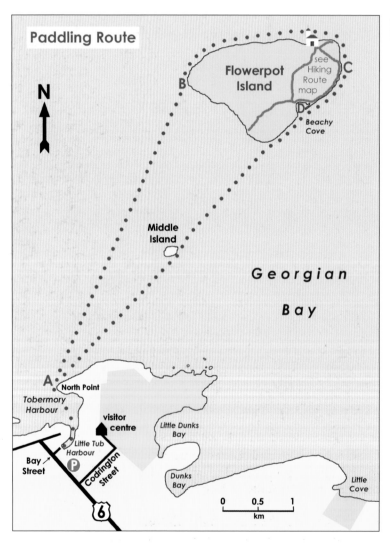

Route Description

1st Segment: Tobermory to Flowerpot Island — Scenic Route (10 km paddle) (see Paddling Route map)

During the summer months, Little Tub Harbour is abuzz with boats — Zodiac tour boats, glass-bottomed sightseeing boats, working fishing boats, sleek sailboats, luxury motorboats, and the *Chi-Cheemaun* (Ojibwe for "big canoe") ferry boat. Make your way north from the launch, dodging this traffic, for 900 m across Tobermory Harbour to North Point **A**. Then set your course for Flowerpot Island **B**, an exposed crossing of 5 km.

Arriving at Flowerpot Island's western tip, begin your tour in a clockwise direction. The wild shoreline on the island's northern side alternates between rounded cobbles and slabs of limestone, whitewashed and polished smooth by waves. In a small cove 2 km along the shore, you will see the red-and-white painted cottages of the Flowerpot Island light station nestled among the cobbles. Then, rounding Castle Bluff at the island's northeastern tip, the flowerpots **C** come into view, set dramatically against the backdrop of Middle Bluff. The shore becomes busy here with sightseers and often with divers exploring the underwater cliff face that drops 90 m from the flowerpots into the icy depths of Georgian Bay.

Beachy Cove lies 900 m farther to the south, its breakwater sheltering a busy tour boat wharf and a smaller dock and beach at the Flowerpot Island campground. Make your way across the cove and pull your canoe or kayak well up onto the sand **D**. There are six wooden tent platforms here and a composting toilet that will be a welcome sight after your morning's paddle. There is also a self-serve fee station where you may buy your day-use permit for the island.

2nd Segment: Beachy Cove to Flowerpots and Cave (1 km hike) (see Hiking Route map)

Pick up the well-marked hiking trail north of the tour boat dock. The trail hugs the shoreline, weaving through the cedars and across the limestone shelves to the flowerpots **C**. Standing directly beneath them, you will find the close perspective accentuates their impressive height (the smaller flowerpot is 7 m tall and the larger, slightly to the north, 12 m). Their extraordinary shape gives them an otherworldly appearance, and it requires no great leap of the imagination to envisage, instead of two geological formations, the two lovers Bounding Deer and Shining Rainbow transformed into stone where their canoe touched the shore.

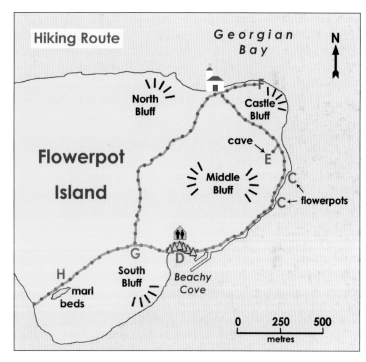

A short trail just beyond the flowerpots leads up the hill to the left. Climb the wooden staircase to a viewing platform inside a massive sea cave **E**. Formed 5,000 years ago when Georgian Bay was part of the much deeper glacial Lake Algonquin, the cave was chiselled into a weak area of the cliff face by waves crashing against the ancient shoreline. Now the shoreline is 14 m lower, and waves are chiselling other cavities into the cliffs — at South Bluff, which you will see as you begin the return paddle to Tobermory.

3rd Segment: Cave to Flowerpot Island Light Station (1 km hike)

Return down the hill from the cave, turn left and continue along the main trail, which cuts inland behind Castle Bluff for 800 m to arrive at a raised cobble beach (another relic of an older, higher shoreline) on the north side of the island. In the cove at the end of the trail, you will find the cottages of the former Flowerpot Island light station. The two-storey cottage was built in 1901 and the one-storey cottage in 1959 to accommodate the lightkeepers' growing families, but both were abandoned in 1987 following automation of the light. Then, after a decade of neglect, the Friends of Fathom Five took over the buildings from the coast guard in 1996 and restored them. Volunteers maintain the property and offer tours for visitors during the summer months. Admission is by donation.

Photographs on display in the cottage show the original 1897 lighthouse perched spectacularly on the edge of the Castle Bluff cliff, 33 m above the water. The lightkeeper lived in the square building attached to the light tower until the cottage on the beach was built. With construction of the modern steel tower in 1969, the old building was abruptly set on fire and pushed over the cliff into the water. The site can be reached via a narrow cement walkway that hugs the cliff edge to the east of the cottages. An observation deck at the end of the walkway **F** offers a splendid view across the busy boating channel between Flowerpot Island and Bears Rump Island, 3 km to the east.

4th Segment: Lighthouse to Marl Beds (2 km hike)

From the observation deck, backtrack along the cement walkway and pick up the trail behind the two-storey cottage. The trail turns inland and climbs over rougher ground across Middle Bluff for 1 km. Many varieties of fern and, in springtime, a dazzling display of wildflowers carpet the forest floor. On the south side of Middle Bluff, a staircase helps you down the cliff, bringing you to a trail junction **G**. If you are feeling weary, a left-hand turn will take you directly back to your canoe or kayak in Beachy Cove **D**, 300 m away. Otherwise, turn right and follow the Marl Trail for 700 m to the island's western shore.

Flowerpot Island's modern light tower on Castle Bluff.

Near the end of the trail, it crosses a patch of cobbles **H**, and a shallow pond becomes visible on the left. Once a narrow cove opening into Georgian Bay, the water was isolated behind a rocky barrier when the lake level dropped. Dissolved limestone trickling from the surrounding hills settled at the bottom of the pond to form marl, a fine-grained lime mud. As the pond gradually seeped away, the marl beds became increasingly exposed. Now the pond water is a murky grey, and its shoreline has the consistency of spongy clay. This harshly alkaline environment is inhospitable to most plants and animals. However, the marl itself, with its excellent binding properties, was once of great commercial value in the manufacture of mortar. In the early 1900s, it was extracted from Flowerpot Island and other beds along the Bruce Peninsula for use at the Portland Cement plant in Owen Sound.

A short distance past the marl beds, the trail ends at a jumble of rocks and driftwood on the island's western shore. You may enjoy a final rest and snack here before your return journey and admire the view across the water (we hope still calm!) to Tobermory and the western islands of Fathom Five National Marine Park.

5th Segment: Homeward (1 km hike plus 6 km paddle)

Return along the Marl Trail for 700 m to the trail junction **G**, and continue 300 m to your canoe or kayak at Beachy Cove **D**. Paddling southwest from the cove, you will see the newly formed caves cutting into the base of South Bluff and beyond them the rocky shore at the end of the Marl Trail. Turn away from the land here, and paddle into open water towards Tobermory. Almost halfway along the route, you will have an opportunity to rest in the lee of Middle Island; do not land, however, as the island is privately owned. From there it is only a 3.5 km push to the Little Tub Harbour launch.

Alternatives

- To shorten the paddling portion of this excursion, you may wish to skip the scenic outward route around Flowerpot Island and paddle directly from North Point to Beachy Cove. This will cut 4 km from the total paddle, reducing it to just over 6 km each way.
- To shorten the hiking portion of the excursion from 5 km to 3.6 km, you can omit the detour down the Marl Trail to the western shore.
- To stretch the excursion into a longer outing, reserve a campsite (well in advance) and stay overnight on Flowerpot Island. This will allow you to explore the flowerpots in relative peace after the tour boats have left for the day and enjoy the island in the moody light of dusk and dawn.

Maps, Publications & Information

- NTS map 41 H/5: Flowerpot Island.
- Nautical chart 223501: Cape Hurd to Lonely Island.
- *Flowerpot Island*, a useful interpretive pamphlet that includes a map of the hiking trails, is available from the National Parks Visitor Centre and the harbourmaster's office in Tobermory.
- Information is available from the Five National Marine Park at www.pc.gc.ca/amnc-nmca/on/fathomfive or by calling (519) 596-2233.

CHAPTER 38

The Wrecks of Fathom Five National Marine Park

OVERVIEW

Fathom Five National Marine Park protects an area of aquatic and shoreline habitat at the tip of the Bruce Peninsula. The park encompasses 22 islands, innumerable shoals, 112 km² of the lake bed, the waters themselves, and the many natural features and historical artifacts they contain. It is Canada's oldest marine park, established in 1971 by the Ontario Ministry of Natural Resources and drawn under the federal banner of Parks Canada in 1987. Fathom Five's popularity and success have made it a model for other marine parks.

The park's fascinating underwater geology is one of its chief attractions for visitors. Escarpment cliffs plunge more than 100 m from the waterline into the icy depths of

Georgian Bay, mirroring the above-water cliffs of Bruce Peninsula National Park. Caves, tunnels, channels and overhangs are sculpted into the rock at various depths, reflecting the fluctuating water levels and shorelines since the last glacier retreated 12,000 years ago. During a low-water era about 6,000 years ago, a river ran from west to east between today's Lake Huron and Georgian Bay, tumbling with the force of Niagara Falls over the escarpment near Middle Island, 3 km northeast of Tobermory. The now submerged riverbed and waterfall were discovered in 1994 by a team of research geologists and marine heritage scientists who were surveying the lake bed by submersible.

Another attraction of Fathom Five Park is the high concentration of shipwrecks. The narrow passage between Lake Huron and Georgian Bay, prone to storms and teeming with islands and shoals, has gained a deservedly menacing reputation. Tobermory's strategic location at the tip of the Bruce Peninsula and its two sheltered harbours, affectionately called Big Tub and Little Tub, made it a popular refuge for mariners. Surveyed and mapped in the early 1800s, Tobermory became a busy port in the latter half of the century as fishing, logging and transportation in the Upper Great Lakes grew with the country's burgeoning population.

When Charles Earl brought his family to Tobermory in 1871, the townsite had not yet been settled, though the harbours were visited frequently by mariners as they rounded the tip of the Bruce Peninsula. Charles hung a lantern from a tree at the mouth of Big Tub Harbour as a beacon for the ships seeking shelter there and so became Tobermory's first informal lightkeeper. His role was made official when he was appointed to tend the lighthouse that was built at the site in 1885. Eventually a trio of lighthouses — Big Tub, Cove Island and Flowerpot Island — reinforced by numerous other navigational markers, formed an efficient network that ensured safe passage for hundreds of vessels around the peninsula. When storms raged across Lake Huron, especially during the legendary November gales, some ships perished nonetheless. Their skeletons are scattered liberally among the Fathom Five islands. At least 27 vessels are known to have been lost in the waters off Tobermory since 1880. Of these, 22 have been located and identified, and the wrecks are now protected and maintained as dive sites.

The paddling excursion in this chapter explores the Fathom Five shipwrecks that lie in Tobermory's harbours and along the west shore of nearby Russel Island. The excursion is possible only in calm weather when the wrecks are easily visible and approach is safe. Your canoe or kayak will require a permit to enter the waters around the wreck sites, available for a nominal fee from the Parks Canada Visitor Centre off Codrington Street in Tobermory. Parks staff will also advise you about weather conditions and the current schedule for visiting the wrecks in Big Tub Harbour. It may be necessary to alter your paddling route to accommodate this schedule, designed to coordinate access for divers, tour boats and private vessels. You might also wish to reverse the route, paddling in a clockwise direction rather than counter-clockwise as described here, to allow for wind and to take advantage of any shelter afforded by islands and headlands.

Distance: **12 km paddle**

(Left) Tobermory's Big Tub lighthouse.

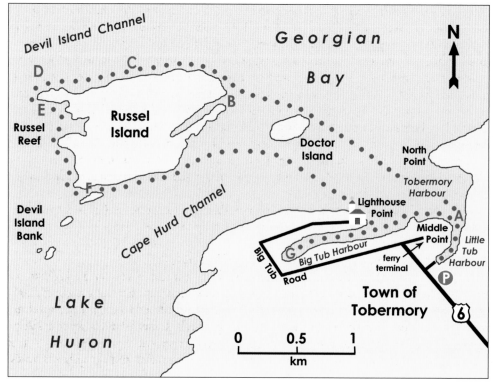

Access

- Exit Hwy 6 onto Bay Street at the bottom of the hill in Tobermory, and drive 100 m to the public boat launch at the end of the road.
- Parking here is for short periods only and extremely limited, so after you have unloaded your canoe or kayak and your day's gear, move your car to one of the free day-use lots in town. The closest is at the community centre 250 m south, on the left side of Hwy 6 near the top of the hill.

Route Description

1st Segment: Tobermory to Russel Island (2.5 km paddle)

During the summer months, Little Tub Harbour is teeming with boats — Zodiac tour boats, glass-bottomed sightseeing boats, working fishing boats, sleek sailboats, luxury motorboats, and the *Chi-Cheemaun* (Ojibwe for "big canoe") ferry boat. Tour boats began to operate from Tobermory in the 1930s, taking wealthy visitors across Georgian Bay to hunting and fishing camps on the north shore. That same decade the daily summer passenger-and-car ferry service commenced between Tobermory and South Baymouth on Manitoulin Island. Today the tour boats' primary business is ferrying summer sightseers and divers to Flowerpot Island and the Fathom Five Park shipwrecks, while the *Chi-Cheemaun*, with a capacity of 143 cars and 638 passengers, shuttles between Tobermory and Manitoulin two to four times daily.

Dodging this traffic, make your way north from the launch to the mouth of Little Tub Harbour. Where Little Tub opens into Tobermory Harbour, you may see activity for about 200 m along the right-hand shore, a popular site for novice divers **A**. Here lie the remains of four small (17 to 20 m) tugboats, workhorses of Tobermory's logging and fishing businesses in the early 1900s. Steam-powered and sturdy, the tugs towed log booms and lumber barges and transported catches of fish in and out of port. From south to north as you paddle out of the harbour, the four tugs are: *John & Alex*, towed out of Little Tub Harbour and released after catching fire at the dock in 1947; *Bob Foote*, believed to have sunk in 1905; *Robert K.*, destroyed by fire in 1935; and *Alice G.*, ripped from her moorings in 1927 during an early December gale. Of these, only the *Alice G.* is still nearly intact, under about 6 m of water. The other tugs have broken apart and their wreckage lies scattered along the shore.

From the wreck site, head northwest for 1.5 km, skirting Doctor Island (privately owned), and continue across the 500 m channel to the eastern tip of Russel Island.

2nd Segment: Wrecks of Russel Island (3.5km paddle)

Russel Island is one of the 22 islands protected within Fathom Five National Marine Park. You may land here to stretch your legs and eat a picnic lunch, but camping and fires are strictly prohibited, and your activities should be confined to the rocky shoreline, leaving the wooded interior undisturbed. As you approach Russel Island, a narrow inlet **B** becomes visible near its eastern tip, offering a sheltered nook where you may wish to rest and explore the shallows. Then make your way around the point and along the island's

The wreck of the Sweepstakes *at the head of Big Tub Harbour.*

northern side. Here spruce and cedar crowd close to the water's edge, and the shoreline angles steeply downwards. Two shipwrecks lie just offshore, but they are too deep to be visible from the surface. Their locations are marked by buoys, and you may see divers in the water around them. The first wreck, about halfway along the north shore, is that of the *Philo Scoville* **C**, a 42 m sailing schooner that ran aground and broke apart during a storm in October 1889. Her four crew were rescued, but their captain, John O'Grady, perished when he fell between the ship and the rocks that she had foundered on.

The second wreck, that of the *James C. King* **D**, lies off the island's northwestern tip. With the advent of steam power, the *King*, originally a 53 m, three-masted sailing ship, had been converted into a lumber barge. On November 29, 1901, the *King* and another barge, the *Brunette*, were under tow behind the steamship *W. L. Wetmore*, all three vessels heavily laden with timber from Parry Sound, when a storm drove them aground on Russel Reef. The *Brunette* was recovered the following day, but the *King* was badly damaged and sank in deep water off the point. Much of the timber cargo was washed ashore and salvaged by tugs the next spring.

The (unfortunately named!) *W. L. Wetmore*, like the *King* she was towing, was too badly battered to salvage. One of Fathom Five's most impressive and accessible shipwrecks, she can be found in the shallows just below Russel Island's northwestern tip, oriented southeast to northwest. The site **E** is clearly marked by buoys; paddlers with a GPS can locate the wreck at UTM coordinates 0444300E, 5012500N. Her 65 m of ribs and planking, solidly constructed from white oak, are easily visible from the surface, as are some railings, a pile of anchor chain and other fittings. But it is her massive boiler rising suddenly from the wreck, almost grasping at the keel of your canoe or kayak as you glide over it, that will send a shiver down your spine.

Looking up from the water and surveying the landscape along Russel Island's western shore, it is not difficult to see why ships might run aground here. The shoreline's pitted rocks slip smoothly into the shallow bay, surfacing — or nearly surfacing — to form the shoals of Russel Reef. And to the southwest, a treacherous bank of tiny islands and submerged rocks stretches for more than a kilometre towards Devil Island. To further complicate navigation here, fluctuating water levels play tricks with the geography. For instance, the small "island" off the northwestern tip of Russel Island seen on current topographic maps has now become a peninsula, a change thankfully recorded on the most recent marine chart for the area.

The last of Russel Island's wrecks, the *John Walters* **F**, nudges the island's southwestern tip, lying in a small channel between Russel Island and a barren offshore rock (located at UTM coordinates 0444840E, 5012060N). The circumstances and even the date of the *John Walters'* wreckage are uncertain; accounts place it anywhere from 1883 to 1899, but most agree that an autumn storm was likely to blame. All that is left of the 23 m, two-masted schooner is a section of hull and some scattered debris. Having run aground so close to shore and near the surface, waves and ice have claimed the rest.

3rd Segment: Russel Island to Big Tub Lighthouse (2.8 km paddle)

With a last glance west past Devil Island to the waters of Lake Huron, follow Russel Island's shoreline east from the *John Walters*. Peering overboard you will be fascinated by the changing architecture beneath the surface, as the shallow, sandy, shell-strewn bottom becomes increasingly rocky and then plunges down an underwater cliff into blackness. Return past Doctor Island and across the Cape Hurd Channel to Lighthouse Point. Gracing the point with its hexagonal wooden tower and cheerful red and white clapboard is the Big Tub lighthouse. Built in 1885 and manned for more than half a century by a succession of unusually unreliable lightkeepers, the light was automated in 1952. At its base a submerged wall has become a favourite haunt of divers, so steer clear of their buoys when rounding the point.

4th Segment: Big Tub Harbour (1 km paddle)

If time, energy and the park's schedule allow, paddle down Big Tub Harbour to visit Fathom Five's two most celebrated and frequently visited wrecks **G**, the *Sweepstakes* and the *City of Grand Rapids*, lying close together in shallow water near the base of the harbour.

In August 1885 the 36 m, two-masted schooner *Sweepstakes* struck a rock off Cove Island. Two weeks later she was towed to Tobermory for repairs but upon arrival the damage was deemed too severe, so she was stripped of serviceable equipment and abandoned. *Sweepstakes* sank in Big Tub Harbour and remains there still, one of the best-preserved wrecks in Fathom Five Park.

The *City of Grand Rapids* was a 37 m steamship that carried passengers and supplies between Owen Sound and villages along the Bruce Peninsula and Manitoulin Island during the late 1800s. While moored in Little Tub Harbour in October 1907, the

The wreck of the John Walters *nudges Russel Island's southwestern tip.*

Grand Rapids caught fire. She was towed out of the harbour to prevent the blaze from spreading to the dock and other vessels and released in Tobermory Harbour. Gradually she drifted west and into Big Tub Harbour, burning to the waterline, her charred hull finally coming to rest at the base of the harbour, just 30 m south of the *Sweepstakes*. The rudder and propeller were salvaged from the wreck in 1968 and are now displayed outside the St. Edmunds Township Museum.

5th Segment: Homeward (2.2 km paddle)

With exploration of the wrecks complete, paddle back up Big Tub Harbour and around Middle Point into Little Tub Harbour. Be careful not to collide with the *Chi-Cheemaun* or one of Tobermory's ubiquitous tour boats as you make your way back towards the launch. Lost in reverie about the ghosts of Fathom Five that you have visited today, you may find it difficult to return to the modern bustle! You may be more inclined to ponder the poetry of *The Tempest*. In the opening act of Shakespeare's play, the romantic hero, Ferdinand, has been shipwrecked on an island and believes that his father, Alonso, the king of Naples, was drowned in the storm. Singing these magic lines to Ferdinand, the spirit Ariel draws him into the drama:

> *Full fathom five thy father lies*
> *Of his bones are coral made*
> *Those are pearls that were his eyes*
> *Nothing of him that doth fade*
> *But doth suffer a sea-change*
> *Into something rich and strange*
> *Sea-nymphs hourly ring his knell*
> *Hark! now I hear them — ding-dong bell*

A restorative fish-and-chip supper at one of the local restaurants, a browse through the wonderfully varied collection of waterfront shops, and an evening stroll along the docks should restore your perspective.

Did You Know?

A fathom is a unit of measure in the imperial system that represents the span of a man's arms when fully outstretched from side to side, a length of 6 ft (1.8 m). The fathom typically refers to nautical measurement, though historically it was also used on land with reference to mine shafts. It derives from the traditional method of measuring depth: a heavy lead plummet attached to the end of a long rope (called a sounding line) would be released overboard and the line let out until the plummet touched bottom; then the line would be hauled up again, arm length by arm length; counting the number of arm lengths gave the depth of the water beneath the ship. With widespread adoption of the metric system and the advent of ultrasonic depth sounding, the fathom is falling into disuse.

Other Things to Do in Tobermory

- *Bruce Trail Cairn*: Located on the walkway above the eastern side of Little Tub Harbour, the cairn was unveiled at the official opening of the Bruce Trail on June 10, 1967. It marks the northern terminus of this famous long-distance hiking trail that winds for 840 km along the Niagara Escarpment from Niagara to Tobermory. If you have enjoyed some of the hikes in previous chapters of this book, your respect for the beauty and ruggedness of the trail will make you appreciate the work of the visionaries who established it and the dedicated volunteers who continue to develop and maintain it. For information and membership, visit www.brucetrail.org.

- *St. Edmunds Township Museum*: Located 4 km south of Tobermory on the northeast side of Hwy 6, the museum is housed in the old St. Edmunds Settlement School, built in 1898. It contains a collection of old photographs, historical documents, relics from life in the township and a fascinating display of marine artifacts and maps. The propeller and rudder from the *City of Grand Rapids* can be found outside by the parking lot.

- *The Big Canoe*: Throughout the summer months, the *Chi-Cheemaun* offers dinner cruises and day-trip return fares for foot passengers wishing to take the ferry across the channel from Tobermory to Manitoulin Island. Its route lies through the islands of Fathom Five National Marine Park and passes close to the Cove Island lighthouse. This elegant Imperial Tower with its cheerful collection of outbuildings and cottages was the first to be built on Georgian Bay in 1858, and in 1991 it was the last to be destaffed. For information visit www.ontarioferries.com.

This cairn marks the Bruce Trail's northern terminus in Tobermory.

Maps, Publications & Information

- Nautical chart 227401: Cape Hurd to Tobermory and Cove Island.
- NTS map 41 H/5: Flowerpot Island.
- Information is available from Fathom Five National Marine Park at www.pc.gc.ca/amnc-nmca/on/fathomfive or by calling (519) 596-2233. Parks Canada publishes an annual diving guide for the Fathom Five wreck sites, which is available at the visitor centre and at local dive shops.

References & Further Information

Paddling & Hiking Associations
- Bruce Trail Association: www.brucetrail.org
- Paddle Canada and *Kanawa* magazine: www.paddlingcanada.com
- Ontario Recreational Canoeing Association: www.orca.on.ca
- Georgian Bay paddling information: www.kayakgeorgianbay.com
- Canadian Canoe Roots: www.myccr.com

Environment & Land Use Information
- Ontario Ministry of Natural Resources: www.mnr.gov.on.ca/MNR
- Ontario Ministry of Natural Resources land use information: www.crownlanduseatlas.mnr.gov.on.ca
- Great Lakes online environmental atlas and resource book (a joint project of Environment Canada and the U.S. Environmental Protection Agency): www.epa.gov/glnpo/atlas
- Georgian Bay Association (also called Greater Bay Area Foundation): www.georgianbay.ca
- Georgian Bay Land Trust: www.gblt.org
- Niagara Escarpment Commission: www.escarpment.org
- Escarpment Biosphere Conservancy: www.escarpment.ca
- Grey Sauble Conservation Authority: www.greysauble.on.ca
- Ontario Nature (formerly the Federation of Ontario Naturalists): www.ontarionature.org
- Nature Conservancy of Canada: www.natureconservancy.ca

Maps & Charts
- Natural Resources Canada's Centre for Topographic Information: www.maps.nrcan.gc.ca
- Department of Fisheries and Oceans' Canadian Hydrographic Service for nautical chart information: www.charts.gc.ca
- *The Bruce Trail Reference: Trail Guide and Maps*, Edition 24 (2006), published by the Bruce Trail Association (www.brucetrail.org)
- Chrismar Mapping Services, publishers of the Adventure Map series of waterproof topographic maps: www.chrismar.com

Camping & Accommodation
- Provincial Parks: www.ontarioparks.com
- National Parks: www.parkscanada.ca, campground reservation service www.pccamping.ca
- Private campgrounds: www.campgrounds.org
- Bed & Breakfast establishments: www.bbcanada.com, www.hometohomenetwork.ca

Outfitters & Retailers
- Killarney Outfitters, Killarney: www.killarney.com
- Killarney Kanoes, Sudbury: www.killarneykanoes.com
- White Squall Outfitters, Parry Sound: www.whitesquall.com
- Swift Canoe & Kayak, Waubaushene: www.swiftcanoe.com
- Sojourn, Barrie: www.sojournoutdoors.ca
- Suntrail Outfitters, Hepworth: www.suntrail.net
- Thorncrest Outfitters, Tobermory: www.thorncrestoutfitters.com
- MEC, Toronto/Ottawa: www.mec.ca
- The Complete Paddler, Toronto: www.completepaddler.ca
- Europe Bound, Toronto: www.europebound.com

Miscellaneous Information
- Environment Canada weather reports: www.weatheroffice.gc.ca
- Great Lakes historical vessels index: www.bgsu.edu/colleges/library/hcgl
- Geocaching sites in Canada (a scavenger hunt for GPS buffs): www.geocaching.com

Index

Page numbers in italic type refer to photographs.